LINCOLN'S
BATTLE
WITH GOD

ALSO BY STEPHEN MANSFIELD

Never Give In:
The Extraordinary Character of Winston Churchill

Then Darkness Fled:
The Liberating Wisdom of Booker T. Washington

Forgotten Founding Father:
The Heroic Legacy of George Whitefield

The Faith of George W. Bush

The Faith of the American Soldier

Benedict XVI: His Life and Mission

The Faith of Barack Obama

The Search for God and Guinness

The Mormonizing of America

LINCOLN'S
BATTLE
WITH GOD

A PRESIDENT'S STRUGGLE WITH FAITH AND WHAT IT MEANT FOR AMERICA

STEPHEN MANSFIELD

THOMAS NELSON
Since 1798

NASHVILLE   DALLAS   MEXICO CITY   RIO DE JANEIRO

Published in Nashville, Tennessee, by Thomas Nelson. Thomas Nelson is a registered trademark of Thomas Nelson, Inc.

All Scripture verses are from the King James Version of the Bible.

Photographs on pages xvi, xix, 6, 38, 55, 76, 115, 125, 129, 135, 156, 168, 169, 172, and 179 are from the Library of Congress.

Photographs on pages 3, 16, 177, and 243 taken by Isaac Darnall.

Photograph on page 87 courtesy of the archives of First Presbyterian Church of Springfield, Illinois.

Photograph on page 138 from Wikipedia.

Thomas Nelson, Inc., titles may be purchased in bulk for educational, business, fund-raising, or sales promotional use. For information, please e-mail SpecialMarkets@ThomasNelson.com.

Library of Congress Cataloging-in-Publication Data

Mansfield, Stephen, 1958-
  Lincoln's battle with God : a president's struggle with faith and what it meant for America / Stephen Mansfield.
      p. cm.
  Includes bibliographical references and index.
  ISBN 978-1-59555-309-6 (alk. paper)
  1. Lincoln, Abraham, 1809-1865--Religion. 2. Presidents--Religious life--United States. I. Title.
  E457.2.M33 2012
  973.7092--dc23
  [B]

                        2012030560

Printed in the United States of America

12 13 14 15 16 QG 6 5 4 3 2 1

To the faculty and students of
Berlin American High School

Berlin, Germany
1966–1994

CONTENTS

CONTENTS

THE LIFE OF
ABRAHAM LINCOLN

A Chronology

1809 **February 12:** Abraham Lincoln is born on Sinking Spring Farm, three miles south of Hodgenville, Kentucky.

1811 The Lincoln family moves seven miles northeast of Hodgenville to a farm on Knob Creek. Abraham is two years old.

1816 **In December,** the Lincolns make a new home along the banks of Pigeon Creek in Indiana, near present-day Gentryville.

1818 **October 5:** Abraham's mother, Nancy, dies of milk sickness.

1819 **December 2:** Lincoln's father, Thomas, marries Sarah Bush Johnston.

1828 **January 20:** Abraham's beloved older sister, Sarah, dies while giving birth. **Spring:** He makes his first flatboat trip to New Orleans and sees for the first time the horrors of slavery.

1830 **In March,** the Lincolns move to Illinois and settle near what is now Decatur.

1831 **In July,** Abraham leaves his family and settles alone in New Salem, Illinois. He comes under the influence of what William H. Herndon calls religious "liberals."

1832 Lincoln serves as captain of a militia in the Blackhawk War. He has his first of several experiences with prostitutes. He runs for the state legislature and is defeated. He reads critics of Christianity such as Volney, Gibbon, and Paine.

1834 Lincoln is elected to the Illinois General Assembly as a representative from Sangamon County. He remains in the assembly for the next twelve years.

1835 Either in this year or the next, Lincoln pens his book on "infidelity," in which he criticizes the Bible and the Christian religion.

1836 **September 9:** The Illinois Supreme Court permits Lincoln to practice law.

1837 **March 3:** Abraham Lincoln enters the first formal protest of his life against slavery, this one in the Illinois legislature.
April 15: At twenty-eight years of age, Lincoln moves to Springfield, Illinois, and shares a room with Joshua Speed. Lincoln becomes the junior law partner of John Todd Stuart.

1838 Lincoln writes "The Suicide's Soliloquy," revealing the depressed state of his soul at the time.

1839 **September 3:** Lincoln begins riding the Eighth Judicial Circuit.
Mary Todd moves to Springfield and meets Lincoln later in the year at a ball.

1840 Lincoln and Mary Todd begin courting.

1841 Lincoln and Todd break off their relationship. Lincoln enters one of the worst "hypos" (depressions) of his life. Friends take razors and knives from his room to guard against suicide.

1842 Lincoln and Todd renew their relationship in secret.
November 4: Abraham and Mary are wed. They take a room at the Globe Tavern boarding house on Adams Street in Springfield.

1843 **August 1:** Robert Todd Lincoln is born to Abraham and Mary. The Lincolns move briefly to a cottage on Fourth Street.

1844 **January 16:** Lincoln purchases the only house he will ever own, at the corner of Eighth and Jackson. The three Lincolns move in on May 1. Lincoln starts his own law firm with Herndon as his junior partner.

1846 **March 10:** Edward Baker Lincoln (Eddie) is born. Lincoln issues his handbill countering the charges of Reverend Peter Cartwright about religious infidelity.
August 3: Lincoln is elected to the U. S. House of Representatives from the Seventh Congressional District of Illinois.

1847 **December 6:** Lincoln takes his seat in Congress.

1848 Lincoln sends Mary and his sons back to Lexington because he believes they "hinder" him in business.

1849 Lincoln proposes a measure to outlaw slavery in the District of Columbia just before completing his congressional term. He happens upon Dr. James Smith's *The Christian's Defence* in his father-in-law's library in Lexington, Kentucky.

1850 **February 1:** Eddie Lincoln dies after fighting a disease—probably tuberculosis—for fifty-two days. He is just shy of his fourth birthday.
December 21: William Wallace Lincoln is born in the Lincoln home.

1851 **January 17:** Thomas Lincoln, Abraham's father, dies.

1852 Mary joins the Presbyterian church in Springfield. Lincoln occasionally attends with her. Reverend Smith, author of *The Christian's Defence*, is the church's pastor.

1853 **April 4:** Thomas (Tad) Lincoln is born in the Lincoln home.

1854 **May 30:** The Kansas-Nebraska Act is signed into law. It allowed popular sover-

eignty to determine slavery in western territories, thus repealing the Missouri Compromise of 1820, which forbade slavery in the former Louisiana Territory.
October 16: Lincoln makes his Peoria speech, the first of a series of antislavery speeches that win him national attention.
November 7: Lincoln is once again elected to the Illinois legislature but withdraws twenty days later to consider a run for the U. S. Senate.

1855 **January:** In deference to his party's interest, Lincoln withdraws from the contest for a U. S. Senate seat.

1856 Rising in the newly reorganized Republican Party, he is considered for vice president at the party's convention.

1857 **In March,** the Supreme Court's *Dred Scott* decision denies that a black man has any rights a white man is obligated to recognize.

1858 **June 16:** Lincoln makes his famous House Divided speech at the Illinois Republican Convention in Springfield. The convention nominates him for the U. S. Senate in a race that Lincoln ultimately loses. Lincoln's series of slavery debates with Stephen A. Douglas occur from August 21 through October 15.

1860 **February 27:** Lincoln gives his famous Cooper Union address in New York.
May 18: Lincoln is nominated for president by the Republican National Convention in Chicago.
November 6: Abraham Lincoln is elected president of the United States.
December 20: South Carolina secedes from the Union.

1861 **February 8:** The Confederate States of America is formed.
March 4: Lincoln is inaugurated the sixteenth U. S. president and delivers his First Inaugural Address.
April 12: Confederate troops bombard Fort Sumter in South Carolina.
April 15: Lincoln issues a call for 75,000 volunteers.
August 12: Lincoln issues the first of nine proclamations of prayer, fasting, and thanksgiving released during his presidency.
July 21: The Battle of First Manassas (Bull Run) is an embarrassing Union loss.

1862 **February 20:** William (Willie) Lincoln dies in the White House, probably of typhoid fever. The battles of Shiloh, Second Manassas, and Antietam occur in this year.

1863 **January 1:** Lincoln issues the Emancipation Proclamation.
In July, the battle of Gettysburg and the fall of Vicksburg occur, both Union victories.
November 19: Lincoln delivers the Gettysburg Address.

1864 **February 22:** Lincoln is renominated for the presidency by his party.
November 8: Lincoln is elected to a second term. General Sherman's troops occupy Atlanta and then take Savannah, Georgia, which Sherman offers to Lincoln as "an early Christmas present."

1865 **January 31:** Congress passes the Thirteenth Amendment and sends it to the states for ratification. By December, it officially abolishes slavery in the United States.
March 4: Lincoln delivers his Second Inaugural Address.

1865   **April 4:** Lincoln visits Richmond, Virginia, two days after the Confederate evacuation. Freed blacks cheer him as a deliverer.
April 9: General Robert E. Lee of the Confederacy surrenders to General Ulysses S. Grant of the Union at Appomattox Court House in Virginia.
April 14: John Wilkes Booth shoots Abraham Lincoln in Ford's Theatre during the play *Our American Cousin.*
April 15: Lincoln dies at 7:22 a.m. in the Petersen Boarding House, across the street from Ford's Theatre.
May 4: Lincoln is buried at Oak Ridge Cemetery in Springfield, Illinois.

INTRODUCTION

～WWW～

FINAL WORDS

AMONG THE MEMORIES OF THOSE WHO LIVED THROUGH that dreadful April day so many years ago was the way the afternoon sunshine quickly descended into evening gloom. With darkness had come fog and a gentle mist that dampened the nation's capital. A chill followed, an unwelcome surprise after the warmth of day. Then there was the moon. It appeared late on that Friday night, leaving the hours just after sunset dark and unusually dreary. It announced itself first in the silvered edges of clouds and then, unhurriedly, came fully, brightly into view. In the years after, more than one man swore that before the night was done, the moon had turned bloodred. If true, it was a fitting banner over the events unfolding below.

At the White House, the Lincolns dined together. The president and First Lady listened as their son Robert, a young officer on General Grant's staff, excitedly described the siege of Petersburg and the magnificence of Lee's surrender at Appomattox. The Lincolns' other son, twelve-year-old Tad, felt slighted by the attention trained on his older brother and misbehaved to correct the injustice. It worked. Mrs. Lincoln scolded him for neglecting his meal and then, prompted by the mention of the Grants, told her husband that she had invited that lovely Clara Harris, daughter of Senator Ira Harris of New York, to accompany them to Ford's Theatre later in the evening. Young Miss Harris had thrilled at the chance to attend the play *Our American Cousin* with the First Family and had assured Mrs. Lincoln that her fiancé, Major Henry R. Rathbone, would cherish the opportunity as well. It was settled, then. The Lincolns would collect the young couple at the Harris home on H Street near Fourteenth.

Lincoln answered the news with a nod, but must have winced inwardly. He knew the truth: Miss Harris and Major Rathbone were to accompany the Lincolns because the more distinguished names in Washington had refused to attend. This, Lincoln had long understood, was his wife's fault. He genuinely loved Mary, but she was not an easy woman to abide. One of her traits in particular haunted his life: she was notoriously jealous. She screamed viciously at any woman who dared even to walk next to her husband. Many a Washington official's wife had been humiliated in public by the enraged First Lady, who thought nothing of making loud and tearful allegations of impropriety no matter who looked on. After one such scene, General Grant's wife swore she would never be in Mary Lincoln's presence again. So the Grants had excused themselves from this night at the theater, as had half a dozen of the city's eminent couples. This left the president of the United States and his First Lady to an outing with a junior officer and his date. It was galling to Lincoln, particularly on this night—when victory was in the air and the president was the toast of the Union. All of Washington knew that Mary's antics kept her husband from the honor due him, and they marveled at Lincoln's love for his wife.

Still, it had been a good day. After breakfast and the usual early visitors, there had been a cabinet meeting, this one attended by the victorious General Grant. As always when Lincoln's cabinet assembled, there was fierce debate. Today, the topic was the way Confederate lead-ers should be treated after the war and what economic aid ought to be offered to the Southern states. Lincoln listened, commented almost absentmindedly from time to time, and then turned with eagerness to General Grant. The president was desperate to know: What had it been like at Appomattox five days before? What kind of man was General Lee, and how had he handled himself in surrendering? With each word Grant spoke, Lincoln grew increasingly peaceful, ever more satisfied. There had been so much horror, so many years. He could be forgiven for reveling in the details of the end.

After a lunch with Mary, he had endured a series of still more meet-ings—with Vice President Johnson, with the assistant secretary of war, and with Nancy Bushrod, a former slave. Before the day's paperwork was done, he had pardoned a deserter who had been sentenced to death. "I think the boy can do us more good above ground than underground," he quipped.

Then came a promised carriage ride with Mary. It was a magical day. The sun's warmth seemed to penetrate the soul while the perfume of flowers filled the nostrils and dogwood trees displayed their beauty like strutting peacocks. The Lincolns rode alone. Only their carriage driver attended them, and this rare privacy encouraged a welcome inti macy. Mrs. Lincoln commented that her husband almost startled her with his cheerfulness. He replied that it was because the war was at a close. "We must both be cheerful in the future. Between the war, and the loss of our darling Willie, we have both been very miserable." It was true, though the mention of the son lost to typhoid a few years before stung the still-grieving Mary. Fortunately, the pain did not linger. The two continued happily toward the Navy Yard, lost in imagining the future and how they would travel and learn to love life again in the years to come.

This was the mood that pervaded as the Lincolns left the White House for Ford's Theatre at 8:05 that evening. From their carriage, they waved to well-wishers along the road in the black, wet night. They were joined by their guests at Senator Harris's home and arrived finally at the theater sometime shortly after 8:30. The play had already begun.

President Lincoln's box at Ford's Theatre

It didn't matter. When the president's party entered the second-story viewing box reserved for them that evening, the orchestra's conductor took note, raised his baton to interrupt the actors on stage, and signaled the start of "Hail to the Chief." The more than sixteen hundred people in the theater exploded into applause. Lincoln bowed in response, his hand over his heart, and then bowed again when those below continued their grateful cheers.

Order returned and the play resumed. Not overly interested in the happenings onstage, the Lincolns quietly continued the flirty intimacy they had kindled earlier that afternoon.

"What will Miss Harris think of my hanging on to you so," Mary asked, referring to her grip on her husband's hand.

"Why, she will think nothing about it," he assured.

This teasing continued. Unnoticed was the figure who had just stepped through the outer door of the president's box. The man was deliberate, even graceful in his movements. He locked the door behind him and then braced it shut with a board he had placed nearby during a visit to the theater earlier that day. Turning then to the inner door, he peered through a hole he had bored just hours before with his pocketknife. He could see what he needed to see: the back of the president's head.

Unaware of the man and enjoying a newfound tenderness with his wife, Lincoln returned happily to the theme he and Mary had touched upon during their lovely afternoon carriage ride. In a gentle whisper, the president assured that after the war, "we will not return immediately to Springfield. We will go abroad among strangers where I can rest."

The figure at the door now stepped silently into the president's box. He paused and took stock of the mere four feet between himself and the president. Slowly, smoothly, the man pulled a .44-caliber Derringer pistol from his pocket and waited. He was listening for lines from the play on the stage below. They would signal his next move.

"We will visit the Holy Land," Lincoln continued, leaning toward Mary so as not to disturb the others.

Now, hearing what he had been waiting for in an actor's words, the stranger—himself an actor named John Wilkes Booth—stepped forward and lifted his pistol toward the president's head.

In the sacred seconds that remained, Lincoln spoke again—before the assassin's shot entered his brain just inches behind the left ear, before the blood and the confusion and the manhunts and the grief, before the ages took him and the great soul left its earthly home to hover over a nation still struggling to be born. Lincoln spoke once more.

"We will visit the Holy Land and see those places hallowed by the footsteps of the Savior," the president said.

And then, nearly as the Derringer ball cracked the air, "There is no place I so much desire to see as Jerusalem."

These, then, are the final, surprising words of Abraham Lincoln in this world.

Or are they? It is natural that some should doubt. The words are rarely included in accounts of Lincoln's assassination. Schoolchildren do not learn them as they do the other facts of Lincoln's life. Indeed, the sentiments are too religious for most teachers to dare include in their lessons. Scholars tend to exclude this episode also, usually because of a similar hesitation about religion.

It is understandable. Lincoln was, after all, a religious oddity. He never joined a church. In fact, he went through periods in his life when he was openly antireligion—even anti-God. In his later years, he spoke often of God but rarely of Jesus Christ. That he was attending a bawdy play on Good Friday—the day Christians set aside to contemplate the crucifixion of their Savior—seems perfectly consistent with the image of Lincoln that has come to us through the years. It is reasonable to doubt that he would call Christ the Savior and declare himself eager to see the Holy Land in the last moments of his life.

Surely, critics will say, to insist that these words are true or that they are any reflection of Lincoln's faith is part of a religious reworking of his life, part of a misguided attempt by the pious to refashion him into a gleaming religious icon of some imagined national religion. Surely this is the fruit of bad research and pitiful scholarship—more myth than history.

Yet there the words are, and they are no invention. They come to us, indirectly, from the only person who could know with certainty: Mary Lincoln. Apparently, in 1882, Mrs. Lincoln reported her husband's last utterances to Noyes W. Miner, the pastor of the First Baptist Church in Springfield, Illinois. Miner reported his conversations with Mary Lincoln in a manuscript entitled "Personal Reminiscences of Abraham Lincoln," now kept at the Illinois State Historical Library. We might be suspicious of such a religiously charged remembrance retold by a clergyman were it not that respected scholarly volumes, such as the oft-consulted *Recollected Words of Abraham Lincoln,* include the Lincoln/Miner version of Lincoln's final words in its pages.[1] Eminent Lincoln scholars—such as Allen C. Guelzo in *Abraham Lincoln: Redeemer President* and Wayne Temple in *Abraham Lincoln: From Skeptic to Prophet*—regard the words as true.[2] The popular Doris Kearns Goodwin alludes to them as well in her best-selling *Team of*

Ford's Theatre in the days just after Lincoln's assassination. Note the guards at the door and the black crepe draped from the windows.

Rivals: The Political Genius of Abraham Lincoln.[3] As important, Dr. James Cornelius, curator of the Lincoln collection at the Abraham Lincoln Presidential Library in Springfield, Illinois, in referring to Mary Lincoln's account of her husband's final utterances, has said, "We believe the words to be substantiated."[4]

So what of it? Why is this important? It is simply that if Abraham

Lincoln did indeed speak of a Savior and a longed-for pilgrimage in his last moments on earth, then there was likely a journey, a progression, some dawning of spiritual reality in his life. In his early years he had been nearly the village atheist. He mocked preachers, wrote against "revealed religion" and carried a Bible about town only to ridicule it. His friend and law partner, William Herndon, said that Lincoln once asked him to remove the word *God* from a speech because Lincoln was sure "no such personality ever existed."[5] Even Mary Lincoln once said, "Mr. Lincoln had no faith and no hope."[6]

Yet against this we have Mary's own account of her husband's dramatic final words, and they do not stand alone. We also have the magnificent Second Inaugural Address, perhaps the noblest American political sermon, given only weeks before the great man's death. It, too, challenges the prevailing view of an atheistic or religiously skeptical Lincoln, and it is unquestionably the fruit of Lincoln's mind. So almost certainly, there was a spiritual journey of some kind in Abraham Lincoln's life, in this man who has nearly come to be regarded as the soul of America, and if so we ought to know it in order to better understand not only Lincoln but our country and even ourselves as well.

What has usually discredited such efforts in the past is that Lincoln's religious life is seldom allowed to speak for itself. Instead, it becomes the repository of religious agendas. This began immediately after his death. That he was killed on Good Friday and at the end of a war that was as much moral crusade as any in history transformed him in memory; in fact, it transformed him by dawn of the Easter Sunday morning two days after his death. He became no longer slain president, but crucified martyr—even crucified savior. Nearly every Christian denomination has claimed him for their own, as have people of religious persuasions as varied as spiritualists, Hindus, and Jews.[7] Each persuasion finds in Lincoln a reflection of itself; each seeks to explain his greatness as a product of its beliefs.

History cannot, should not, be treated in such a way. Those who believe in a sovereign God who rules history should be humble enough before the face of their Creator to report the past as it was, no matter how disturbing, and to always understand themselves as feeling their way along the contours of providence. To invent, to contort history into neatly packaged spiritual lessons, does disservice to the very idea of God's sovereignty. Similarly, those who do not believe in a divine being but rather in the processes of history also have an obligation to the past. If man's story in this world is all the truth we have, then how much heavier is our responsibility to it, how much more sacred our devotion to fact?

Perhaps more than most figures from the past, Lincoln's life demands this fidelity to history as it was lived. He always surprises, always resists confinement to the forms and definitions imposed upon him. He lived in an age still foreign to us. He was a complicated soul, an innovative mind, and an oppressed spirit. He was raw and earthy and poetic. He could be ambitious and enraged and cold. He rose from a spare cabin to the White House, and did so in an age of titanic conflict, of near incomprehensible change. We can strive to know what we may of Lincoln. We can hope to understand. Yet never can we confine him; never can we seek to make him conform. His story, particularly the story of his faith, ought to be written with respect for these mysteries in honor of both the man and the nation he served.

This book, then, is intended to explore Lincoln's life with Mary's recollection of his final words in mind and with his grand Second Inaugural Address ringing in our ears. Lincoln seems to have made a religious journey of some kind. It was, perhaps, the product of a struggle, a battle—with preachers, with doctrines, with the Bible, with providence, with religious politics, perhaps even with God himself. What can we know of that battle, and what meaning does it have for our time?

ONE

~~~~~~

A MOTHER'S LEGACY

I T WAS ON A DAY EARLY IN THE 1850s WHEN ABRAHAM Lincoln, then a rising Springfield lawyer, was traveling with his partner, William Herndon, to try a case in a county nearby. The matter to be decided before the court had in part to do with inherited traits, with what a man received from his ancestors and what was uniquely his own. Something about this theme stirred Lincoln and, while his buggy rattled and jerked over rutted roads, he began to speak of his childhood.

Herndon would never forget the moment. Lincoln seldom revealed much of himself and certainly never spoke of his early life. A friend had called him the most "shut-mouthed" man he ever knew.[1] It was true, and it frustrated journalists and biographers no end. When J. L. Scripps of the *Chicago Tribune* proposed to write Lincoln's story, he found his subject mystified at the thought of it. "Why, Scripps," Lincoln said, "it is a great piece of folly to attempt to make anything out of me or my early life. It can all be condensed into a single sentence, and that sentence you will find in *Gray's Elegy*: 'The short and simple annals of the poor.' That's my life, and that's all you or anyone else can make out of it."[2]

The subject of the trial had bored into him, though, and in time he decided to open his soul to his friend. "Billy, I'll tell you something, but keep it a secret while I live. My mother was a bastard, was the daughter of a nobleman, so called of Virginia. My mother's mother was poor and credulous, and she was shamefully taken advantage of by the man. My mother inherited his qualities and I hers."[3]

It was not the kind of thing a man disclosed casually, and Herndon listened silently, struck by the sadness in his friend's voice. After a long pause, Lincoln continued. He believed, he said, that from his Virginia grandfather and thus from his mother he received "his power of analysis, his logic, his mental activity, his ambition, and all the qualities that distinguished him" from the other members of his family.[4] But he was wrestling with how these traits had come to him. Almost pleadingly, he turned to Herndon and asked, "Did you never notice that bastards are generally smarter, shrewder and more intellectual than others? Is it because it is stolen?"[5]

Finally, and in a melancholy tone that would stay with Herndon all his life, Lincoln ruefully said, "All that I am or hope ever to be I get from my mother. God bless her."[6]

We can forgive Lincoln his view of heredity. It now seems primitive, almost bigoted, but it was typical of his age. Of greater importance is what these words reveal of him and his early world—the grinding lot of the poor, their misuse by the powerful, their ignorance and shame, their uncertainty about past and future. These images are far from the Disneyesque, Americana versions of Lincoln's life now so familiar, but they are consistent with the grief and tormenting loneliness that had filled his childhood years. He was haunted by these memories, as he was by much else, and it is revealing that amid so much agony in remembrance he was certain of one thing: his mother made him who he was.

Nancy Hanks Lincoln likely evoked such tender memories in her

Abraham Lincoln's boyhood home in Indiana

son because though hers was a hard and toilsome life—she died withered and toothless at the age of thirty-four—she lived her years with exceptional grace. She was taller than most females of her age, but she was thin—some guessed 120 pounds—and gave the impression that she "inclined to consumption," meaning that she had the cough and raspy breathing associated with tuberculosis.[7] She had dark skin, brown hair, and gray eyes that were long remembered. Her prominent forehead and sharp facial features are reflected in the later pictures of her son.

It adds texture to the traditional portrait of Nancy Lincoln to learn that she was one of the best wrestlers in Kentucky. It also helps to remind us how far removed frontier life was from our own. Apparently, in rural regions of early nineteenth-century Kentucky, wrestling was not a sport for males only. Usher Linder, a Lincoln family friend, recalled in his memoirs that Nancy Lincoln

> was said to be a very strong-minded woman, and one of the most
> athletic women in Kentucky. In a fair wrestle, she could throw most
> of the men who ever put her powers to the test. A reliable gentleman

told me he heard the late Jack Thomas, clerk of the Grayson Court, say he had frequently wrestled with her, and she invariably laid him on his back.[8]

She was also known for her fine singing and gift for reciting verse. We can imagine how her melodic voice must have filled the Lincolns' rude cabin in the wilderness, wrapping her children in love. While the family worked, she recounted Bible stories and recited bits of poetry. This, surely, was the beginning of her son's literary sense. And he adored her. She was "highly intellectual by nature, had a strong memory, acute judgment, and was cool and heroic," he recalled.[9] She left his life and this world when he was nine, but it is a testament to the depth of her love that he attributed all the good that came afterward to her care.

Among the legacies that Nancy Hanks left the world in her son, there are three that are important to us in pondering his faith. They will seem, initially, disparate and unrelated, but each coalesces with the others to form the early framework of what would become Abraham Lincoln's religious life. Fortunately, they are also among the more fascinating elements of his personality and character.

⁒

It is odd, perhaps, that Abraham would describe his mother, Nancy, as "highly intellectual." She could not read, or at best could not read well. She had learned to make out sentences in the Bible, and this awed illiterate neighbors, but it was nothing like knowing an alphabet and thus having the key to language and literature. Still, Lincoln knew what he was saying. Nancy was smart, insightful, and quick to learn, and she retained what she knew. She lived in a world of hearing rather than reading, of the oral transmission of knowledge. Listeners were expected to memorize. Nancy could recite long passages of the Bible, speeches from Shakespeare, tales from *Aesop's*

Fables, and haunting accounts of burning Protestants from Foxe's *Book of Martyrs*. She had also mastered favorite passages from the Declaration of Independence and the Constitution, and these likely informed Abraham's earliest political sensibilities. He saw her as intellectual because she skillfully and wisely articulated the world to him. She explained the ways of men and the meaning of moss on a certain side of a tree and the purposes of providence in terms that gave him an enduring map of the world.

Her intellectual legacy is best found in her son's magnificent intellectual achievements. It was Nancy who first instilled a love of learning in young Abraham and she who insisted he go to school when he could. He had already briefly attended two schools by the time he left Kentucky at the age of seven. One was run by Zachariah Riney, the other by Caleb Hazel, surely names that ought to live long in American educational history. When the family moved to Indiana in 1816, Nancy again sent young Abe off to school as often as possible, first under the tutelage of Azel Dorsey, whose school was a mile and a half from the Lincoln farm. He attended Dorsey's off and on until he was ten, then occasionally the school of an Andrew Crawford until he was fourteen, before studying under a Mr Swaney in his seventeenth year.

None of this schooling was consistent or in any way thorough. Lincoln himself said,

> There were some schools, so called; but no qualification ever required of a teacher, beyond "readin', writin', and cipherin'" to the Rule of Three. If a straggler supposed to understand Latin happened to sojourn into the neighborhood, he was looked upon as a wizard.[10]

Carl Sandburg, the most poetic of Lincoln historians, has written,

> The Schoolmasters were paid by the parents in venison, hams, corn, animals skins, and other produce. Four miles from home to school

and four miles to home again Abe walked for his learning, saying later that "all his schooling did not amount to one year."[11]

It was, nonetheless, beneficial, and it kept a love of knowledge burning brightly in Abraham's mind. It was also a monument to Nancy's insistence that her son achieve what she could not.

That young Abe attended school at all is confirmation that Nancy won her running battles with her husband. Thomas Lincoln was a hulking, demanding, disapproving man who valued his son's physical strength but cared little for his mind. He interpreted Abe's literary bent as laziness. Little infuriated him as much as seeing the boy under a tree with a book while chores waited. He feared that neighbors would notice and conclude that Abe was slothful and not worth hiring. This was a threat to the family's well-being. By law Abe owed the fruit of his labors to his father until he was twenty-one. Thomas intended to see that the boy produced

Thomas Lincoln, c. 1850

and was not beyond using beatings to make his wishes known. After 1818, when Nancy died of the dreaded milk sickness, she was no longer there to protect her son from his father's rage.

By then, though, it was nearly too late to stop what was coming.

Abe's mind awakened; he quickly learned to read. He then learned to write. This delighted him so much that he not only practiced with a piece of coal on a shovel by firelight, as the popular and true story goes, but he wrote on the entire Lincoln home. Thomas often returned in the evenings to find words written in chalk on the log walls of his cabin, on the family's plates, on tools, and on any stone surface flat enough to use. Then came books. Once Abraham Lincoln learned their power, he began the journey toward becoming an exceptional man.

His early literary life has become legend, and yet what has been recounted is largely true. Though books were few on the frontier, they were cherished, owned, and traded even by those who couldn't read them but who understood their worth. Abe read the Bible and then borrowed *Aesop's Fables, Pilgrim's Progress, Robinson Crusoe,* Grimshaw's *History of the United States,* and Weems's *The Life of George Washington.* He also devoured *The Kentucky Preceptor,* William Scott's *Lessons in Elocution,* and Caleb Bingham's *The American Speaker* and *Columbian Orator,* these last two promising to "improve youth and Others in the Ornamental and Useful Art of Eloquence." These books we know he read for certain. There were dozens of others whose titles are lost to us. What we can know is their effect. Sandburg wrote that for Lincoln, "books lighted lamps in the dark rooms of his gloomy hours."[12] They also introduced him to the world beyond his father's farm.

Reading began to make young Abe a man of reason and reflection. He began to suspect the superstitions he was taught, to question the myths handed down. Like many devoted readers, he felt more at home in that otherworld of thought and ideas, of history and epic lives, than he did in the world defined by the cabin, the barn, the sickle, and the ax. He was more enamored of Weems's Washington than he could ever be of his father, more delighted in the invisible presence of Shakespeare's Puck than he was with the characters at the general store. But books were beyond just an escape. They charted a path. They taught that thought, reason, and rational processes were doors to—what?—achievement, perhaps. Or at the least deliverance from Thomas's home. Maybe even to some form of power and fame.

It is important to mention here that with his mother's gift of intellect and love of knowledge came a poetic sense as well. He lived in a world of slang, twangy speech, bad grammar, and odd dialects. When he discovered reading, and thus vocabulary, he grew fascinated with the meaning and euphony of words. He rolled new terms around his mouth, meditated on dictionary definitions, and tried out these new tools, sometimes clumsily, on townspeople who stared at him blankly. To this love of the meaning of words he wed a gift for their grace and beauty. This came more naturally—from his people's English roots and the poetry, storytelling, and song of the early American experience. It would take time to mature in him, but when it did he would write poetry of impressive beauty and would give the world some of its most enduring phrases: "mystic chords of memory," "the better angels of our nature," "to bind up the nation's wounds." If it is true, as we are told by experts, that authors write guided by a voice in their minds, a narrative voice that first awakens when a child is read to early in life, then it is to Nancy Hanks that much of the credit is due for the literary legacy of Abraham Lincoln. Truly, there is a line to be drawn from a rugged cabin in the Indiana woods filled with the music of a mother's voice and the hallowed words of the Gettysburg Address.

What came of all of this also was a mastery of the skills of self-education. He gained early the confidence that he could learn what he needed to know on his own: through books, by observation, and by enlisting mentors. It served him well. In time, he would become a lawyer, ascend in politics, and reach the presidency informed by an aggressive program of self-education, all having never set foot in a classroom beyond his eighteenth year. Even when he was commander in chief during the tactically complicated Civil War, he masterfully counseled his generals based on what he had learned from a few military texts—texts he had usually read only a short time before. He became his own university. In this, he joined Jefferson, Franklin, and Washington—among dozens of other eminent Americans—in achieving greatness by first mastering the art of self-education. This, too, was Nancy Lincoln's gift to her son, and it would have a defining effect not only on his rise to power but also upon the religious seasons that came to define his life.

⤬

A second legacy from Nancy might seem more a curse than a gift, but it may have helped to give us the Lincoln our nation reveres. She would pass on to him her own struggle with depression, with that enveloping darkness that lurks, for some, ever at the soul's door. This would merge with a Lincoln family heritage of mental illness to become a force in Abraham that he fought to subdue all his days. It would leave him scarred, and it would even deform parts of his personality, but by striving to master it and by remembering what he had experienced in those hours of suffocating gloom, he emerged a man of greater wisdom, wit, and humanity.

It was said by those who knew Nancy that her life was "beclouded by a spirit of sadness."[13] Herndon, Lincoln's friend, law partner, and biographer, wrote that her face "was marked with an expression of melancholy which fixed itself in the memory of everyone who ever saw or knew her."[14] It is tempting to believe that this was simply fruit of the life she led. It was true she passed most of her days in bleak frontier settlements, the wife of an unsympathetic man and chained to mindless, soul-numbing work. Sandburg wrote that when she died, she had only "memories of monotonous, endless everyday chores."[15] Then, too, there was the lifelong cloud of her illegitimacy. Lesser burdens were known to drive some frontier women insane. But something darker, more ominous, tortured her, and it was more than what we now call "the blues." A resident despondency, a permanent grief, dwelled in her; it is not going too far to believe that this reached what would now be termed depression, and that Abraham absorbed this same "spirit of sadness" into his soul.

If he did, that spirit intermingled in him with the Lincoln family heritage of mental instability. The Lincoln men were nearly all considered melancholy, but some had problems far more extreme. A great-uncle once told a court of law that he was troubled by "a deranged mind." Mood swings, drinking, and even violence troubled others in the family. Onlookers spoke of "Lincoln characteristics." They meant vast mood swings and a desperate, almost forced sense of humor. Abraham's first cousin had a daughter who was committed to the Illinois State Hospital for the Insane. The jury who sent her there reported that her disease had already tortured her for thirteen years by the time she appeared before them. At that hospital, a worker noted, "Her father was cousin to Abraham Lincoln, and she has features much like his." A historian writing late in the 1800s reported that the Lincolns "suffered from all the nervous disorders known. Some were on the ragged edge." A family member described these mental dysfunctions as "the Lincoln horrors."[16]

Abraham Lincoln avoided the extremes of his family's psychological deformities, but he still suffered from a dark, draining, despair-inducing force that seemed at times to bore into the center of his being. Shortly after Lincoln's death, Herndon described his slain friend as "a sad looking man: his melancholy dripped from him as he walked."[17] Townspeople reported that he was indeed the saddest-looking man they had ever known. Lincoln's friends stood what we now call "suicide watch" more than once, and Lincoln himself said that he was careful not to carry a pocketknife lest he sink into a depression—his word for it was *hypo*—and harm himself.[18] During one episode of his life, he reported, "I am now the most miserable man living. If what I feel were equally distributed to the whole human family, there would not be one cheerful face on the earth. Whether I shall ever be better I cannot tell; I awfully forbode I shall not."[19] Friends who loved him when he was jovial and joking avoided him when he was in a hypo. He could suck the color from the world, no matter the joy of the occasion. To a young girl he knew, he wrote this bleak verse:

> *To Rosa—*
> *You are young, and I am older;*
> *You are hopeful, I am not—*
> *Enjoy life, ere it grows colder—*
> *Pluck the roses ere they rot.*[20]

The poor girl had only asked Lincoln to sign her autograph book. He couldn't help himself. His depression was spilling over. It was this dark spirit that moved intimates to describe him in terms first used of the suffering Messiah. Lincoln, they said with a shake of the head, "was a man acquainted with grief."[21]

Though he did not seem troubled by depression in his childhood, the emotional chemistry of his later melancholy was undoubtedly formed during that time. It is not hard to find potentially defining inci dents. An infant brother died when Lincoln was three. He might have been too young to understand, but in the manner of children, he likely felt more than he could comprehend of the grief in his home. Then there was the influence of Nancy herself. He would have steeped in her "spirit of sadness" whether he understood its source or not. Always there was the distance and disapproval of his father, the effect of which on a young man's soul is nearly too devastating to describe.

Always, too, there was death. Most traumatic of all was the death of his mother. Historian Fawn Brodie has concluded that "his mother's death was related to Lincoln's life-long tendency to melancholy."[22] This seems likely. It has long been the insistence of psychologists that "bereavement in childhood is one of the most significant factors in the development of depressive illness in later life," and that "a depressive illness in later years is often a reaction to a present loss or bereavement which is associated with a more serious loss or bereavement in child-hood."[23] If this is true, there is no question that Nancy's death—both the fact of it and the manner of it—was traumatic enough to have dug a well of grief that overflowed into the rest of Lincoln's days.

It occurred two years after the family moved from Kentucky to their new farm in Indiana. Abraham was nine. What was then called milk sickness suddenly struck the Lincolns' tiny community along the banks of Pigeon Creek. Few illnesses were as feared, for there was no cure and it claimed thousands of lives. Later, researchers discovered it was caused by drinking milk from cows that had eaten white snakeroot; this led to tremetol poisoning. In Lincoln's day, milk sickness was evil and mysterious, called variously "the puking fever," "river sickness," and "fall poison." Once infected, a victim first felt weary, then experienced trembles; these progressed to pain, numbness, and cramps. Nausea would set in, and then both emotional depression and a burning sensation in the pit of the stomach. Vomiting and convulsions followed. The skin turned pale and cold. The breath grew short, the heartbeat irregular, and finally the victim slipped into a coma.

In late September 1818, Nancy contracted the disease. It took her a week to die. Young Abraham watched as, in Sandburg's words, "there came to Nancy Hanks Lincoln that white coating of the tongue; her vitals burned; the tongue turned brownish; her feet and hands grew cold and colder, her pulse slow and slower."[24] She knew she was dying. Already her aunt and uncle had been cut down by the sickness and were buried in a clearing nearby. She knew she would follow them soon. Calling Abe to her side, she weakly placed a hand on his head and told him to be kind and good, to love his family, and to worship God.[25] She passed away on October 5. Young Abe helped his father hew the casket and lower his mother into the ground.

Grief was heavy upon the little family, made worse for the children by Thomas's decision to return to Kentucky to find a wife. He left Abraham and his older sister, Sarah, in the hands of their twenty-year-old cousin and was gone for months. The children had long given their father up for dead when he returned with a new wife, Sarah Bush Johnston. Abe and his sister were thin, dirty, filled with fear, and barely comprehending. Stepmother Sarah immediately got about the cleaning and mending necessary to transform the by then filthy cabin into a cozy home. She helped Thomas's children through their pain and on with their lives. Lincoln spoke of her with affection all his days.

Still, his mother's death wounded him, and in a way that was worse for not being visible. Years later, another episode in his life exposed a toxic and unseen ocean of grief, which may give credence to the theory that depression in later life is related to early anguish over the death of a loved one. This second episode was his storied relationship with Ann Rutledge.

Lincoln first met Ann Rutledge when he moved to New Salem in 1831 and began taking meals in her family's boardinghouse. He could not help noticing her. She had bright blue eyes, billowing blonde hair and was witty and intelligent. Her laughter lifted his gloom. In August of 1835, Ann became ill. Lincoln visited her frequently as she lay weak and miserable in the family cabin. On the twenty-fifth, she died.

All who knew her grieved, but something in Lincoln's grief invaded his sanity. Friends first noticed it when Lincoln told them he was haunted by the thought of rain falling on Ann's grave. He pulled away from company, became indifferent to his surroundings, and descended somewhere inside himself. He then mentioned to a friend he was thinking about suicide. This is when the suicide watch began, and friends soon learned to fear for the effect of storms or fog on Lincoln's mind. Finally, those who cared for him locked him up to keep him from harming himself. "That was the time the community said he was crazy," an acquaintance recalled.[26]

Lincoln's collapse would be understandable if he and Ann had been deeply in love and committed to each other. But it is possible, even likely, that this was not true. In fact, it is possible the entire extent of Lincoln's relationship with Rutledge has been exaggerated through the years. As Joshua Wolf Shenk points out in his masterful *Lincoln's Melancholy*, it is probable that a love affair was assumed by friends and neighbors only after Rutledge's death and only after Lincoln's agonized response seemed to suggest the two might have been passionately in love. In truth, many in New Salem who would have known of any such love affair had never even heard of a relationship between the two. Only after Ann's death did they conclude otherwise and only because Lincoln was so distraught. Rutledge's brother, Robert, recalled that Lincoln "became plunged in despair, and many of his friends feared that reason would desert her throne. His extraordinary emotions were regarded as strong evidence of the existence of the tenderest relations between himself and the deceased." In other words, after Ann's death and after Lincoln's implosion, friends assumed there must have been deep feeling. Yet a neighbor of the Rutledges reported, "I did not know of any engagement or tender passages between Mr L and Miss R at the time. But after her death . . . he seemed to be so much affected and grieved so hardly that I then supposed there must have been some proximate cause."[27]

It is likely that this death of a friend when Lincoln was in his mid-twenties summoned grief and anguish that had first filled him years before—when, as a frightened nine-year-old, he watched his mother die an excruciating death in a bleak cabin in the wilderness. It is a pattern that would repeat itself often in his life, for he would know many deaths—of a mother, a sister, sons, comrades, and hundreds of thousands more in the war he could not prevent. He would be haunted by the thought of rain falling on graves all his days. And the darkness came, as it had for his ancestors and for the mother whose heartache spilled into his life.

Nonetheless, Lincoln's story is, in part, that of a man who beat back the spirits that came for him in the night. He might well have been crushed by his woes, by the death of the first son and then the second, by the madness of his wife, or the hatred of his foes—even by the devils in his thoughts. He did not yield, though, not ultimately. As important, he mined the valleys of depression for what riches he could find. He emerged to see life differently from other men, to understand and feel as though he were looking in from outside of human existence. For that is what depression is—a way of seeing and feeling life as though from another, tormented world. This ability to outlast the darkness was one more gift from his mother, and it, too, would shape the brand of faith he eventually made his own.

Of all the gifts Nancy Lincoln bequeathed her son, surely her faith was chief among them. We should recall that her last words to him—with her feeble, milk-sick hand upon his head—were "worship God." It is likely this charge came back to him again and again through the years. We know her other words of faith did. A friend recalled Lincoln saying that "his instruction by [his mother] in letters and morals, and especially the Bible stories, and the interest and love he acquired in reading the Bible through this teaching of his mother, had been the strongest and most influential experience in his life." Lincoln also said that throughout his life, "when he read certain verses which he had in early boyhood committed to memory by hearing her repeat them as she went about her household tasks, the tones of his mother's voice would come to him and he would seem to hear her speak those verses again."[28] Clearly, Nancy Lincoln's expressions of faith lived brightly in Abraham's mind.

Yet it may well have been his mother's unique brand of faith, combined with his broader exposure to the fiery religion of the frontier, which pushed Lincoln away from the spiritual vision of his parents and, for a season, even from belief in God. To understand how this was so requires that we understand the unique religious movements then sweeping the American West.

The dense woods of Abraham Lincoln's youth

As the United States stepped from the century of its birth into the new and promising nineteenth century, religious leaders looked about with concern. America was in spiritual decline, they believed. It had been so since the Revolution, a war that had nearly destroyed the founding faith of the country. In the devastation of those days, pastors were killed. Colonial Bibles and hymnals were burned. Churches were turned into riding stables or houses of prostitution. Seminaries were abandoned. With the institutions of faith destroyed, the high tide of religious fervor that helped carry the colonies into battle dwindled to a trickle by war's end.

It did not help that some of the most beloved figures of the Revolution became outspoken critics of Christianity in the years that followed. In 1784, Ethan Allen, the hero of Fort Ticonderoga, published a book entitled *Reason, the Only Oracle of Man*, in which he viciously attacked traditional Christianity. Allen was joined by Thomas Paine, beloved by patriots for his tract *Common Sense*, which had movingly made the case for American independence in

1776 when many a colonist was still unsure. In 1794, Paine published *The Age of Reason*, a venomous assault on biblical Christianity. He argued that "the Christian mythologists, calling themselves the Christian Church, have erected their fable which for absurdity and extravagance, is not exceeded by anything that is to be found in the mythology of the ancients."[29] The book of Genesis, he wrote, is filled with "downright lies" that "drops to the level with the Arabian Tales, without the merit of being entertaining."[30] The Christian gospel he regarded as "a fable of Jesus Christ"; the virgin birth he thought "blasphemously obscene."[31]

American Christianity was weak and under attack. The opening of the frontier dealt another blow. The promise of riches, adventure, and distance from the restrictions of the East drew men to the wild but gave them no redeeming vision. As Henry Adams wrote in 1800:

> The Pilgrims of Plymouth, the Puritans of Boston, the Quakers of Pennsylvania, all avowed a moral purpose and began by making institutions that consciously reflected a moral idea. No such character belonged to the colonization of 1800. From Lake Erie to Florida, in a long, unbroken line, pioneers were at work, cutting into the forests with the energy of so many beavers, and with no more express purpose than the beavers they drove away.[32]

In 1798, the General Assembly of the Presbyterian Church stated the case more desperately.

> We perceive, with pain and fearful apprehension, a general dereliction of religious principle and practice among our fellow-citizens, a visible and prevailing impiety and contempt of the laws and institutions of religion, and an abounding infidelity which in many instances tends to Atheism itself . . .
> The eternal God has a controversy with this nation.[33]

Moved by these concerns, the Christian denominations urged their members to pray and to hope for a return to God. In the language of the faithful, this meant revival—a passionate return to the living God. And revival came. Led by men of grit and fire, mass spiritual awakenings began to occur throughout the nation. There was one at Yale University led by Timothy Dwight, a grandson of Jonathan Edwards. Others arose throughout New England. Outpourings also occurred in the Southern states and were reported as far away as Canada. Yet it was in Kentucky, in the years just before Abraham Lincoln was born, that the most raw and dramatic revivals occurred, and these would set the stage not only for Lincoln's journey of faith but also for the course of religion in the American West.

It began in Logan County, an area so corrupt it had earned the name Rogues' Harbor. Murderers, horse thieves, highway robbers, and counterfeiters had settled there in large numbers, just out of reach of the law. The U.S. Congress knew of such places but felt powerless to regulate them, complaining that "the immunity which offenders experience attracts as to an asylum, the most vile and abandoned criminals, and at the same time deters useful and virtuous persons from making settlements in such society."[34]

A buckskinned Presbyterian preacher named James McGready decided to see what he could do. He was a cross between Billy Graham and Daniel Boone, a blend of frontiersman and prophet that became familiar in the American West. In 1798, he began to preach in Logan County and eventually drew enough souls to sustain three churches, one by each of the three rivers that flowed through the area—the Muddy, the Red, and the Gasper. McGready had bigger things in view, though, and determined to call his three congregations to prayer for a widespread work of renewal. He asked his followers to commit to prayer every Saturday evening and Sunday morning and to fast the third Saturday of each month. He also asked them to bind themselves together in a covenant of prayer:

When we consider the Word and promises of a compassionate God, to the poor lost family of Adam, we find the strongest encouragement for Christians to pray in faith—to ask in the name of Jesus for the conversion of their fellow men. . . . With these promises before us, we feel encouraged to unite our supplications to a prayer-hearing God, for the out-pouring of His Spirit, that His people may be quickened and comforted, and that our children, and sinners generally, may be converted.[35]

Little happened for a year, but in July of 1799, at the Red River congregation, excitement began to rise as "some of the boldest, most daring sinners in the county covered their faces and wept bitterly" in repentance.[36] A few months later, at a quarterly communion service, still more notorious rebels were converted, but these were not the sweet, organ-music-accompanied events of later years. Men wept out their repentance with agonizing groans and shouted their spiritual victories. When conviction rested heavily upon these rough, illiterate, hard-drinking souls, they often shook or writhed or fell to the ground as though dead. It was the way of hard-boiled frontier religion and would be for decades to come.

By 1800, the renewals under McGready's leadership had become widely known. In June of that year, other ministers joined together to help with the work. They were needed. More than five hundred people gathered that summer, many from miles away, and simply camped on the church grounds during the days of the protracted meetings. The "camp meeting" was born, as was the raucous kind of religious experience that would envelop Abraham Lincoln's world.

On the last day of the three-day meeting, the assembled worshipers celebrated communion and then waited until "the spirit fell." After a time of silence, hundreds began to weep. A Methodist minister from Nashville was charged with making a final appeal for conversions. He found he couldn't. As he tried to exhort the congregation to "let the

Lord Omnipotent reign in their hearts and submit to Him, and their souls should live," chaos broke out. A woman began shouting. The minister left his pulpit to quiet her. As he went, several Methodist friends pulled him aside for a warning: "You know these people. Presbyterians are much for order, they will not bear this confusion. Go back and be quiet." The minister started to return to his pulpit but as he did, the same force that caused the woman to shout fell upon him: "The power of God was strong upon me. I turned again and losing sight of the fear of man, I went through the house exhorting with all possible ecstasy and energy.[37] The dam had broken. Some parishioners lay on the floor, motionless. Others screamed for mercy. Still others shook and gyrated. It was the beginning of the Logan County Revival.

Word spread. The curious began arriving from all over Kentucky, and by late July a field had been cleared for yet another mass meeting. McGready and his fellow ministers were overwhelmed when more than ten thousand people attended. By comparison, the largest city in Kentucky at that time was Lexington, and it was a mere eighteen hundred souls. The revival was the largest event in the state. And the most unusual. As one observer recalled, while McGready and others preached,

> many, very many, fell down as men slain in battle and continued for hours together in an apparently breathless and motionless state, sometimes for a few minutes reviving and exhibiting symptoms of life by a deep groan or a piercing shriek or by a prayer for mercy fervently uttered. The gloom cloud that had covered their faces seemed gradually and visibly to disappear, and hope in smiles brightened into joy.[38]

All of this was precursor to the historic camp meeting that took place the following year. In 1801, Barton Stone, a McGready convert and a pastor at Cane Ridge, determined to clear a vast space for a meeting of unprecedented size. Even he, though, could not have anticipated that more than twenty-five thousand people would attend, nearly an eighth of the state's population.[39] For four days, the faithful roamed the great field that Stone and his helpers had cleared and listened to a variety of preachers who spoke from elevated stands. Half a dozen ministers spoke at once; the field being so large that none could interfere with the other. Again, as in Logan County, the effects of the meeting were dramatic.

Recalling this amazing scene years later in his biography, Stone catalogued the unusual manifestations that were common at Cane Ridge. There was the falling exercise, in which a person would "with a piercing scream, fall like a log on the floor, earth or mud, and appear as dead." Then there was a phenomenon called "the jerks." Stone insisted that in this manifestation a man's head "would be jerked backward and forward, or from side to side, so quickly that the features of the face could not be distinguished . . . I have seen the person stand in one place, and jerk backward and forward in quick succession, their head nearly touching the floor behind and before." There was also the dancing exercise, the barking exercise—in which "a person affected with the jerks, especially in his head, would often make a grunt, or bark, if you please, from the suddenness of the jerk"—and the laughing exercise. Understandably, there was the running exercise, in which "persons feeling something of these bodily agitations, through fear, attempted to run away." More pleasant was the singing exercise, which came from a person "in a very happy state of mind" singing "entirely from the breast."[40] Though Stone conceded that "there were many eccentricities, and much fanaticism in this excitement," he was also sure that "the good effects were seen and acknowledged in every neighborhood."[41]

Stone, of course, was an advocate of the revival. The report of a skeptic would be helpful too. James B. Finley attended Cane Ridge to criticize. He left unchanged but impressed.

The noise was like the roar of Niagara. The vast sea of human beings seemed to be agitated as if by a storm. I counted seven ministers, all preaching at one time, some on stumps, others in wagons . . . some of the people were singing, others praying, some crying for mercy in the most piteous accents, while others were shouting most vociferously. While witnessing these scenes, a peculiarly-strange sensation, such as I had never felt before, came over me. My heart beat tumultuously, my knees trembled, my lip quivered, and I felt as though I must fall to the ground. A strange supernatural power seemed to pervade the entire mass of mind there collected. Soon after, I left and went into the woods, and there I strove to rally and man up my courage.

After some time, I returned to the scene of the excitement, the waves of which, if possible, had risen still higher. The same awfulness of feeling came over me . . . I saw at least five hundred swept down in a moment, as if a battery of a thousand guns had been opened upon them, and then immediately followed shrieks and shouts that rent the very heavens. My hair rose up on my head . . . I fled into the woods a second time, and wished I had stayed at home.[42]

However sincere the participants in this revival were, however genuine these manifestations, it was natural that such oddities would draw spectators. They came by the thousands, and with them came peddlers, whiskey dealers, gamblers, speculators, hucksters, and even prostitutes. The camp meeting was the biggest event on the frontier, entertainment if not spiritual renewal for a people whose lives were filled with dreary, withering toil. It was little surprise that those not "touched by the spirit" might set up camp, take a swig from a jug, and enjoy the show with their neighbors.

This was far from the pure intentions of the revival's founders. When camp meetings became both entertainment and profitable business, they ceased to be of spiritual impact. There would always be genuine seasons of religious renewal, of course, some so powerful as to influence the course of American history. Yet where revivals became spectator sport, ministers worked ever harder to keep interest. In the pursuit of attention, their methods became extreme; their doctrines became warped; their egos became inflated. The style of the revivals—but rarely the spiritual content—became something to emulate, even by salesmen and carnival barkers, and the revivals sometimes descended to little more than traveling shows. Competition set in and then division. Barton Stone's sad summary of this troubled decline is telling: "These blessed effects would have continued, had not men put forth their hallowed hands to hold up their tottering ark, mistaking it for the ark of God."[43]

It was just as revivals like Red River and Cane Ridge were defining frontier religion that Abraham Lincoln entered the world. His parents absorbed the tenacious, fiery, sometimes rigid frontier brand of religion through their Baptist faith. When Abraham was born in 1809, the Lincolns were members of Little Mount Baptist Church. When they moved to Indiana in 1816, they joined the Pigeon Creek Baptist Church, which Thomas and his son helped build. Among a strict sect, the Lincolns were stricter still. They were "Separate Baptist," their conflict with "Regular Baptist" having largely to do with the matter of a creed. Separate Baptists wanted to add nothing to the pristine gospel of Christ and the church he founded—not a creed or a missionary organization or a Sunday school or a paid and educated clergy or even musical instruments in worship. They were often called "Hard Shell Baptists," both for their stubbornness and for their unshakable devotion to the doctrine of predestination. For them, free will did not exist. God had chosen who would be saved as surely as he determined daily events and the course of nations. There was no violating his sovereign choosing, and a man should be willing even to be condemned to hell in honor of divine predestination.

The Lincolns' stout religion merged with the ways of the camp meeting to produce a spirituality that was demanding, emotional, and full-throated. Herndon gives us a window into this culture by describing a scene that he believed portrayed Thomas and Nancy Lincoln just before they were married. Some historians dispute this, though nearly all agree that the scene does depict the kind of religion the Lincolns practiced.

It was at a camp-meeting . . . when a general shout was about to commence. Preparations were being made. . . . To the right a strong, athletic young man, about twenty-five years old, was being put in trim for the occasion, which was done by divesting him of all apparel except shirt and pants. On the left a young lady was being put in trim in much the same manner, so that her clothes would not be in the way, and so that, when her combs flew out, her hair would go into graceful braids. She, too, was young, not more than twenty perhaps. The performance commenced about the same time by the young man on the right and the young lady on the left. Slowly and gracefully they worked their way towards the centre, singing, shouting, hugging and kissing, generally their own sex, until at last nearer and nearer they came. The centre of the altar was reached, and the two closed, with their arms around each other, the man singing and shouting at the top of his voice,

> *"I have my Jesus in my arms*
> *Sweet as honey, strong as bacon ham."*[44]

Young Abraham's exposure to this type of religion was unfiltered. It was practiced in his home. It pervaded his community. It was discussed in the newspapers and in smoky whittling circles when the day's work was done. He also experienced it as it passed by his world. The Lincolns' home at Knob Creek in Kentucky was near the path of the famous Cumberland Trail, which ran from Louisville to Nashville.

Along that road moved a universe of unfamiliar lives that must have fascinated seven-year-old Abe. As Sandburg describes it, the boy would have seen

> covered wagons with settlers heading south, west, north, peddlers with tinware and notions, gangs of slaves or "kaffles" moving on foot ahead of an overseer or slave trader on horseback, and sometimes in dandy carriages congressmen or legislative members going to sessions at Louisville.[45]

There would also have been, certainly, preachers and itinerant revivalists and mobile camp meetings that likely set up shop for a few days not too far from the Lincolns' front door. Each would have made an impression on Abe's eager mind.

That mind had an impressive capacity for memorization, particularly of sermons. Those who knew him during his Indiana years often recalled how he would take a break from work by getting up on a stump and repeating almost word for word the sermons he had heard in the weeks before. He not only captured the language but the mannerisms, the inflections, even the quirks of each minister. This hilarity lasted until Abe's offended father ordered it stopped lest his son commit the sin of sacrilege.

In later years, Lincoln made it clear that he had rejected the faith of his father. When an artist guessed just by examining Lincoln's face that he had once been a Hard Shell Baptist, the surprised president said, "You are right, my father was a member of the Baptist Church, but I am not."[46] It is difficult to know whether this rejection was more a matter of religion or the need for distance from his father. Eminent Lincoln scholar Allen Guelzo has written that "on no other point did Abraham Lincoln come closer to an outright repudiation of his father than on religion."[47] The two had a painful relationship that drove Abraham out of his boyhood home as soon as it was legal and nearly kept him from seeing Thomas again for the rest of his life. This may explain why an adolescent Abraham rarely went to church with Thomas and why he distanced himself from the man's weepy, loud, legalistic brand of faith as early as possible. Besides, Abe might have thought, if Thomas Lincoln could not keep from whipping his son and if he could not try to understand the boy's eager, hungry mind, and if he worked him like a slave just for the money it would bring—how real could the man's religion truly be?

The truth is, Thomas's type of religion had little chance of success with Abe anyway. At the age when he might have joined a church for himself, the younger Lincoln was already a reader, already immersed in the habits of thought, analysis, and reflection that would mark him the rest of his days. This turned him from the wild, dramatic expressions of camp-meeting religion. He was drawn to the character of Washington, not to rough rubes who "got the spirit" and barked the night away. He was stirred by the saga of America and by the cadences of Shakespeare and Burns, not the rantings of a revival preacher or the babblings of some fool possessed by the jerks. He longed for a loftier plane, one his books revealed, and he did not find it at the explosive revival service or the sweaty, shouting Hard Shell Baptist church.

Did Lincoln reject Christianity out of offense with his parents' brand of faith? Yes, at least for a season, as we shall see. Yet even in his early days, there were signs that to reject the faith of Thomas was not necessarily to reject faith in God. Though many historians make much of Lincoln's early aversion to church and his literary, more secular ways, they neglect to consider the part of his heart that surfaced only when Thomas was not around. His stepsister, Matilda Johnston, recalled that when their parents were at church, the children—grateful for some hours of freedom and peace—would not immediately begin to play. Instead, "Abe would take down the bible, read a verse—give out a hymn—and we would sing."[48] Then, sometimes, he would teach. This is not evidence of a lifelong faith, of course, but it is indication that in those early years Lincoln avoiding his father and church was not the same as Lincoln avoiding faith. He was wrestling, certainly, but he was also feeling his way—toward truth, toward inspiration, toward some sort of answer for his soul.

And this, too, was a gift from Nancy Hanks Lincoln.

TWO

‒‒‒〰‒‒‒

LINCOLN'S ALMA MATER

ABRAHAM'S CHILDHOOD ENDED LEGALLY AND SYMBOL-ically in 1830. He was twenty-one and no longer owed servitude to his father. It is a testament to his character that as miserable as he was in his father's house, he did not leave his family immediately. Instead, he helped move the Lincoln clan to Illinois and then left them for a life of his own.

That critical year is framed by two journeys, both of which embedded images in Lincoln's soul that never left him. These were the famous flatboat journeys that carried young Abe down the Ohio and Mississippi rivers to New Orleans. There he beheld for the first time the famed St. Louis Cathedral, standing a short distance across Jackson Square from where Lincoln's boat docked to offload its wares. The thrilling, ornate structure spoke to him of a world beyond what he had known. He also saw the stark misery of slavery—the chains, the vile inspection of bodies, the screams as families were ripped apart, the haunting look on African faces. A friend later said of Lincoln in New Orleans, "Slavery ran the iron into him then and there."[1]

What he saw in the great Southern city usually receives the attention, but perhaps as intriguing is what passed through Lincoln's mind during those long, unhurried, hypnotizing days on the river before he arrived. It was 1,627 miles from New Salem to New Orleans. Lincoln covered that distance four times just as he was stepping into adulthood. It meant many languid days to thoughtfully laze through, many hours of staring into the current from a sixteen-by-four-foot flatboat on which there was little else to do. Perhaps the river became for him, as it has for many a man, a metaphor of his life: his past spinning away behind him, his future unsettlingly near.

If so, he may have let the two decades he had lived run through his mind. He would not have remembered much of his life in Kentucky. His family left for Indiana when he was only seven, though it is likely that memories of the wider world passing by on the Cumberland Trail near his home stuck in his mind. He would have remembered more of Indiana, of course. The woods, the years learning his father's carpentry trade and the awakening of his love of learning and books would have filled his memory.

So, too, would his sufferings. The death of his mother was too horrible to contemplate for long. Then, years later, there was the loss of his best friend—his sister, Sarah. Perhaps he could still feel, in that strange type of memory the body seems to retain, the great convulsions and sobs that racked him when he heard she was gone.

On the second of his two voyages, he might have thought back on the horrifying storm that had hit central Illinois only the year before. No man who lived through it ever forgot. The Lincolns had barely moved into the area from Indiana when a snowfall began that did not let up until it was three feet deep. Then came freezing rain, which fell and hardened until a thick crust of ice—in most places too dense to break—imprisoned the snow underneath. The temperature dropped below zero and remained there for two weeks.

It all happened so quickly that travelers were stranded. Men in their fields, blinded by snow that fell as though from a shovel, simply clung to the tails of their animals and trusted the beasts to get them home. Families were sealed into their cabins for weeks after and only ventured out when starvation threatened. Those less fortunate froze in the wild and sometimes were not discovered until the spring thaws.

Abe must have shaken his head at the memory. Storms like that one were part of life in the West, but, God, it was hard to hew a coffin for a child or lay the frozen body of a husband before his already destitute wife.

God. He surely thought about God too. But which God? Which God of all that he had seen was his? Was it the God of the explosive, exhausting revival? Or perhaps it was the God of his father's blustery, Calvinistic certainties? Maybe it was the God he sensed on a Sunday morning, when his parents were away and he spoke gently of the Scriptures after he and the other children had sung. It is hard to say. He was, as he drifted down the Ohio and the Mississippi, still trying to decide.

We cannot know with certainty anything that an Abraham Lincoln newly in his twenties might have pondered during those seemingly unending river days. It would be pleasant to think that he recalled scenes and ideas from his books. It would be natural to believe that he turned over and over again in his mind the painful image of his father. It would not be too far removed from the truth, surely, to believe that he remembered his many hours of mindless labor and resolved again to escape that life forever.

We cannot know with certainty. What we do know—and perhaps it is enough—is that when Lincoln came to journey's end, he had not ceased to believe that New Salem was the beginning for him, was the first stepping-stone of his destiny. He was right about this, of course, though not even a mind such as his could have envisioned what that village on the Illinois frontier would come to mean to him.

❧

Before we consider what New Salem gave to Lincoln, though, we should first consider what kind of man it was who strolled into that village in 1831. He was, by all accounts, a peculiar figure. He was tall, of course, but also exceptionally gangly for his height. His hair was unkempt, his face was strong-featured but homely, and he had startlingly long arms with massive, powerful hands. He wore a low-crowned, broad-brimmed hat, threadbare pants, a ragged shirt, frayed suspenders, and farm-boy shoes. None of it fit properly. He tended to lope rather than walk—"like an Indian," townspeople said. Onlookers were amazed that he read books as he passed them on the streets and did so while mumbling aloud. *Odd, rough,* and *ragged* were the terms most used of him during his early New Salem days. Lincoln simply described himself as "driftwood."

His coarse exterior belied the sophistication of his interior life. He had seen much, more than many frontier men of his day, and he had worked to understand what he saw. He did not let the words he read or the politician's oratory or the preacher's pleading float meaninglessly above his head. Instead, he forced himself to know, to define, to wrestle new ideas to the ground. He was also intimate with suffering; the experience had savaged him but left him tender and kind, slow to despise and condemn. Then there was what came from pushing back against his father's demands. It had instilled toughness in him and made him cautious about anything society expected him to embrace uncritically. This included religion. By the time he ambled into New Salem, he had rejected the wildness of camp meeting religion and found it hard to hide his disdain for most preachers. He still wondered about God, though, and thought often about what his mother seemed to know of a Savior's grace.

It would have been easy for onlookers to assume he was a man of few ambitions. It wasn't so. He burned with a desire to rise in the world. In later years he told a friend, "You know better than any man living that from my boyhood up my ambition was to be President."[2] One of the earliest samples of his handwriting is from a verse he scribbled in a friend's copybook: "Good boys who to their books apply / Will make great men by and by."[3] A mystical sense of destiny swirled about him. Nearly everyone who knew him in his youth recalled his certainty that he was made to play a role in important events. He saw confirmation of this in any variety of omens, signs, and formulas. So did a girl who lived not too far away. When her grandmother chastised her for being noisy and asked, "What on earth do you suppose will become of you if you go on this way?" the girl responded, "Oh I will be the wife of a President some day."[4] Her name was Mary Todd.

❦

New Salem lay on a bluff of the Sangamon River, some twenty miles northwest of Springfield. In those days, the village held much promise. It boasted a mill, a location along the Sangamon where the water was deep enough for steamboats, and visionary souls who dreamed of a great trading center on the site one day. Lincoln, armed with dreams of his own, likely felt at home among a people looking eagerly to the future. As William Herndon wrote much later, "Looking back over his history we are forced to conclude that Providence or chance, or whatever power is responsible for it, could not have assigned him to a more favorable refuge."[5]

Herndon was likely right, though it is a truth lost in the frequent portrayal of New Salem as something close to a Hollywood set. It was, in this view, merely the physical backdrop to Abraham's inevitable rise, peopled by a cast of crusty characters who colorfully adorned the great man's rustic years. They were illiterate rubes whom Lincoln impressed with his ability to read and his ambition to reach for more than New Salem townsfolk could even envision. We think this because it is hard to imagine that a remote village on the frontier could be much more, but this belies one of the great truths of early American life—a truth that profoundly shaped the mind of Abraham Lincoln.

We should remember that the early English settlers in the New World left England accompanied by fears that they would pursue their "errand into the wilderness" and become barbarians in the process. Loved ones at home wondered how a people could cross an ocean and live in the wild without losing the literacy, the learning, and the faith that defined them. The early colonists came determined to defy these fears. They brought books, printing presses, and teachers with them and made the founding of schools a priority. Puritans founded Boston in 1630 and established Harvard College within six years. After ten years they had already printed the first book in the colonies, the Bay Psalm Book. Many more would follow. The American colonists were so devoted to education—inspired as they were by their Protestant insistence upon biblical literacy and by their hope of converting and educating the natives—that they created a near-miraculous culture of learning.

This was achieved through an educational free market. Colonial society offered "Dame schools," Latin grammar schools, tutors for hire, what would today be called "home schools," church schools, schools for the poor, and colleges for the gifted and well-to-do. Enveloping these institutions of learning was a wider culture that prized knowledge as an aid to godliness. Books were cherished and well-read. A respected minister might have thousands of them. Sermons were long and learned. Newspapers were devoured, and elevated discussion of ideas filled taverns and parlors. Citizens formed gatherings for the "improvement of the mind"—debate societies and reading clubs and even sewing circles at which the latest books from England were read.

The intellectual achievements of colonial America were astonishing. Lawrence Cremin, dean of American education historians, estimated the literacy rate of the period at between 80 and 90 percent.[6] Benjamin Franklin taught himself five languages and was not thought exceptional. Jefferson taught himself half a dozen, including Arabic. George Washington was unceasingly embarrassed by his lack of formal education, and yet readers of his journals today marvel at his intellect and wonder why he ever felt insecure. It was nothing for a man—or in some cases a woman—to learn algebra, geometry, navigation, science, logic, grammar, and history entirely through self-education. A seminarian was usually required to know Greek, Hebrew, Latin, French, and German just to begin his studies, instruction which might take place in a log classroom and on a dirt floor.

This culture of learning spilled over onto the American frontier. Though pioneers routinely moved beyond the reach of even basic education, as soon as the first buildings of a town were erected, so, too, were voluntary societies to foster intellectual life. Aside from schools for the young, there were debate societies, discussion groups, lyceums, lecture associations, political clubs, and always, Bible societies. The level of learning these groups encouraged was astounding. The language of Shakespeare and classical literature—at the least Virgil, Plutarch, Cicero, and Homer—so permeated the letters and journals of frontier Americans that modern readers have difficulty understanding that generation's literary metaphors. This meant that even a rustic Western settlement could serve as a kind of informal frontier university for the aspiring. It is precisely this legacy and passion for learning that shaped young Abraham Lincoln during his six years in New Salem. Some historians have even called the village his alma mater. Yet we could easily miss the depth of New Salem's imprint upon Lincoln's life if we think only in terms of the caricature of the frontier town and a Hollywood-inspired image of the bumpkins who supposedly walked its streets.

⁘

It was his churning ambition that drove Abraham to learn, and in New Salem—while he tended store, carried the mail, and learned the art of surveying—he sought out mentors and the presence of the learned to augment his self-education. It was fortunate that willing teachers were abundant in the gritty frontier village. A schoolmaster helped him work through *A Compendium of English Grammar*; another friend taught him mathematics and philosophy. He immersed himself in Shakespeare, too, and often sat fishing with a friend who shared this love, the two of them reciting verses from the Bard to the fishes. He consumed history, poetry, and newspapers with eagerness. Always he read the Bible, and he did not shrink from the rigors of legal commentaries and the most technical writing about science. The discipline of self-education made him fearless about learning. It was nothing for him to sit up an entire night to master some new intellectual challenge. He was inspired by a fresh understanding of how knowledge could give him power to rise in the world. A schoolteacher who knew him during these years recalled, "Abraham Lincoln was the most studious, diligent strait forward young man in the pursuit of a knowledge of literature than any among the five thousand I have taught in the school."[7]

His reading made him rethink religion. Already he had voyaged into Gibbon's *Decline and Fall of the Roman Empire*, which blamed Christianity for the fall of Rome. He had also discovered the Scottish poet Robert Burns, who likely played a greater role in Lincoln's attitudes toward religion than any other writer. The parallels between Burns and himself must have been obvious to the young Illinois shopkeeper. Both were born into poverty. Both were bound to life on a farm. Both despised the drudgery of physical labor. Both were moody, plagued by depression, and cherished the bawdy and the raw. In Burns, Lincoln found a kindred soul as well as a guide for distancing himself from Christianity. As a friend from that time told Herndon, "Lincoln used to quote Burns. Burns helped Lincoln to be an infidel . . . at least he found in Burns a like thinker and feeler."[8]

This same friend identified one Burns poem in particular, "Holy Willie's Prayer," as "Lincoln's religion." It is easy to see why. Both Burns and Lincoln recoiled from the presumptive arrogance of hyper-Calvinism, those proud souls who were confident they had been chosen by God and yet who dared to rejoice in the predetermined punishment of their fellow man. Burns captured Lincoln's disgust perfectly in his satirical poem, long regarded as one of his best.

The Willie of the poem is a drunken man who has no doubt he is among the elect, the chosen of God, but who takes great pleasure in the certainty that many around him are going to hell.

> *O Thou, Wha in the heavens dost dwell,*
> *Wha, as it pleases best Thysel',*
> *Sends ane to heaven an' ten to hell,*
> *A' for Thy glory,*
> *And no for ony gude or ill*
> *They've done afore Thee!*
>
> *I bless and praise Thy matchless might,*
> *When thousands Thou has left in night,*
> *That I am here afore Thy sight,*
> *For gifts an' grace*
> *A burning and a shining light*
> *To a' this place.*
>
> *What was I, or my generation,*
> *That I should get sic exaltation,*
> *I wha deserve most just damnation*
> *For broken laws,*
> *Five thousand years ere my creation,*
> *Thro' Adam's cause?*
>
> *When frae my mither's womb I fell,*
> *Thou might hae plunged me in hell,*
> *To gnash my gums, to weep and wail,*

In burnin lakes,
Where damned devils roar and yell,
Chain'd to their stakes.

Yet I am here a chosen sample,
To show thy grace is great and ample;
I'm here a pillar o' Thy temple,
Strong as a rock,
A guide, a buckler, and example,
To a' Thy flock.

The poem ends with Willie asking God not to hear the prayers of his enemies.

Lord, in Thy day o' vengeance try him,
Lord, visit them wha did employ him,
And pass not in Thy mercy by 'em,
Nor hear their pray'r,
But for Thy people's sake, destroy 'em,
An' dinna spare.

But, Lord, remember me an' mine
Wi' mercies temp'ral an' divine,
That I for grace an' gear may shine,
Exdell'd by nane,
And a' the glory shall be thine,
Amen, Amen! [9]

Lincoln absorbed this poem and made it his own. He memorized it, perfected a Scottish accent for reciting it, and gave performances of it whenever occasions allowed. Friends delighted in his renditions but wondered at his almost sinister pleasure in each verse. He was likely trying to deal the deathblow to his father's brand of faith. He had heard words like Willie's in Thomas's prayers and pronouncements and had grown to despise what he perceived to be his father's cal-lousness and religious pride—in fact, the spiritual arrogance of all who believed in absolute predestination and yet who vainly assumed they were among the chosen few.

Thomas Paine

He was helped in his move away from Christianity not only by what he read in Gibbon and Burns but also by the influence of his intellectual New Salem friends. He had joined a debate society that met twice a month in an old store, and this put him in contact with a bookish crowd who were unlike any he had known before, who possessed the American passion for self-education but rejected the traditional faith that had inspired this passion at the country's beginning. As Herndon recalled,

In 1834 . . . he was surrounded by a class of people exceedingly liberal in matters of religion. Volney's "Ruins" and Paine's "Age of Reason" passed from hand to hand and furnished food for the evening's discussion in the tavern and village store. Lincoln read both these books and thus assimilated them into his own being.[10]

We can picture young Lincoln reading the English pamphleteer Paine and the French avant-garde statesman Volney between customers at his store, under a tree while nibbling a bit of bread and cheese, or at night in bed, his long legs stretched up the wall of his second-story room.[11] We can picture him eagerly anticipating another discussion at the tavern, another argument by a friend's stove or a customer's wagon. He was doing what young men do—trying on ideas as a man tries on clothes, seeing what fit, what it felt like to exercise the powers of his mind.

In Paine he must have found the courageous reasoning of an inflamed intellect; in Volney the poetic ecstasies of a lover of mankind. Paine explained that he first doubted Christianity when as a boy he heard a sermon on "the subject of what is called redemption by the death of the Son of God." He "revolted at the recollection of what he had heard, and thought to himself that it was making God Almighty act like a passionate man who killed His son when He could not revenge Himself in any other way."[12] How this must have resonated with Lincoln, who surely believed his own father would never have hesitated to sacrifice his son.

Paine boldly proclaimed a new creed to replace the ones inspired by the "myth" of Christianity: "I believe in one God, and no more; and I hope for happiness beyond this life. I believe in the equality of man; and I believe that religious duties consist in doing justice, loving mercy, and endeavoring to make our fellow creatures happy."[13] For churches Paine had no patience: "All national institutions of churches, whether Jewish, Christian or Turkish, appear to me no other than human inventions, set up to terrify and enslave mankind, and monopolize power and profit."[14] The only place of worship Paine sought was one Lincoln, in the iconoclasm of youth, would have understood. "My own mind," Paine insisted, "is my own church."[15]

Volney's Ruins; or, Meditation on the Revolutions of Empires and the Law of Nature was a lyrical, wistful reflection upon ancient civilizations that called the religions of the world "arbitrary . . . not demonstrable and often absurd."[16] Though Volney usually maintained a lofty, airy tone—befitting the literature of the age—he could sometimes descend into the angry rant. Of the biblical story of Adam and Eve he roared, "What! because a man and woman ate an apple six thousand years ago, all the human race are damned? And you call God just? What tyrant ever rendered children responsible for the faults of their fathers! What man can answer for another's actions: Is not this subversive of every idea of justice and reason?"[17] Volney concluded that man had simply created religion as a means of answering the demands of nature.

> Hence originated fatal doctrines, gloomy and misanthropic systems of religion, which painted the gods malignant and envious, like their despots. Man, to appease them, offered up the sacrifice of all his enjoyments: he environed himself in privations, and reversed the laws of nature. Conceiving his pleasures to be crimes, his sufferings expiations, he endeavored to love pain, and to abjure the love of self; he persecuted his sense, hated his life; and a self-denying and antisocial morality plunged nations into the apathy of death.[18]

Uninspired as Lincoln had been by the Christianity he had seen, he gratefully drank in Volney and Paine. He had known only the religion of the haughty, self-assured hyper-Calvinist or the exuberant camp meeting extremes. He had found both wanting. Paine and Volney—along with Burns and Gibbon before them—pointed a way out of the confusion of perpetual skepticism into a clear and always rational faith: the existence of God, love of mankind, the cathedral of the mind. This was what they gave Lincoln, and he loved them for it. He eagerly shared his discoveries in their writings with anyone in his shop or on the footpaths of New Salem who was willing to listen. He was a man possessed by new ideas, and they seemed to him a revelation. He even adopted the manner of expression of both these intellectuals. Paine had said that the virgin birth was little more than the story of a woman being "debauched by a ghost" and was "blasphemously obscene." Lincoln went as far. Friends later heard him call Christ "a bastard" and the Bible a book of contradictions.[19]

◦◦◦

Lincoln's views became so well-known—not hard in a small village where everything newsworthy was debated in tavern and store—that he gained a reputation as an "infidel." He was hardly alone. Many in the community seemed to be with him. As Herndon later said of Lincoln's fellow frontier freethinkers,

> They were on all occasions, when opportunity offered, debating the various questions of Christianity among themselves; they took their stand on common sense and on their own souls; and though their arguments were rude and rough, no man could overthrow their homely logic.[20]

Feeling the need to declare himself further—or perhaps impress the learned New Salem elite—Lincoln decided to write a booklet arguing his newfound ideas. This became known in memory as his "little book on Infidelity," the one in which he attacked the divinity of Christ and the inspiration of the Bible. Herndon called it "an extended essay." Lincoln intended it for publication, perhaps in a magazine. It was very much in the style of Thomas Paine, after all—taking stories from the Bible and exposing their foolish inconsistencies—and the booklet might show Lincoln as a man worldly and grown beyond his dirt-floor cabin roots. He had great hopes for the good it might do.

Friends were mortified. While Lincoln read from the booklet to anyone who would listen and passed the unfinished work about town, those who knew his dreams and potential realized what the existence of such a thing might mean. Lincoln remained naive. Most others knew that a man could not write a book against religion—or, as Herndon said, "against Christianity, striving to prove that the Bible was not inspired and therefore not God's revelation, and that Jesus Christ was not the son of God"—and hope to rise in a largely Christian society.[21]

The solution to this crisis was provided by Samuel Hill, Lincoln's friend and employer. As Herndon later recalled,

> Lincoln and Hill were very friendly. Hill, I think, was a skeptic at that time. Lincoln, one day after the book was finished, read it to Mr. Hill—his good friend. Hill tried to persuade him not to make it public—not to publish it. Hill at that time saw in Mr. Lincoln a rising man, and wished him success. Lincoln refused to destroy it— said it should be published. Hill swore it should never see the light of day. He had an eye to Lincoln's popularity—his present and future success; and believing that, if the book were published, it would kill Lincoln forever, he snatched it from Lincoln's hand, when Lincoln was not expecting it, and ran it into an old-fashion tin-plate stove, heated as hot as a furnace; and so Lincoln's book went up to the clouds in smoke.[22]

The existence of this little booklet would be hotly debated years later both during Lincoln's political campaigns and in battles over his religious legacy after his death. Whatever claims were made, there was no denying that Lincoln had indeed written such a thing. Too many citizens of New Salem had seen it and too many were willing to speak of it to reporters after Lincoln achieved fame. Perhaps Samuel Hill had indeed done his friend a favor.

At the time, Lincoln was incensed by Hill's presumption in burning his writings and was still spoiling for a religious fight. Perhaps to appease Lincoln's wrath, Hill allowed Lincoln to use his name in attacking a local clergyman. The man's name was Peter Cartwright, and he was everything Lincoln despised about preachers. He was a circuit-riding Methodist who mixed religion with local politics and high-handedly tried to dictate moral behavior. Cartwright had also attacked Hill in print. Lincoln resented it bitterly.

Hill let Lincoln return fire in his name. Writing that if Cartwright had stood for true religion then Lincoln might have left the man alone, he said that instead the circuit rider was "a most abandoned hypocrite." Lincoln complained that "the people in this country are in some degree priest ridden" and that men like Cartwright prosper "only by the contributions he has been able to levy upon and collect from a priest ridden church." Echoing complaints about the wealth of clergymen that have endured through the centuries, Lincoln described Cartwright's huge farm and then wrote, "It will not do to say he has earned it by the 'sweat of his brow.'" Moreover, Lincoln had heard Cartwright threaten to turn the Methodist Church against any candidate he opposed. "For a church or community to be priest ridden by a man who will take their money and treat them kindly in return is bad enough in all conscience," Lincoln wrote, "but to be ridden by one who is continually exposing them to ridicule by making a public boast of his power to hoodwink them, is insufferable." Cartwright, Lincoln charged, had "two sets of opinions, one for his religious, and one for his political friends; and to plat them together smoothly, presents a task to which his feverish brain is incompetent."[23]

That Lincoln wrote his "Infidelity" and then raged in such terms against Cartwright tells us how far he had come. He had only arrived in New Salem in 1831. He was not then an eager participant in church or Christian events but he had also not yet turned against the informal Christianity of his youth. Now, less than three years later, he had not only become convinced that the Bible was uninspired, that Jesus Christ was not divine, and that the Christian Church was a lie, but he had gone so far as to publicly chastise a leading clergyman as a charlatan. The phrase *priest ridden*, which he used repeatedly, is language from

Paine, from the French Revolution, and from the anticlericalism of the Enlightenment. Lincoln's venom for Cartwright was part of a broader disgust with preachers and with religion in general. Obviously, Abraham Lincoln had become the Thomas Paine of New Salem—through his reading of anti-Christian books, through the encouragement of those Herndon called the religious "liberals," and through his own disappointment with the Christianity he had known.

There was, though, another source of his rage. Herndon said as much in his claim that the entire matter of the booklet and the outburst against Cartwright was simply Lincoln possessed by grief. "Poor, patient, suffering, cross-bearing, sublime Lincoln!" Herndon wrote to a friend. "Did not God roll him through His furnace? Take all this . . . and you will perceive that Lincoln's work on infidelity—burnt up by his friends—was a blast, Job-like, of despair. Now does not melancholy drip from this poor man?"[24] Clearly, Herndon thought that Lincoln's angry assault on Cartwright and religion in general came from Lincoln's utter Job-like resentment of God. He may have been right. Lincoln certainly had room for complaint. He had suffered much, not unlike Job. There were the many deaths he had known. There was the demon of depression that dogged his steps. There was the haunting of rain falling on graves.

Yet Lincoln's "blast" was not just a roar of grief over his sufferings but also a roar of rage against a God he thought had abandoned him. A close friend would later recall that Lincoln had written the booklet on infidelity "through the spirit of his misery, through the thought and the idea that God had forsaken him, and through the echoes of Lincoln's mental condition, suffering, a burden of wild despair."[25] We shall see this resurface often in Lincoln's life. For some uncertain reason, Lincoln began early in his life to feel that he was cursed, that "God had forsaken him." He never explained this fully himself, but it is mentioned numerous times in the recollections of his friends and deserves to be considered. Most of these friends tell of Lincoln's feelings in order to explain the intensity of his disbelief in God. It may be that he was actually living out the inner duplicity of the atheist's confession: "There is no God—and I hate him." Perhaps Lincoln was not as certain about his atheism as he seemed. Perhaps instead he did believe in God but also felt that this God had rejected him and left him to suffer alone. It may have been so devastating to him that he embraced "infidelity" as a defense against the pain of his curse, of whatever it was he thought made him displeasing to heaven. Of course, it all may have been little more than his depression driving his perceptions of spiritual things. Whatever the cause, believing himself cursed made God his enemy, the cause of his sufferings, the unjust deity who punished a man without even explaining why. A battle had begun, then, between Lincoln and this capricious God who caused him so much pain. If Herndon was right about this feature of his friend's thinking—and there is good reason to believe he was—it explains much about Lincoln's tortured journey of faith.

Not surprisingly, Lincoln's newfound rational religion did not bring him relief. The wife of a friend, who had listened carefully to his views, once asked him, "Do you really believe there isn't any future state?" He replied, "I'm afraid there isn't. It isn't a pleasant thing to think that when we die that is the last of us."[26] We can imagine how this thought must have tormented him. It meant that all who had left him—his younger brother, his mother, his sister, Anne Rutledge, and dozens of other friends and family—simply were no more. They had become dust, living only in the memory of those who knew them. But these living beings, too, would die, and so, then, would the memory of the people Lincoln loved. This thought haunted him, disturbing his sleep and picking at the reservoirs of grief and depression in his soul.

Understandably, he started to fixate on death. Even apart from his religious reflections, the cast of his life might naturally have turned him in this direction. Without belief in an afterlife, a resurrection, death became oppressive, a horrid specter of obliteration looming at the end of his days. He reached for comfort in poetry and discovered a piece by William Knox that he grew to love, that became part of him as few other words would. It was called "Mortality," and it captured—in language Lincoln thought the most beautiful he had heard—what he believed about death.

> *O why should the spirit of mortal be proud!*
> *Like a fast flitting meteor, a fast flying cloud,*
> *A flash of the lightning, a break of the wave—*
> *He passes from life to his rest in the grave.*
>
> *The leaves of the oak and the willow shall fade,*
> *Be scattered around, and together be laid;*
> *As the young and the old, and the low and the high,*
> *Shall moulder to dust, and together shall lie.*
>
> *The child that a mother attended and loved;*
> *The mother that infant's affection who proved,*
> *The husband that mother and infant that blest,*
> *Each—all are away to their dwellings of rest.*
>
> *The maid on whose cheek, on whose brow, in whose eye,*
> *Shone beauty and pleasure—her triumphs are by;*
> *And the memory of those that beloved her and praised,*
> *And alike from the minds of the living erased.*

All the deaths Lincoln endured in his life are summoned in the mournful phrases of this poem. It is no surprise it grew dearer to him with the passing years. Friends knew he might quote it in its entirety at nearly any moment. He made it part of his eulogy for President Zachary

Taylor in 1850 and recited it just months before his own death in 1865. We can almost hear him slowly, sadly reciting the final stanza:

> 'Tis the wink of an eye, 'tis the draught of a breath,
> From the blossom of health to the paleness of death,
> From the gilded saloon to the bier and the shroud—
> O why should the spirit of mortal be proud?[27]

This wrestling with a graceless vision of death overlaid a season that ought to have been rewarding for him. Having lost a race for state legislature once before, he ran again in 1834 and won. He thus joined his Whig comrades in Vandalia, the Illinois state capital in those days, and quickly earned a reputation for storytelling, for industriousness, and for backroom dealing. Though he did not join his fellow representatives in their drinking escapades—he said alcohol made him feel "flabby and undone"—he was the soulful, entertaining fellow the others most wanted to be with when a day's politicking was done. This popularity made him influential while his keen mind made him effective. He supported Henry Clay's "American System" of state-funded internal improvements, spoke out against slavery, and helped move the Illinois capital from Vandalia to Springfield. He had proven himself and so won election again in 1836, 1838, and 1840. He did not run in 1842, but in 1846 he won a seat in the U.S. Congress. He was but a short season from the rube he had been when he first set foot in New Salem in 1831, yet he had matured and achieved as much as some men do in a lifetime.

His success did not make him happy. He was in serious debt, having invested unwisely in a New Salem store that eventually failed. Returning from the legislature in 1837, he told a friend that while his fellow politicians had much to look forward to, "it isn't so with me. I am going home . . . without a thing in the world. I have drawn all my pay I got at Vandalia and have spent it all. I am in debt . . . I don't know what to do."[28] Soon his hypo returned, awakened almost certainly by this debilitating financial pressure.

Some historians believe that the familiar darkness also returned on the wings of fear that he had contracted syphilis. He once admitted to Herndon that he had been with a prostitute in Beardstown during his militia service in the Blackhawk War and that it was not the only time he indulged.[29] He was certain he had the disease. If so, he would not have been alone. As Joshua Shenk has written, "as many as half of the men in Lincoln's day had some kind of sexually transmitted disease, and even more feared that they did. According to a leading physician of the time, fear of syphilis was a typical feature of hypochondriasis."[30]

Finally, there was simply the fear of failure that haunts most men in their twenties and thirties. Realizing that he could not live forever as a store clerk, surveyor, and state legislator, he had decided to move to Springfield to become a lawyer. This was daunting and surely stirred his insecurities. He was but six years from his father's farm, and now he was planning to declare himself against men from esteemed universities in the raucous battle of wits that gave frontier courtrooms their reputation. He was not sure he could do it and confessed as much to friends.

His condition at this moment has been perfectly described by the novelist Thomas Keneally.

So here is Lincoln in the spring of 1837: tortured in equal and abundant measure by self-doubt and ambition, ill-clothed, rough mannered, hard up, possessed of his peculiarly American powers of articulation and charm, burdened by what now would be considered clinical depression, plagued by exultant vision, yearning for and terrified by women, raucous in joke telling, gifted in speech, abstinent in drink, profligate in dreams. No man ever entered Springfield, a town that would become his shrine, as tentative, odd-seeming, and daunted as Abraham Lincoln.[31]

Though Keneally does not mention it, Lincoln was also a man of discarded faith. He had entered New Salem certain that the camp meeting and the usual ranting preacher were not for him. Yet he had still believed in God and had still found meaning in the pages of Scripture. In New Salem he was mentored by skeptics and steeped in anti-Christian rationalism. He drank deeply of the Enlightenment stream, and it left him venomous toward clergy and spiteful of belief in Jesus Christ. Some torrent in his soul—perhaps anger at the losses he had endured or resentment of the hypo that haunted him or his anger over God's curse—joined with the intellectual currents of Gibbon, Paine, Volney, and Burns to make him spew against the gospel of Christ. He shocked his friends with his vehemence, friends who already lived among a disbelieving tribe.

And he was not done: not with his anger, not with his rejection of God, not with his determination to declare himself publicly against his parents' faith. In Springfield, he would find the larger stage that his surging infidelity required. It is not a story often told in the traditional, distilled Lincoln tale, but it cannot be omitted. Not only is it true but it does much to explain the man who later wrestled with God and himself during a war for the soul of the nation, the man who questioned and then rearticulated the purposes of God for the United States.

⚶

Before following Lincoln to Springfield, it would be instructive to consider some of the events that occurred in the wider world while the future president became an "infidel" on the shores of the Sangamon River.

In the same year Lincoln drifted into New Salem, an August lunar eclipse signaled to a black man in Virginia that the moment had come. He was a slave on a tidewater plantation, and now this night seemed the perfect time. The heavy work of harvest was yet a month off and the white families had decided to attend spirited camp meetings elsewhere. There was a disturbing lull in the life of Southampton County, and this is what gave Nat Turner his opportunity. He had long dreamt of this day, the day on which the trumpet would sound and the slaves of the South would arise. He was God's chosen instrument to make it so. Hadn't he fasted and meditated for hours in the woods? Hadn't he seen visions of "white spirits and black spirits engaged in battle . . . and blood flowing in streams?"[32] Yes, it was true. God had made his will known.

On the night of August 22, Turner led seven others to the home of his owner, Joseph Travis. Quietly, skillfully, the intruders slit the throats of the still-slumbering family within. It was but a beginning. Spurred by Turner's apocalyptic preaching, the band of ex-slaves moved on to the next plantation, and then the next. Over the following two days, Turner gathered some seventy-five insurgents and made his way toward the county seat of Jerusalem, killing fifty-five whites as he went. Turner and his mob never reached Jerusalem, though. The state militia and armed townsmen stopped the raid three miles from the capital and then chased the escaped slaves into the swamps and gunned them down from horseback. Turner eluded capture for two months, and this sent panic throughout the Southern states. Finally, the most dreaded man in America was caught, tried, and hanged. To make sure his remains weren't used for a martyr's relics, the body was given to doctors, who melted it down into grease.[33] The South breathed a sigh of relief . . . for the moment.

Earlier in the same year, a journalist named William Lloyd Garrison issued the first edition of his newspaper, the *Liberator*. It came with a promise: "I am in earnest—I will not equivocate—I will not excuse—I will not retreat a single inch—and I will be heard."[34] This was Garrison's way of calling for complete and immediate emancipation of all slaves. It was a summons heard first in Boston and then throughout the nation, but it was new, radical, unheard-of. Prior to Garrison, slavery had always been regarded as a national problem. No one expected the

South to bear the burden of solving it alone. And besides, wasn't slavery dying out? Wouldn't it suffer a natural death over several generations? Why demand immediate freedom for all slaves now? What justification was there for the North to pressure the South into eradicating a system both helped to build? Such reasoning was lost on Garrison, though. Declaring war on moderation, he wrote,

> Tell a man whose house is on fire, to give a moderate alarm; tell him to moderately rescue his wife from the hands of the ravisher; tell the mother to gradually extricate her babe from the fire into which it has fallen; but urge me not to use moderation in a cause like the present . . . The apathy of the people is enough to make every statue leap from its pedestal and to hasten the resurrection of the dead.[35]

Tragically, the work of Turner and Garrison galvanized the South. As late as 1827, most antislavery societies and all four of the nation's abolitionist papers were located in Southern states. After Turner and Garrison, any good that Southern abolitionists might have done was lost. In the panic that ensued, it became a crime to teach a slave to read. Abolitionist literature was banned from the U.S. mail. Since Nat Turner was called the Preacher, black ministers were no longer allowed to hold religious services. Trusted slaves were viewed with suspicion, and many who had never known a chain found themselves bound hand and foot. The genteel ways of the Old South were lost in the paranoid panic of an armed camp awaiting assault. Presbyterian theologian and historian Robert L. Dabney wrote soon after,

> Before the Abolitionists began to meddle with our affairs, with which they had no business, I remember that it was a common opinion that domestic slavery was at least injudicious, as far as the happiness of the master was concerned. I do believe that if these mad fanatics had let us alone, in twenty years we should have made Virginia a free

State. As it is, their unauthorized attempts to strike off the fetters of our slaves have but riveted them on the faster.[36]

As though in indictment of both North and South in the United States, a Christian in England tried to show the way. In 1833, the second year of Lincoln's six in New Salem, the British Parliament outlawed slavery in its dominions with the stroke of a pen. The champion of this cause had been William Wilberforce. John Wesley, founder of the Methodist Church, had written the final letter of his life to Wilberforce, urging the politician to fight the evils of slavery. At risk of his fortune, his health, and his reputation, Wilberforce did. Though he died just three days after hearing that passage of the Slavery Abolition Act was assured, Wilberforce had already shown the West how to escape the curse that slavery had become.

Some nations listened. Others, like the United States, did not.

The decades of rage and offense that followed led to an American war more costly in lives and devastation than anyone in the early 1830s could have imagined. And it all grew from events that occurred while Abraham Lincoln read Volney and Paine along the shores of the Sangamon River. These were transitional years, both for Lincoln and for the nation. They brought visions of divine purpose into conflict. They brought visions of national purpose into question. They witnessed an intertwining of destinies only the passing years would fully reveal. And they guaranteed payment in blood for national ills the nation's statesmen could not bring themselves to pay in any other way.

THREE

〰〰〰

THE "INFIDEL"

IT WAS SPRING OF **1837.** ABRAHAM LINCOLN WAS JUST then in his second term as an Illinois state legislator. He had also become a lawyer and was moving to Springfield, the state's new capital, to open a law office and position himself for what he hoped would be a storied political career. It had already begun. He was gaining the reputation of a well-spoken, intelligent politician possessed of a strong moral sense. His fellow legislators used words like *clever* and *destined* to describe him.

It all sounds impressive. It wasn't. Nor was he.

A friend from the time described Lincoln as "a long, gawky, ugly, shapeless man." On the day he moved to Springfield, he rode the fourteen miles from New Salem on a borrowed horse and carrying everything he owned—a few law books and some clothing—thrown into saddlebags with room to spare. Nothing about him signaled the greatness yet to come.

Upon arriving in town, he made for the store where his friend

Joshua Speed worked as a clerk. He was looking for lodging, he said, and asked what the furniture for a single room would cost. Speed put pencil to paper and determined that seventeen dollars would do the job.

"It is probably cheap enough," Lincoln replied. "But I want to say that cheap as it is I have not the money to pay. But if you will credit me until Christmas, and my experiment here as a lawyer is a success, I will pay you then. If I fail in that I will probably never be able to pay you at all."

Speed later recalled, "His voice was so melancholy that I felt for him. I looked up at him and thought then as I think now, that I never saw so gloomy and melancholy a face."

Eager to help the forlorn figure before him, Speed made a proposal: "I think I can suggest a plan by which you will be able to attain your end, without incurring any debt. I have a very large room, and a very large double-bed in it; which you are perfectly welcome to share with me if you choose."

"Where is your room?" Lincoln asked.

"Upstairs," Speed replied.

Upon hearing this, Lincoln, without a further word, climbed the stairs to the floor above, set his saddlebags down, and returned "beaming with pleasure and smiles."

"Well, Speed, I am moved," he announced.[1] This was Abraham Lincoln's beginning in Springfield.

⁊҈Ҩ

Nine years later, after he had married the daughter of a prominent family and risen to such notoriety that he was preparing to run for the United States Congress, Lincoln wrote to a friend,

> It would astonish if not amuse, the older citizens of your County who
> twelve years ago knew me a strange, friendless, uneducated, penniless

boy, working on a flat boat—at ten dollars per month to learn that I have been put down here as the candidate of pride, wealth, and auto-cratic family distinction.[2]

It is obvious from these words that Lincoln recognized the rapid pace of change in his life. It is one of the surprising features of his story, yet it often goes unnoticed in deference to the "country boy rising slowly" mystique that tradition prefers.

We should recall that in 1831 Lincoln trudged into New Salem fresh from his father's farm—poor, poorly spoken, and with barely a friend in the world. Six years later, he had read voraciously and enlisted mentors to refash-ion himself an educated man. He had been elected to the state legislature, had largely completed the course of study allowing him to practice law, and had undergone a dramatic religious revolution fueled by his mastery of some of the most respected authors of the day.

Despite his achieve-ments during these short six years, he then rode into Springfield in 1837 in a condition he himself described as "strange, friendless, uneducated,

Mary Todd Lincoln, wife of Abraham Lincoln, in 1846

penniless." He was overstating, of course, but he wasn't far from the truth. Five years later, he had risen as a politician and lawyer to a height that attracted even the deeply ambitious Mary Todd. They married in 1842. Four years later, in 1846, he was elected to Congress. Twelve years after, he gained national prominence in a series of debates with Stephen A. Douglas. Two years earlier he had found himself being nominated as the newly organized Republican Party's candidate for vice president of the United States. He was not chosen at the convention, but what mattered was that he had reached such stature. His later ascent to the presidency, then, did not seem outlandish when it occurred. All of this took place in the two decades since he had ridden into Springfield with no more than the books under his arm and the clothes on his back.

Such a rise might not seem that unusual today, in our age of instant celebrity, live global media, and at-the-ready star-maker machinery. Yet it was a surprisingly rapid ascent for Lincoln. Not only did he live in a far different world from ours, of course, but he also had against him several features of his own mind and personality. The first of these was his depression.

※

The gloom Speed noticed in the face of his friend betrayed a condition of soul that ever threatened to destroy Lincoln's life. Nothing confirms this like a poem he likely wrote in 1838, within a year of arriving in Springfield. Speed mentioned the poem briefly in an interview he gave after Lincoln's death, but it was lost to us for 139 years until a scholar named Richard Lawrence Miller rediscovered it. Though the poem was unsigned when it appeared in the *Sangamo Journal*, historians have concluded Lincoln must be its author because of its date, style, and topic.

The poem is titled "The Suicide's Soliloquy." It presents itself as a suicide note found "near the bones" of someone who has taken his own life deep in a forest near the Sangamon River. What convinces experts that it is Lincoln's work are not only its gruesome, tortured reflections but also that it was published on August 25, 1838, three years to the day after Ann Rutledge died.[3]

Here, where the lonely hooting owl
Sends forth his midnight moans,
Fierce wolves shall o'er my carcase growl,
Or buzzards pick my bones.

No fellow-man shall learn my fate,
Or where my ashes lie;
Unless by beats drawn round their bait,
Or by the ravens cry.

Yes! I've resolved the deed to do,
And this place to do it:
This heart I'll rush a dagger through
Thou I in hell should rue it!

Hell! What is hell to one like me
Who pleasures never knew
By friends consigned to misery,
By hope deserted too?

To ease me of this power to think,
That through my bosom raves,
I'll headlong leap from hell's high brink
And wallow in the waves.

Though devils yell, and burning chains
May waken long regret;
Their frightful screams, and piercing pains,
Will help me to forget.

Yes! I'm prepared, through endless night,
To take this fiery berth!
Think not with tales of hell to fright
Me, who am damn'd on earth!

Sweet steel! Come forth from out of your sheath,
And glist'ning, speak your powers;
Rip up the organs of my breath,
And draw my blood in showers.

I strike! It quivers in that heart
Which drives me to this end;
I draw and kiss the bloody dart,
My last—my only friend![4]

If these are indeed Lincoln's words, then they tell us that in his twenty-ninth year, just as he was rising as lawyer and lawmaker, he was pondering suicide. It is little surprise. He had done so before. He considered killing himself just after the death of Ann Rutledge. Friends had scurried to prevent it. It was not the last time they had to keep Lincoln from suicide. A few years after this poem was published, he thought of ending his life again, this time during the convoluted mess that was his courtship with Mary Todd.

The details of this affair are beyond the scope of a book on Lincoln's faith, but the episode does reveal much of Lincoln's mind at the time.

Mary Todd moved to Springfield in 1839. She was not the beauty some of her relatives were, but her intelligence, wit, and flirtatious energy drew men in swarms. She and Lincoln famously met at a ball, where he told her he wanted to dance with her in the worst way. After a stumbling tour of the dance floor, she confirmed to all that he certainly had danced with her in the worst way she had ever known. The couple courted and became engaged. It did not last long. The ever-tortured

Lincoln broke off the engagement early in 1841, and many Lincoln scholars have suspected it was because he had fallen in love with Mary's relative, the stunning Matilda Edwards.

This was not the light matter it often is today. As Jean Baker, author of the authoritative *Mary Todd Lincoln: A Biography* has written, "In nineteenth-century America a matrimonial pledge was as legally binding a contract as any commercial agreement, and the right of the rejected to seek damages was a familiar litigation."[5] Lincoln knew this, of course. As a lawyer he had experience with such cases.

His vacillation, the possible lawsuit, and the imagined public humiliation brought on another season of the hypo. It was one of the worst of his life. Speed remembered that Lincoln "went Crazy as a Loon," that friends had to "remove razors from his room—take away all Knives and other such dangerous things—it was terrible."[6] Nearly as bad as the depression itself were the methods used to treat it. Lincoln was placed under a doctor's care and, as Joshua Shenk has written, if that doctor "followed the standard course with Lincoln, he would have bled him, purged and puked him, starved him, dosed him with mercury and pepper, rubbed him with mustard, and plunged him in cold water."[7]

Adding to his suffering, Lincoln's condition became public. One of the Springfield papers made sport of his condition. Letters to the editor asked about his emaciated state. The affair of Miss Edwards and Miss Todd swirled in town gossip. Before long Lincoln was writing the words now regarded as the enduring tribute to his lifelong battle with the hypo:

> I am now the most miserable man living. If what I feel were equally distributed to the whole human family, there would not be one cheerful face on the earth. Whether I shall ever be better I can not tell; I awfully forebode I shall not. To remain as I am is impossible; I must die or be better, it appears to me.[8]

The resolution of the affair was nearly as strange as its beginning. Mary had taken note of Lincoln's affection for Matilda and released him from his obligations. There was a period of icy separation and then the two resumed corresponding. This led to visits in a friend's home. Suddenly one morning, Mary announced they would be wed by the end of the day. After summoning her Episcopal pastor and a few friends, the two were married in a prominent relative's living room before the sun had set.

Friends recalled that at the wedding Lincoln looked "as if being driven to slaughter."[9] We will never fully know why. Some scholars have suggested he was worried about syphilis. Others have suspected that in the couple's renewed affection, events had progressed to the point that Mary feared she could be pregnant, making a wedding urgent. Scholars who hold this view cite the fact that Robert, the Lincolns' first child, was born forty weeks to the day from the date Abraham and Mary wed. Most students of Lincoln simply conclude he was in love with someone else and afraid of marriage but felt obligated to Mary Todd. The more important mystery may be that his political career ever survived such public revelations of his inner torment.

❧

It is also a mystery that his political ascent survived his religious views. He had not moved away from the beliefs he absorbed from Gibbon, Paine, Volney, and Burns, nor the mentoring in Enlightenment thought he acquired in New Salem. This put him far outside the mainstream of American society and particularly out of step with the religious consensus in Springfield.

The term most used of him in these years is *infidel*. His friend James Matheny recalled, "when Lincoln first Came to Springfield in 1837," he would "pick up the Bible—read a passage—and then Comment on it— show its falsity—and its follies on the grounds of *Reason*—would then show its own self made & self uttered Contradictions and would in the End—finally ridicule it and as it were Scoff at it."[10] John Stuart, another friend, recalled "Lincoln went further against Christian beliefs—& doctrines & principles than any man I ever heard: he shocked me—Lincoln always denied that Jesus was the Christ of God—denied that Jesus was the son of God as understood and maintained by the Christian world."[11] By all accounts, in Springfield Lincoln continued to call Christ a "bastard," continued to speak of a churched society as "priest ridden," and continued to call Christianity a myth.

That Lincoln pushed his religious ideas whenever opportunity allowed reminds us of Churchill's dictum that "a fanatic is one who can't change his mind and won't change the subject." Lincoln was clearly angry, inflamed, unyielding. His fiery animosity against religion at this stage of his life makes us wonder if the fuel of this heat wasn't some other hatred entirely. Perhaps it was rage against his father, or perhaps it was spite for the preachers he had known. It may have been anger with God for the many deaths he had endured.

When he was going through the worst of the engagement crisis, he visited the home of Joshua Speed's parents to rest. Seeing his distress, Joshua's mother, Lucy Speed, gave Lincoln a Bible and told him it would comfort his stormy soul. Later, Lincoln wrote Joshua's half sister and asked her to "tell your mother that I have not got her 'present' with me; but that I intend to read it regularly when I return home. I doubt not that it is really, as she says, the best cure for the 'Blues' *could one but take it according to truth.*"[12] Even in the mention of a kind gift, he could not keep himself from expressing his religious doubts. Still, the memory of the gift was precious to him. Decades later President Lincoln autographed a picture of himself and inscribed it, "For Mrs. Lucy G. Speed, from whose pious hand I accepted the present of an Oxford Bible twenty years ago."[13]

That he could not keep his convictions private hurt him in his early career. Matheny recounts, "In 1834 & 5, my father being a strong

Methodist—a Kind of minister and loving Lincoln with all his soul hated to vote for him because he heard that Lincoln was an Infidel—All these things were talked about in 1845 & 6 & 7—Many Religious—Christian Whigs hated to vote for Lincoln on that account."[14] Suspicion of his beliefs would follow him the rest of his life. He had done it to himself, though. He had been brash and belligerent in his criticism of Christianity, and this in a churched and deeply Bible-loving society.

Nevertheless, the barbs of criticism hurt. In 1843, the year after he married, Lincoln tried to win his party's nomination for the Seventh District's congressional race. He was not chosen, and religion played a role in it.

As he wrote a friend, "My wife has some relatives in the Presbyterian and some in the Episcopal Churches, and therefore, wherever it would tell, I was set down as either the one or the other, whilst it was everywhere contended that no Christian ought to go for me, because I belonged to no church."[15] He was wounded by the experience and recalled it often with bitterness. He seems almost naive in his surprise. Religion shaped politics as much as did alcohol and rhetoric on the American frontier. Lincoln knew this and should not have expected to declare war on the faith of the voters and then to enjoy their political support. Religious suspicions would always hover over his political career.

⌘

The unsettling truth was that when not in seasons of revival-inspired unity, the American West was often a religiously contentious place. It was not unusual for Christian denominations to fight each other with venom and for preachers to treat religious hatred as a measure of righteousness. The Methodists and Baptists in particular were legendary for Christian infighting. One historian has written, "As they lined up as the chief contenders for converts, the two denominations, eyeing each other suspiciously, developed attitudes of extreme antagonism and tore into each other's ranks with abandon, casting aside all courtesy and ethics."[16] It was routine for churches to interrupt each other's services and to assault each other's beliefs as though laying siege to the kingdom of darkness itself. Methodists routinely chanted:

> *I'll tell you who the Lord loves best—*
> *It is the shouting Methodist!*

The Baptists retorted:

> *Baptist, Baptist, Baptist*
> *Baptist till I die.*
> *I'll go along with the Baptists*
> *And find myself on High.*[17]

Among preachers who led such frontier clashes, Reverend Peter Cartwright—the clergyman Lincoln had excoriated in the name of Samuel Hill at New Salem—was a legend. He was a rugged, sometimes violent, often opinionated, rifle-toting circuit rider who could be harsh and condemning in his views. Sandburg recounted two stories revealing of the man's character: "A deacon once spoke a cold, precise, correct prayer and Cartwright had to say, 'Brother, three prayers like that would freeze hell over.'" This has often wrung a laugh through the years since, but the second story portrays a less-endearing Cartwright: "When a presiding elder at a church meeting in Tennessee whispered to Cartwright, pointing out a visitor, 'That's Andrew Jackson,' the reply was: 'And who's Andrew Jackson? If he's a sinner God'll damn him the same as he would a Guinea [negro].'"[18]

The good reverend bombarded non-Methodist Christians with equal fire. When he once determined to establish a church near present-day Hendersonville, Tennessee, he positioned himself directly across the street from the local Presbyterian church. Cartwright so loudly thrashed the Presbyterians and their doctrines that thirteen Presbyterians left their church and joined the new Methodist congregation across the street. In 1845, the Presbyterian Synod of Tennessee complained of the "too successful misrepresentation of the doctrines and polity of Presbyterianism made by the Methodists."[19]

It was just a year after this episode that Cartwright declared himself the Democratic candidate for the Illinois Seventh Congressional District. His opponent was Abraham Lincoln. Cartwright's biographer, Robert Bray, has written, "Throughout his career Cartwright either could not or would not clearly distinguish church from state, religion from civic life, preaching from politicking—especially when he was concurrently doing both himself."[20] In his well-honed manner, the preacher's tactics against Lincoln were intended not to wound but to destroy. He had done his research. Cartwright men trotted out every statement against Christianity Lincoln had ever made and added others of their own: Lincoln's wife was an Episcopalian. Lincoln embraced drunkards as good Christians. Lincoln hated Christ.

Knowing he was vulnerable—and still bruised by his race for the nomination in 1843—Lincoln decided to write a handbill that answered Cartwright's charges. It was not widely distributed, but it is important as a statement of Lincoln's views and political tactics at the time.

> To the Voters of the Seventh Congressional District
>
> Fellow Citizens:
>
> A Charge having got into circulation in some of the neighborhoods of this District, in substance that I am an open scoffer at Christianity, I have by the advice of some friends concluded to notice the subject in this form. That I am not a member of any Christian Church, is true, but I have never denied the truth of the Scripture; and I have never spoken with intentional disrespect of religion in general, or of any denomination of Christians in particular. It is true that in early life I was inclined to believe in what I understand

is called the "Doctrine of necessity"—that is, that the human mind is impelled to action, or held in rest by some power, over which the mind itself has no control; and I have sometimes (with one, two or three, but never publicly) tried to maintain this opinion in argument—The habit of arguing thus however, I have, entirely left off for more than five years—And I add here, I have always understood this same opinion to be held by several of the Christian denominations. The foregoing, is the whole truth, briefly stated, in relation to myself upon this subject.

I do not think I could myself, be brought to support a man for office, whom I knew to be an open enemy of, and scoffer at, religion. Leaving the higher matter of eternal consequences, between him and his maker, I still do not think any man has the right thus to insult the feelings, and injure the morals, of a community in which he may live. If, then I was guilty of such conduct, I should blame no man who would condemn me for it; but I do blame those, whoever they may be, who falsely put such a charge in circulation against me.[21]

Among the intriguing portions of this handbill are the statements that simply are not true. Lincoln had indeed denied the truth of the Scriptures. He had unquestionably scoffed at religion in general. He had certainly insulted the religious convictions of his community. These are affirmed by numerous witnesses, as we have seen. That Lincoln chose to dissemble, to distort the truth of his religious convictions, lent credence to the later claim that he frequently toyed with the religious, saying what was not true and offering himself as a candidate for conversion to keep those who might have been his fiercest critics bound to him by compassion. We shall explore this view further in time, but what we can know with certainty here is Abraham Lincoln—Honest Abe—distorted his religious convictions for political gain in the race of 1846.

His decision to distance himself from the "doctrine of necessity" is also revealing. He had long quoted Shakespeare's *Hamlet* to summarize his thinking about the causes of events: "There's a divinity that shapes our ends, Rough-hew them how we will" (act 5, scene 2). Mary Todd Lincoln told Herndon in later years that "Mr. Lincoln's maxim and philosophy was—'What is to be will be and no cares of ours can arrest the decree.'"[22] He believed, as he said in his handbill, there is a force that controls the human mind—and thus human action—over which human beings have no control. Clearly, he had been unable to fully escape his parents' Calvinism, though his version of "necessity" was nothing religious or spiritual but rather an impersonal force that worked in the world.

Lincoln scholar Allen Guelzo has written that "virtually all of the major deistic or 'infidel' literature published in America in the late eighteenth and early nineteenth century incorporated some form of determinism, largely as a way of accounting for order in the universe without invoking a personal God to create and provide for it."[23] This seems to explain Lincoln well. He wanted to keep a comforting belief in the idea that events have a cause but distance himself from the disturbing idea that this cause could be God. He called this his "superstition" and only sheepishly admitted it to friends.

He claimed that he had stopped arguing for the doctrine as early as 1841. Many of his Springfield friends, though, thought it was the sum of what he believed during all the years they knew him, well past 1841. Jesse Fell, his friend at that time, claimed Lincoln's views "were eminently practical," and included a belief "in a Superintending & over-ruling Providence, that guides & controls the operations of the world; but Maintained that Law and order, & not their violation or suspension; are the appointed means by which this providence is exercised."[24]

If this is accurate and if we can take at least some of the statements in the handbill as true, there had been a mellowing in Lincoln's religious views. The Abraham Lincoln of New Salem boldly declared all religion false. The Lincoln of the handbill says he would never vote for a man who scoffs at religion. The Lincoln of New Salem thought Christianity a hoax. The Lincoln of the handbill appeals to the beliefs of several Christian denominations in his defense. The Lincoln of New Salem and the early days in Springfield was an infidel, an atheist, by testimony of his closest friends. The Lincoln of Jesse Fell's description is a man who believes in a God who exerts some degree of sovereign rule in human affairs.

⌘

This mellowing is confirmed in a conversation Lincoln had with the mother of his friend Henry Rankin in the year of his congressional race. Mrs. Rankin did not recount this conversation until long after the president's death and may have been inspired by a hope to present Lincoln in terms favorable to the religious sentiments of the time. Still, the tone is so clearly Lincoln's and the sentiments expressed so near that of the handbill that it is likely the truth.

During a visit in the summer of 1846, Mrs. Rankin asked Lincoln about Peter Cartwright's charge of infidelity.

> Mrs. Rankin, you have asked me a question opening up a subject that is being thrust into this congressional campaign and which I have resolved to ignore. It is one having no proper place, or call for an answer by me, in the political present or future before us. I will not discuss the character and religion of Jesus Christ on the stump. That is no place for it, though my opponent, a minister of His gospel, thinks it is.

Then, noting the confidence he had in Mrs. Rankin and his "private circle of friends," Lincoln went further.

At the time you refer to, I was having serious questionings about some portions of my former implicit faith in the Bible. The influences that drew me into such doubts were strong ones, men having the widest culture and strongest minds of any I had known up to that time. In the midst of those shadows and questions, before I could see my way clear to decide on them, there came into my life sad events and a loss that you were close to and you knew a great deal about how hard they were for me; for you were at the time, a mutual friend. Those days of trouble found me tossed amidst a sea of questionings. They piled big upon me, experiences that brought with them great strains upon my emotional and mental life. *Through all, I groped my way until I found a stronger and higher grasp of thought, one that reached beyond this life with a clearness and satisfaction I had never known before. The Scriptures unfolded before me with a deeper and more logical appeal, through these new experiences, than anything else I could find to turn to, or ever before had found in them.*

I do not claim that all my doubts were removed then, or since that time have been swept away. They are not. Probably it is to be my lot to go on in a twilight, feeling and reasoning my way through life, as questioning, doubting Thomas did. But in my poor maimed, withered way, I bear with me, as I go on, a seeking spirit of desire for a faith that was with him of olden time, who, in his need, as I in mine, exclaimed: "Help thou my unbelief."

I do not see that I am more astray—though perhaps in a different direction—than many others whose points of view differ widely from each other in the sectarian denominations. They all claim to be Christian and interpret their several creeds as infallible ones. Yet they differ and discuss these questionable subjects without settling them with any mutual satisfaction among themselves.

I doubt the possibility or propriety of settling the religion of Jesus Christ in the models of man-made creeds and dogmas. It was a spirit in the life He laid stress on and taught, if I read aright. I know I see it to be so with me.

The fundamental truths reported in the four gospels as from the lips of Jesus Christ, and that I first heard from the lips of my mother, are settled and fixed moral precepts with me. I have concluded to dismiss from my mind the debatable wrangles that once perplexed me with distractions that stirred up, but never absolutely settled anything. I have tossed them aside with the doubtful differences which divide denominations—sweeping them all out of my mind among the nonessentials. I have ceased to follow such discussions or be interested in them.

I cannot without mental reservations assent to long and complicated creeds and catechisms. If the church would ask simply for assent to the Savior's statements of the substance of the law: "Thou shalt love the Lord thy God with all thy heart, and with all thy soul, and with all thy mind, and thy neighbor as thyself," that church would I gladly unite with.[25]

We should keep in mind that Rankin recounted this conversation forty-three years after it was supposed to have occurred. More than a few historians have been dubious about the recollection. Still, if this is indeed Lincoln in the summer of 1846, then there has been—as his handbill already signaled—a definite shift from the Lincoln of 1837. He is certainly no Christian and not only has doubts about the claims of the Bible but also disappointments with the wrangling of churches. Who does not? Yet he does believe in God, does call Jesus Christ the Savior, does hold the Scriptures as being a reliable moral guide, does yearn to be part of a Christlike church, and does hope for a day of greater faith. This is significant change, but what is its source? Perhaps it has come from his occasional visits to Mary's Episcopal church. Perhaps its seeds were planted by the brand of intelligent, orthodox Christians he encountered for the first time in Springfield. Perhaps it has simply come from his own reading of Scripture, as he seemed to indicate to Mrs. Rankin. Whatever the case, he appears to have emerged from his season of "infidelity" and moved toward a less skeptical view of Christian truth.

He is ever the nonconformist, however. A story recounted by Sandburg captures this, and even if it didn't happen quite as described, it is still the enduring picture of Lincoln's manner that has come to us from the campaign of 1846. Apparently, during the heat of the congressional race, Lincoln went to hear Cartwright preach. During the sermon, the preacher insisted that all who wanted to go to heaven stand. Lincoln didn't. Cartwright urged the congregation again, cutting his eyes to Lincoln. Again, the lanky visitor did not stand. Finally, exasperated, Cartwright sarcastically asked Lincoln directly just where he thought he was going. This time, Lincoln stood: "I came here as a respectful listener. I did not know that I was to be singled out by Brother Cartwright. I believe in treating religious matters with due solemnity. I admit that the questions propounded by Brother Cartwright are of great importance. I did not feel called upon to answer as the rest did. Brother Cartwright asks me directly where I am going. I desire to reply with equal directness: I am going to Congress."

And so he did. Lincoln defeated Cartwright in the race of 1846— 6,340 votes to 4,829.[26]

ஒ௸

It was typical of Lincoln that while a political victory he had long pursued finally graced his life, his mind turned to heartrending themes. In 1844 he had taken time to visit his boyhood home along the banks of the Pigeon River in Indiana. Though his family had moved elsewhere, this was where Abraham had lived for fourteen years, from the age of seven until the age of twenty-one when he set out on his own. To return now as a thirty-seven-year-old man, to see the transformations and ravages of time, filled him with the tender sadness of remembrance. He spoke with aging friends and marveled at their etched faces. He walked among the graves of friends and felt the familiar haunting.

By 1846, despite the distractions of politics, he found himself in a "poetizing mood" and wrote verses that captured what he had felt when he revisited the scene of his youth. The words are important not only as a window into Lincoln's reflections during that all-important year but also as an expression of his maturing literary skill. The poem is among the finest to come from the pen of a future American president. Lincoln must have had some sense of the quality of his work. He sent the verses to a friend and asked that he have them published, which they were the following year.

> *My childhood's home I see again,*
> *And sadden with the view;*
> *And still, as memory crowds my brain,*
> *There's pleasure in it too.*
>
> *O Memory! thou midway world*
> *Twixt earth and paradise,*
> *Where things decayed and loved ones lost*
> *In dreamy shadows rise,*
>
> *And, freed from all that's earthly vile,*
> *Seem hallowed, pure, and bright,*
> *Like scenes in some enchanted isle,*
> *All bathed in liquid light.*
>
> *As dusky mountains please the eye,*
> *When twilight chases day;*
> *As bugle-notes that, passing by,*
> *In distance die away;*

As leaving some grand waterfall,
We, lingering, list its roar—
So memory will hallow all
We've known, but know no more.

Near twenty years have passed away
Since here I bid farewell
To woods and fields, and scenes of play,
And playmates loved so well.

Where many were, how few remain
Of old familiar things;
But seeing them, to mind again
The lost and absent brings.

The friends I left that parting day,
How changed, as time has sped!
Young childhood grown, strong manhood gray,
And half of all are dead.

I hear the loved survivors tell
How nought from death could save,
Till every sound appears a knell,
And every spot a grave.

I range the fields with pensive tread,
And pace the hollow rooms;
And feel (companion of the dead)
I'm living in the tombs.[27]

Having completed this haunting poem, Lincoln paused for a season and then decided to enshrine in verse a particularly painful memory from his Indiana travels. A childhood friend, Matthew Gentry, had suddenly, inexplicably gone insane when Lincoln was sixteen. Seeing Matthew again and hearing of his wild behavior through the years—he had maimed himself, fought with his father, and tried to kill his mother—was painful. Lincoln was unable to forget the "mental night" to which his old friend was condemned, unable to stop Matthew's "mournful song" from sounding again and again in his ears. Mindful of his own family's history of mental illness and ever tortured by the specter of depression, Lincoln was tormented by Matthew Gentry's fate.

> *But here's an object more of dread*
> *Than ought the grave contains—*
> *A human form with reason fled,*
> *While wretched life remains.*
>
> *Poor Matthew! Once of genius bright,*
> *A fortune-favored child—*
> *Now locked for aye, in mental night,*
> *A haggard mad-man wild.*
>
> *Poor Matthew! I have ne'er forgot*
> *When first, with maddened will,*
> *Yourself you maimed, your father fought,*
> *And mother strove to kill;*
>
> *When terror spread, and neighbours ran,*
> *Your dang'rous strength to bind;*
> *And soon, a howling crazy man*
> *Your limbs were fast confined.*
>
> *How then you strove and shrieked aloud,*
> *Your bones and sinnews bared;*

And fiendish on the gazing crowd,
With burning eye-balls glared—

And begged, and swore, and wept and prayed
With maniac laughter joined—
How fearful were those signs displayed
By pangs that killed thy mind!

And when at length, tho' drear and long,
Time soothed thy fiercer woes,
How plaintively thy mournful song,
Upon the still night rose.

I've heard it oft, as if I dreamed,
Far-distant, sweet, and lone—
The funeral dirge, it ever seemed
Of reason dead and gone.

To drink its strains, I've stole away,
All stealthily and still,
Ere yet the rising God of day
Had streaked the Eastern hill.

Air held his breath; trees, with the spell,
Seemed sorrowing angels round,
Whose swelling tears in dew-drops fell
Upon the listening ground.

But this is past; and nought remains,
That raised thee o'er the brute.
Thy piercing shrieks, and soothing strains,
Are like, forever mute.

Now fare thee well—more thou the cause,
Than subject now of woe.
All mental pangs, by time's kind laws,
Hast lost the power to know.

O death! Thou awe-inspiring prince,
That keepst the world in fear;
Why dost thou tear more blest ones hence,
And leave him ling'ring here?[28]

We see a familiar Lincoln in these words. He is still fixated on grief, loneliness, and loss. He does not mention the joys of his youth—the adventures and pranks, the excitement of a boy or the transforming fire of dawning manhood, even the books and the thrill of discovery. Instead, every spot is a grave. The dead loom larger than the living. Death itself is not a gentle end to lives woven by the hand of God. Instead, it is an "awe-inspiring prince" who rules by fear and tears the dead from the living. Clearly, whatever softening toward God and Christianity Lincoln may have undergone—if his campaign handbill and the conversation with Mrs. Rankin are any guide it had not lifted the shadows circling his soul or given him a loving, sovereign Deity to replace his icy doctrine of necessity.

⁂

His term in Congress was brief and relatively uneventful. He was seated in December 1847 and was out of office, because of his party's policy of rotating each congressional seat, by early August of 1849. His opposition to the U. S. war with Mexico was unpopular and moved political enemies to call him a Benedict Arnold. He also urged the abolition of slavery in the District of Columbia, a moral stand more appreciated in later history than at the time.

Abraham Lincoln, Congressman-elect from Illinois (1848)

Overall, his months in Congress were a disappointment to him, and he likely let his frustrations spill out on Mary. Just three months after arriving in Washington, he found Mary and the boys such a distraction that he sent them to her father's home in Lexington. It did not help. The true distraction had been elsewhere, perhaps in the war between ambition and self-doubt that raged in his soul, and within months of sending his wife away, he apologized. "In this troublesome world we are never quite satisfied," he wrote her on April 16, 1848. "When you were here, I thought you hindered me some in attending to business; but now, having nothing but business—no variety—it has grown exceedingly tasteless to me . . . I hate to stay in this old room by myself." Still, there had obviously been some bad behavior on Mary's part, perhaps outbursts of her volcanic jealousy. When she sent letters pleading to return to him, he wrote, "Will you be a good girl in all things, if I consent? Then come along, and that as soon as possible. Having got the idea in my head, I shall be impatient till I see you."[29]

We cannot know if his disappointment with Washington politics and the wearying discord in his home moved him to reflect more deeply on religion. It had clearly been on his mind prior to taking office. On a speaking tour that allowed him to visit Niagara Falls, he wrote in sweeping biblical imagery of the "wonder" and "charm" of the great waters: "When Columbus first sought this continent—when Christ suffered on the cross—when Moses led Israel through the Red-Sea— nay, even when Adam first came from the hand of his Maker—then as now, Niagara was roaring here."[30] Though these words give us no certainty about Lincoln's religion, they do indicate that he no longer regarded the Bible as myth. He mentions three miraculous events— creation, the crucifixion of Jesus, and the escape of Israel from Egypt through the Red Sea—which no "infidel" or consistent "religious skep- tic" would refer to without a sneer of disbelief. Given that he had once been under the tutelage of Paine, Volney, Gibbon, and Burns—and if we assume that he was not merely pandering to the religious sentiments of his audience—this is further evidence that Lincoln was in the midst of a subtle religious shift in the late 1840s.

Even if he was not—even if religion had not crossed his mind since he dispensed with Peter Cartwright in the election of 1846—what came next did change his thinking about Christianity and did become one of the most defining events of his life. It occurred in the wake of his father-in-law's death on July 17, 1849. Robert Smith Todd, a good man who thought much of Lincoln, fell to cholera at the age of fifty- nine and left a second wife and four daughters to settle his disputed financial affairs. All turned to Lincoln, now an experienced lawyer just months out of Congress, to resolve the infighting and the lawsuits. This is how the Lincoln family came to live for a time in Robert Todd's home, and it is also what placed Abraham Lincoln in the Todds' library in the fall of 1849.

By that year Lexington, Kentucky, was already known as the Athens of the West for its rich cultural life and the intellectual achievements of its citizens. Bookish networks that served the cause of self-education thrived; this meant a successful businessman like Robert Todd had opportunity to read widely and assemble an impressive library. It is easy to imagine that when the day's filings and mediating were done,

Lincoln took refuge in this calm, quiet room in the Todds' home. We are certain that he read portions of numerous books there because, perhaps forgetting himself, he routinely scribbled comments in margins and notes on flyleaves.

One of the volumes he took from the shelves and began reading with fascination was by a Reverend James D. Smith. Lincoln would have immediately recognized the name, and perhaps this was why he first noticed the book. Smith was the pastor of First Presbyterian Church at the southeast corner of Third and Washington streets in Springfield. Since the city did not yet number even five thousand people, Lincoln certainly knew who Smith was. If he did not choose the volume because he knew its author, it is likely he was intrigued by the title: *The Christian's Defence, Containing a Fair Statement, and Impartial Examination of the Leading Objections Urged by Infidels Against the Antiquity, Genuineness, Credibility and Inspiration of the Holy Scriptures; Enriched with Copious Extracts from Learned Authors.*

✽

If Lincoln knew anything of Smith's story, he may have felt some connection to it. Both were large, powerful men. Both had mothers who died early: Lincoln's of the milk sickness when he was nine and Smith's when she was giving birth to him on May 11, 1798. Both were religious skeptics in their early years who were mentored by the works of Volney and Paine. Both enjoyed mocking the antics of preachers.

Smith's life eventually took a different course. He moved from Glasgow to New York in 1820 to establish himself in business. He failed both there and in Cincinnati and by 1824 had moved to southern Indiana to teach school and write. As a brash "confirmed Deist," he loved to attend camp meetings to heckle the ministers and mimic the wild manifestations. When he arrived in Indiana, though, he heard Reverend James Blackwell preach and was so moved that he converted to faith in Jesus Christ and became a Christian. Having once despised revivals, he became a revivalist and was ordained by the Logan Presbytery of the Cumberland Presbyterian Church in Kentucky on October 13, 1825.

He was a revivalist Presbyterian, but he also had a scholarly bent. While he pastored churches in Kentucky and Tennessee, he started a periodical, edited the works of James McGready, and published a collection of hymns. A few years later he completed a history of the Cumberland Presbyterian Church. He was a founder of Cumberland College in Lebanon, Tennessee, and likely earned a doctorate there but eventually left the Cumberland Presbyterians to join the "regular" Presbyterians. The issue that led to this change was likely free will. The Cumberland Presbyterians favored free will over the strong predestination stand of traditional Presbyterians. Learned, fiery, and personable, Smith appealed to the congregation of First Presbyterian Church in Springfield when he was asked to speak there and later was chosen as their pastor in March of 1849, just about the time Abraham Lincoln was leaving the U.S. Congress to return home and practice law.

Smith's book was the fruit of a debate he had been part of in 1841. He was known for his skilled, sometimes bombastic defense of the Bible, and in 1839 and 1840 he gave a series of popular lectures in Columbus, Mississippi, bearing titles like "The Natures and Tendencies of Infidelity" and "The Evidences of Christianity." A well-known skeptic named C. G. Olmsted challenged Smith to a debate and suggested topics like, "Were the writers of the different books of the Bible inspired men? Did the facts which they detail occur? Was Jesus Christ miraculously begotten? Did he perform miracles? Did Jesus rise from the dead?"[31] Smith agreed to the challenge and threw himself into his preparation, even writing friends in England for drawings of Egyptian monuments to use as evidence for the sojourns of the Jews described in the biblical book of Exodus.

The debate between Smith and Olmsted lasted eighteen nights.

By all accounts, Olmsted was outgunned. Smith was a sharp mind and a big personality skilled in the use of grand, dramatic gestures. He was often compared with the orator Daniel Webster. His only failing was his insistence upon attacking Olmsted personally. As a witness to the debates later wrote, "The defeat would have been more complete, had Mr. S omitted some of his personal allusions, and had he suppressed his natural inclination to sarcasm. Indeed his blasts of sarcasm were truly withering. His opponent, finding that he could not cope with him in this respect, retreated, and took shelter under the sympathies of his audience."[32] This failing aside, so thorough was Smith's victory that his supporters began pleading for his arguments in print. In 1843, Smith complied. *The Christian's Defence* was published and distributed on a limited basis to those eager souls who had paid subscriptions in advance. A copy eventually made its way to Robert Todd's library, where, six years later, Abraham Lincoln pulled it from the shelves.

⁓

Lincoln began reading Smith's book in Lexington, but since it ran to a lengthy two volumes, he could not complete it. He returned to Springfield on November 15 and quickly sought out Thomas Lewis, a fellow lawyer who was also an elder at First Presbyterian Church. Lewis later recalled, "Mr. Lincoln said to me that when on a visit somewhere he had seen and partially read a work of Dr. Smith on evidences of Christianity, which had led him to change his view of the Christian religion, and he would like to get that work and finish the reading of it, and also to make the acquaintance of Dr. Smith. I . . . took Dr. Smith to Mr. Lincoln's office, Dr. Smith gave Mr. Lincoln a copy of his book, as I know, at his own request."[33]

What was it that attracted Lincoln to Smith's work? He had surely come across Christian apologists before. Clearly, none had won him.

Now he was so enamored of a work on this topic that he was eager not only to read it but to own it and meet its author. It is likely that the main draw of Smith's work for Lincoln was the author's insistence upon an unrelenting examination of evidence. Lincoln had known more of the shouting, sweaty preacher who appealed to sentiment than the cool, thoughtful Christian orator.

Smith reached to the lawyer in Lincoln by making a case for Christ and the Bible as an attorney might plead his case before the bar. Smith also must have impressed Lincoln with his intellectual courage. He took on religious skeptics directly, quoting their works and answering them methodically. In one section he cleverly used statements from Volney's own travel journals as support for the accuracy of the Bible. In another he used Roman writers and early church fathers to make his case for the authenticity of Scripture. This fearless, learned approach surely won Lincoln.

He likely admired, also, how farsighted Smith was on the matter of race. Most skeptics of that time used racist arguments to refute the idea that all men might have come from a common ancestor like Adam. Smith argued that the differences between the races were only "skin-deep," that blacks and whites were essentially the same apart from the matter of color.[34] He was ahead of his time in this thinking. Lincoln was with him. He had not heard many preachers speak in such terms, and he wanted to hear more.

Lincoln took Smith's gift home, read it, and kept it on the shelves with the rest of his tiny but treasured collection of books. His son, Robert, remembered seeing Smith's work many times in his family's home at Eighth and Jackson.[35] Lincoln's brother-in-law, Ninian W. Edwards, recalled that Lincoln told him, "I have been reading a work of Dr. Smith on the evidences of Christianity, and have heard him preach and converse on the subject, and I am now convinced of the truth of the Christian religion."[36] Smith also believed Lincoln was converted to Christianity through his ministry and writing. Less than two years after Lincoln was assassinated, Smith told Herndon, "It is a very easy matter to prove that while I was Pastor of the 1st Presbyterian Church of Springfield, Mr. Lincoln did avow his belief in the Divine Authority and Inspiration of the Scriptures." Referring to his book, Smith explained that "the preparation of that work cost me long and arduous mental labor, and if no other effect was ever produced by it, than the influence it exerted upon the mind of that man whose name thrills the heart of every patriotic American, I thank God that I was induced to undertake the work. Immediately after the above avowal Mr. Lincoln placed himself and family under my pastoral care, and when at home he was a regular attendant upon my ministry."[37]

This episode in Lincoln's life has been fiercely debated by scholars. Most allow that Lincoln might have embraced a broader view of God and the Bible under Smith's influence but argue that he certainly did not become a Christian in any meaningful sense. Typical is British scholar Richard Carwardine:

It is, then, quite possible that Lincoln's intellectual development within a Presbyterian institutional framework in Springfield made him much more receptive to the idea of the inspiration of Scripture. It is also possible that he had embraced a more Christological theology, now using the terms "Lord" and "Savior" in more than just a humanist sense. It is possible, but the weight of evidence is against it.[38]

Views like Carwardine's are rooted in more than an academic's suspicion of religion. Statements from Lincoln's Springfield friends lend credence to such doubts. Fellow lawyer and intimate Jesse Fell insisted, "I have no hesitation whatever in saying, that whilst he held many opinions in common with the great mass of Christian believers, he did not believe in what are regarded as the orthodox or evangelical views of Christianity."[39] James Matheny was not only a friend and fellow lawyer but also a groomsman at Lincoln's wedding. He believed that Lincoln's entire involvement with Smith was part of a "sharp game" he was playing with the clergy.

> Lincoln knew that he was to be a great man—was a rising man—was looking to the Presidency &c. and well knowing that the old infidel, if not Atheistic charge would be made & proved against him and to avoid the disgrace—odium and unpopularity of it tramped on the Christian toes saying—"come and Convert me"; the Elders—lower & higher members of the churches, including Ministers &c flocked around him & that he appeared openly to the world as a seeker—that it was noised about that Lincoln was a seeker after Salvation &c in the Lord—that letters were written more or less all over the land that Lincoln was soon to be a changed man &c and thus it was he used the Revd Jas Smith of Scotland.[40]

Less cynically, a year after his father's death, Robert Lincoln told William Herndon, "I have to say that I do not know of Dr. Smith's having 'converted' my father from 'Unitarian' to 'Trinitarian' belief, nor do I know that he held any decided views on the subject as I never heard him speak of it."[41]

෴

Even if these recollections are true—and some of Lincoln's friends dramatically revised their accounts of his faith in later years, as we shall discover—there was still a change of some kind happening in Lincoln's life, and it was deepened by a tragedy that befell him early in 1850.

Just weeks after the Lincolns returned from Lexington, as Abraham met Smith and finished reading *The Christian's Defence*, three-year-old Eddie fell ill. Doctors thought at first he suffered from diphtheria, but as the sickness raged on for weeks, this became unlikely. Finally, the dreaded diagnosis came: "consumption"—pulmonary tuberculosis. Consumption was an apt term, though, for victims of the disease seemed to slowly, horribly waste away. Their suffering was terrifying and cruel, particularly to those who stood by helplessly. There was high fever and violent coughing that left lifeless exhaustion in its wake. Then the coughing would resume. Depression set in, and anorexia. The disease killed more Americans in the 1850s than any other sickness except cholera. Half its victims were under the age of five.[42]

Doctors did not know what to do but did what they knew. They began by bleeding the victims, a common answer to nearly every malady in that age. Then emetics and purgatives were used. So, too, were anticoughing medicines that were mostly made from opium. Sufferers were fed a diet of panada, oatmeal gruel, and rice jelly. Little of this brought relief.

Eddie coughed and sweated and vomited for fifty-two days. Finally, on February 1, 1850, he died. Abraham and Mary were understandably undone and called for Springfield's Episcopal minister, Father Charles Dresser. Mary was only a nominal Episcopalian, but Dresser had married the Lincolns and perhaps could be of comfort. Word quickly came that Dresser was out of town. This turned the Lincolns to the only other clergyman who had impacted their lives in any memorable way: Reverend James Smith.

At eleven o'clock the next morning, Smith conducted Eddie's funeral in the Lincolns' home and then followed the casket the fourteen blocks to Hutchinson Cemetery to speak final words over the boy's body. Perhaps something he said prompted the poem that appeared in the *Illinois Daily Journal* a few days later. Either Abraham or Mary wrote it, and though it is filled with the religious sentimentality of the Victorian age, it does, perhaps, hint at the spiritual themes that brought them comfort at the time—themes likely suggested by Smith's funeral sermons.

Those midnight stars are sadly dimmed,
That late so brilliantly shone,
And the crimson tinge from cheek and lip,
With the heart's warm life has flown—

The angel of Death was hovering nigh,
And the lovely boy was called to die.
The silken waves of his glossy hair
Lie still over his marble brow,

And the pallid lip and pearly cheek
The presence of Death avow.
Pure little bud in kindness given,
In mercy taken to bloom in heaven.

Happier far is the angel child
With the harp and the crown of gold,
Who warbles now at the Savior's feet
The glories to us untold.

Eddie, meet blossom of heavenly love,
Dwells in the spirit-world above.
Angel Boy—fare thee well, farewell
Sweet Eddie, We bid thee adieu!

Affection's wail cannot reach thee now
Deep though it be, and true.
Bright is the home to him now given
For, "of such is the kingdom of heaven."[43]

It is more likely that this is from Abraham's pen than from his wife's. Mary had become hysterical, as she would time and again when faced with death throughout her tortured life. She could not have composed such verses just days after her son's passing. It was Abraham who wrote this tribute and he who worried about a wife driven to the edge of sanity by sorrow. We can imagine him tenderly comforting her but then slipping away alone to stand at lot number 409 in the Hutchison Cemetery and grieve for his dead son.

In his heartbreak, he turned to the counsel of Reverend Smith. The two spent time together, discussed Christian truth by the hour, and Smith recommended books the anguished father devoured. If Lincoln did not emerge from this season a stalwart Christian, he had at a minimum begun to think differently about God. Years later, Mary, who admitted her husband's religious infidelity in his early days, reported,

> From the time of the death of our little Edward, I believe my husband's heart, was directed towards religion & as time passed on—when Mr. Lincoln became elevated to Office—with the care of a great Nation upon his shoulders—when devastating war was upon us—then indeed to my own knowledge—did his great heart go up daily, hourly, in prayer to God—for his sustaining power.[44]

John Todd Stuart recalled that after Eddie's death,

> Dr. Smith and Mr. Lincoln had much discussion in relation to the truth of the Christian religion, and . . . Dr. Smith had furnished Mr. Lincoln with books to read on that subject, and among others one had been written by himself, some time previous, on infidelity; and that Dr. Smith claimed that after this investigation Mr. Lincoln had changed his opinion, and became a believer in the truth of the Christian religion.[45]

We cannot know with certainty the degree of religious change that came about in Lincoln's life during this time. We can, though, see evidence that a meaningful transformation was under way. Not long after Eddie's death, the Lincolns—grateful for Smith's ministry at their time of grief—began attending First Presbyterian Church. It brings a smile to consider that at first they sat in the "amen corner" of the church, where the pews were free and agreement with the sermon was often boisterous.

Reverend James D. Smith of Springfield First Presbyterian Church

In time, they rented a pew—the custom of the time—and grew to love Smith's ministry so dearly that Mary, with her husband's permission, joined the church in 1852. This would have come only after the elders of First Presbyterian met with Mary to assure she had an "experimental religion." This meant that they wanted to know if she had actually experienced the grace of God and the work of his Spirit, something more than intellectual assent to doctrine. She apparently satisfied the elders. They accepted Mary Lincoln as a member and issued a letter saying as much. Three years later, the Lincolns had their son Thomas baptized at First Presbyterian. He was the only one of the Lincolns' children to be baptized, probably because he was the only child born after Smith entered their lives.

Abraham often attended services with Mary, paid his "pew tax," and gave liberally to the church's ministries. He also gave to other churches. When the Baptists raised funds to build a meeting house, Lincoln gave. When the Evangelical Lutherans built a building at Sixth and Madison in Springfield, Lincoln gave again. He even helped pay the salary of the minister of the First Baptist Church for a season.[46] When Reverend Noyes Miner arrived in Springfield, Lincoln gave him the free use of his horse and carriage for several years to encourage the man's ministry. Even if Lincoln had not turned fully to Christianity as Smith and others insisted, he had at least begun to value the good that Christian ministers did. No longer would he complain of a "priest ridden" people as he had in his battles with Peter Cartwright.

Equally telling is a letter Lincoln wrote when word reached him that his father lay dying. It was addressed to his stepbrother on January 12, 1851.

> I sincerely hope Father may yet recover his health; but at all events tell him to remember to call upon, and confide in, our great, and good, and merciful Maker; who will not turn away from him in any extremity. He notes the fall of a sparrow, and numbers the hairs of our heads; and He will not forget the dying man, who puts his trust in Him . . . but that if it be his lot to go now, he will soon have a joyous [meeting] with many loved ones gone before; and where [the rest] of us, through the help of God, hope ere-long [to join] them.[47]

Some scholars have complained there are no references to Jesus Christ in this letter and so insist that it cannot be evidence of a Christian conversion in Lincoln's life. Perhaps, but this misses the point. If this letter is a genuine reflection of its author, it means that not only is Lincoln no longer an infidel or an atheist; he is also no longer a skeptic so far as God, his providence, the resurrection, and the reality of heaven are concerned. This is confirmation of the dramatic shift then under way in Lincoln's life. It was signaled by the handbill in the congressional race of 1846. It was confirmed in the conversation with Mrs. Rankin. It is hinted at even in the words Lincoln chose in describing Niagara Falls. It is certainly affirmed in the testimony of Reverend Smith, Mary Lincoln, Ninian Edwards, and John Stuart, among others. Then, of course, there is Lincoln's support for religion and religious leaders in Springfield, as well as his words of comfort for his father.

⁓

Had Lincoln become a Christian? We cannot know definitively. We do have reason to suspect, though, that something had changed in his ongoing battle with God. Perhaps there was only a slight thaw in an otherwise hostile cold war. Lincoln, certainly, was not as he had been. He was no longer the village atheist. He was no longer the man aflame with Enlightenment ideas of atheism or infidelity. He was no longer an unceasing critic of the Bible. He no longer sat with Paine and Volney and agreed that the religious were "priest ridden," that the Christian Church was a hoax, or that the Bible was the work of mythologists. Instead, he had become, at a minimum, a believer in the existence of God, in heaven, in the value of Christian ministry, in the Bible as a wise guide to human conduct, and in life after death. A process of spiritual broadening had clearly begun.

And what of those from Lincoln's Springfield years who were certain their friend remained a skeptic all his days? Many, in time, reversed themselves. James Matheny—who had charged Lincoln with playing a "sharp game" by convincing religious people that he was open to conversion merely to win their votes—later said, "While I do believe Mr. Lincoln to have been an infidel in his former life, when his mind was as yet unformed, and his associations principally with rough and skeptical men, yet I believe he was a very different man in later life; and that after associating with a different class of men, and investigating the subject, he was a firm believer in the Christian religion."[48] William Herndon had so insisted Lincoln was a religious skeptic that it sometimes led to public feuds. Yet in later life, when he had mellowed a bit, Herndon admitted that Lincoln "believed in God," that he "would go to church as other men do," and that he was "a deeply and thoroughly religious man."[49]

This leads us to the conclusion that the Lincoln of the New Salem and early Springfield years is not necessarily the Lincoln of later life. A progression had begun, a journey toward a belief in God and an understanding of that God's nature. This would not end all of Lincoln's spiritual wrestling. He would still feel himself cursed. He would still be frustrated with churches and preachers, still be unsure of the ways of Providence, still be disgusted with the evils men sanctioned from the pages of Scripture. He had also not settled his questions about Jesus Christ. Yet he was in motion, migrating, on something of a pilgrimage toward truth.

This is not a Lincoln we are usually allowed to see in the pages of textbooks and the writings of historians. Lincoln's faith is usually frozen as of his early Springfield years and never allowed to mature. This makes him ever the skeptic, ever religiously uncertain and unsure. It is an injustice, for the truth is that Lincoln was, in fact, a religious pilgrim, and his spiritual journey is among the more fascinating and defining realities of his life.

༄

There is still a vital question that lingers over the subject of Lincoln's religion: Why, after Smith's ministry and years in a Presbyterian church and hours of reading the Bible, was Lincoln not definitively converted (perhaps the language should be *born again* or *saved*)? He may well have been, though at this stage in his life it does not seem likely. But why? Why is there no statement from Lincoln that he had fully committed himself to Jesus Christ? Why does his acceptance of Christianity seem to come in bits and pieces, one doctrine at a time—the sovereignty of God from one source, the truth of Scripture from another? Never in these years do we have a full, unreserved statement of Lincoln's entire acceptance of the Christian faith. Given how much time he spent reading and discussing Christianity and given how close he was, by his own admission, to what most orthodox Christians believed, why did he seem to keep himself just short of conversion?

Scholars have pointed to his intellectualism or factors like his distrust of the often stilted Christianity of his day as possible causes for Lincoln's slow, hesitant, qualified journey into Christianity. Yet another reason, one that is rarely mentioned, is so revealing of Lincoln's mind and tortured soul that it should not be missed. If it is true, it explains much of Lincoln's perspective on his faith and exposes an ongoing struggle with God that may even, in turn, have shaped his understanding of a subject as vast as the American Civil War.

We have already seen that Lincoln was troubled by his suspicion that he was the son of an illegitimate woman. He had told Herndon in the early 1850s, "My mother was a bastard, was the daughter of a nobleman, so called of Virginia. My mother's mother was poor and credulous, and she was shamefully taken advantage of by the man. My mother inherited his qualities and I hers."[50]

Today the knowledge that a man's mother was illegitimate would lead us to think no differently of the man himself. It was not so in Lincoln's time. Heredity was still a divinely governed, mystical force. First sons were still considered superior to second sons in parts of Europe; morality and character were thought to be inherited; and men spoke of the lightest family trait as being "in the blood." This is why Lincoln told Herndon in that same conversation that he was sure "his power of analysis, his logic, his mental activity, his ambition, and all the qualities that distinguished him" came from the "nobleman" who had wronged his mother.[51] He assumed, as did many of his generation, the upper classes were populated by those of superior gifts. He also assumed that the illegitimate were somehow inferior. "Did you never notice," he asked Herndon, "that bastards are generally smarter, shrewder and more intellectual than others? Is it because it is stolen?"[52] He was a product of his times in believing that what good qualities an illegitimate man might have were somehow acquired improperly, that they were not gifts originally intended for him by his Maker.

Once we understand how the illegitimate were often perceived in Lincoln's day, we can begin to understand why he was tortured by the circumstances of his mother's birth. We can also begin to understand how he might have begun attributing his illegitimacy to God, begun seeing it as the reason for the divine rejection he thought he had long endured. Herndon believed "rumors of bastardy" convinced Lincoln "that God had cursed and crushed him especially."[53] As Allen Guelzo explains,

> It was not the smart-tongued "infidelity" of his New Salem days which, in the 1850s, kept Lincoln from following Mary Lincoln into a church fellowship that would otherwise have had every reason to welcome him with but few questions asked. It was Lincoln's sense of being helpless and unworthy in the estimate of the glowering Father who offered nothing but demands for a perfection Lincoln could not honestly claim for his own. This was far more terrifying than the passivity which is supposed to be the flip side of "necessity," and it is this which accounts for the new edge of plaintiveness that creeps into Lincoln's comments on religion in the 1850s.[54]

Lincoln would not have been the first man to long for divine acceptance but to think himself unworthy of it. Martin Luther certainly did. So did John Wesley and George Whitefield, to name but a few. These men felt themselves too given to sin to warrant the salvation of God. Lincoln's difficulty was not that he thought himself too unclean to please a holy God but rather that he thought God had cursed him before Lincoln had even emerged from the womb. This may be why he spoke as one who longed for a salvation that would never be his. He was the son of a bastard. The kingdom was shut tight against him. This was why he could not believe as other men did.

Joshua Speed confirmed this when he said that Lincoln "tried to be a believer, but his reason could not grasp and solve the great problem of redemption as taught."[55] Again, Lincoln said this even more forcefully in his talk with Mrs. Rankin in 1846. "Probably it is to be my lot," he told his friend's mother, "to go on in a twilight, feeling and reasoning my way through life, as questioning, doubting Thomas did. But in my poor maimed, withered way, I bear with me, as I go on, a seeking spirit of desire for a faith that was with him of olden time, who, in his need, as I in mine, exclaimed: 'Help thou my unbelief.'"[56]

Yet why did Lincoln believe he bore the mark of Cain—that he, like Job, had been chosen for punishment? Why was he "maimed" and "withered" while seeking true faith? If Herndon is correct, it is because he took his mother's illegitimacy as a sign of God's judgment, as evidence of a curse that kept him from fulfilling the only condition of divine acceptance: faith. It is important to note that Lincoln would not have found this reasoning in the sermons of Reverend Smith or, for that matter, in the theology of any other pastor he grew to trust. The evangelical gospel of men like Smith and Miner offered salvation—divine love and forgiveness—to all who repented, believed, and followed Christ's teaching. None were denied the kingdom because of some defect of birth. Lincoln had concocted this on his own, creating it entirely from his own sense of humiliation. He had translated his sense of shame to a theological level by believing that God rejected him for a wrong that occurred before he was even born.

⁓

In searching for the reason that a man of Abraham Lincoln's gifts would come to believe he was cursed, we must also consider both his atrocious relationship with his father and his battle with depression. It is natural that human beings should perceive God in terms of their earthly fathers. For most people, "God" is simply "father" written large. The only reference they have for "father" is human fathers, and so they come to expect of God a universal version of what they have already known. This means that often their religious struggles to love and obey God spring from their psychological struggles to surmount the wounds and deformities of living with imperfect human fathers.

If this is true, then it is no wonder that Lincoln thought himself unwelcomed by a cruel and demanding God. Thomas Lincoln had never understood his bright, quixotic son. He punished the boy well into his teenage years, lacerated him with criticism, condemned him with scripture, and forced him to work so tirelessly that Lincoln later told his audiences he had once been a slave. Meanwhile, Thomas was negligent in his son's care. He thought nothing of abandoning his two children for months without word, leaving them without adequate provisions and in the hands of an immature, irresponsible twenty-year-old cousin. The two Lincoln men argued often, endured lengthy seasons of stony silence, and parted company almost as soon as the law allowed. Abraham rarely saw his father thereafter; when the older man died, Lincoln did not attend the funeral and did not bother to mark the grave with a stone. He also did not name a son after his father, the custom of the time, until two years after the man was dead.

If Abraham expected of God what he had experienced from Thomas Lincoln, it is no wonder he concluded that some combination of his sins, his heredity, his theological uncertainty, or even his innate personality angered God and caused him to turn away. Thus he was ever doomed to be a "questioning, doubting Thomas."

Lincoln's depression certainly made him feel cursed as well. The nature of depression is cruel, capricious, and commanding. While other men walk the streets at peace and in seeming harmony with the world, those who suffer depression feel themselves singled out for abuse. Their disease is a marauding foe that declares war on the soul and siphons from it hope, meaning, love, and the resilience necessary for rebounding against the agonies of a pitiless world. The light fades, and it is painful even to exist. Depression is so all-encompassing that life is defined by it: sufferers often think of it as the label fate has placed over their lives. In other words, depression is in every sense a curse to those who endure it, a curse of rejection from life itself. Add to this ever-present specter the death of nearly everyone Lincoln cared about in his early life, and it is not difficult to see how he might come to think of his life as absent the grace and goodness others knew. And who would be withholding that grace and goodness but the same God who had strewn his life with graves and left him mired in suicidal hypos time and again. Of course that God would never accept him or give him the gift of faith others seemed to receive without effort. Of course no matter how eagerly he strived to believe, belief would elude him. This was the prerogative of a sovereign God who did as he wished with human life. What was Lincoln to do but accept his fate and hope for a change of the divine mood?

The truth may be that Lincoln's hesitation to commit himself unreservedly to the Christian gospel may not have been solely because of nagging theological questions but also because of nagging certainties about his repugnance to God. This would have shaped everything about his religious life. One does not love a God who rejects a man because he is a bastard's son; one obeys him and keeps his distance. One does not feel the joy of undeserved mercy; one feels the press of prescribed duty. One does not think of such a being as Father and Savior and friend, but rather as "Supreme Being" and "Ruler of Nations."

There is in Lincoln's life, then, an ongoing battle—for understanding one's fate, for living in the glare of divine rejection, for unqualified submission, and, perhaps, for eventual acceptance. If Herndon was right and Lincoln thought himself cursed because of his mother's illegitimacy, then beginning to believe in God as he had in recent years meant he had only begun to believe in his foe—the God who marred him from birth and withheld affection. He now had to fight to understand this God's will, both for himself and, in time, for a nation just then beginning to destroy itself in hate.

FOUR

〰〰〰

ON WINGS OF GRIEF

IT WAS FEBRUARY 11, 1861. THE DAY WAS COLD AND wet, a dismal, dreary setting for the scene. Poet Sandburg tells us, "Chilly gray mist hung the circle of the prairie horizon."[1] Some were grateful that the wet weather hid the tears.

Lincoln had been busy in the days before. Crowds had flooded into Springfield to see him. He had to navigate them. He also had to navigate the thorny issue of whether he would stay in partnership with William Herndon. Friends urged against it. Herndon was a heavy drinker, an embarrassment. It wouldn't do. Lincoln decided to keep the firm as it was. He would not abandon his friend. He insisted the Lincoln and Herndon sign remain in place, gently swinging on its rusty hinges.

There was also packing to do. Clothes, furniture, household goods, and, of course, books—it all had to be prepared. And there was livestock to sell. He wouldn't need them. What he wrote in his own hand on his luggage told the tale: "A. Lincoln. The White House, Washington D.C." On November 6, he had been elected president of the United States.

Now, it was time to leave for Washington by train. The destiny he had dreamed of as a boy now called.

Yet all was not as he had imagined. He was under the heavy burden of watching the country come apart. His election had signaled many in the South that their days in the American union were at an end. A banner at an Alabama rally proclaimed, "Resistance to Lincoln is Obedience to God." It was the slogan of the Southern mood. Already Southern states had left the Union; already a Confederate States of America had been formed. The spirit of impending war filled the land—revealed in the boasts of angry men, in the worries of mothers, in the way nervous friends passed each other on the streets.

The time had come. Lincoln was scheduled to leave at eight o'clock that morning. He arrived early at the redbrick Springfield station, accompanied by some fifteen men. Mary and the children were not with him. They would come soon after. Hundreds gathered to cheer him, but now, with news of the nation's fragmenting, there was little sense of joy. The crowd was solemn, almost in mourning. Lincoln entered the station and began greeting friends. He was moved by the moment and by the heaviness in the people, and decided to speak. He walked out onto the platform toward the train prepared for him. Then he stepped up to the rear platform of a train car and gestured to the crowd. All became silent. Without having prepared any remarks in advance, he began to speak.

> My friends—No one, not in my situation, can appreciate my feeling of sadness at this parting. To this place, and the kindness of these people, I owe every thing. Here I have lived a quarter of a century, and have passed from a young to an old man. Here my children have been born, and one is buried. I now leave, not knowing when, or whether ever, I may return, with a task before me greater than that which rested upon Washington. Without the assistance of that Divine Being, who ever attended him, I cannot succeed. With that assistance

I cannot fail. Trusting in Him, who can go with me, and remain with you and be every where for good, let us confidently hope that all will yet be well. To His care commending you, as I hope in your prayers you will commend me, I bid you an affectionate farewell.[2]

The words were remembered by most as the sincere, even prophetic utterance of a president who would return to that same Springfield train station four years and three months later in a casket, the slain martyr of a war-purged nation.

Not all would remember the moment this way.

One historian has written that such a large portion of Springfield's citizens doubted Lincoln's religious sincerity that his farewell address "was regarded by many as an evidence both of his weakness and of his hypocrisy, . . . and was tossed about as a joke—'old Abe's last.'"[3]

This was typical of the suspicion that surrounded Lincoln's faith, particularly during the presidential campaign of 1860. Words that from another man would have been taken as sincere and even holy were taken as a cynical joke when spoken by Lincoln. A journalist reported that only three out of twenty-three ministers in Springfield intended to vote for Lincoln.[1] This was nothing new. Ministers had long criticized him for being an infidel. He was used to it. He had cut his political teeth on the tactics of Peter Cartwright. Still, for a politician who believed in God and occasionally went to church to be opposed by the majority of his hometown's clergymen—well, it was scandalous. If it was true, it amounted to an indictment in the minds of many—an indictment of Lincoln's faith, of his honesty, and even of his basic morality.

⤜⤜

It was a plague that would never fully lift from Lincoln's life, and it had only gotten worse since his spiritual turning under Reverend Smith. When he had simply been a skeptic, he might have been out of step with the religious mores of society, but he was not open to the charge of being a hypocrite. Yet since he had begun to believe in God and some Christian truths, few in Springfield had believed it, and many had thought he was simply playing politics. Certainly Lincoln could not have been a genuine believer, they thought. He had been too much the outspoken infidel. He was too much the "shut mouthed" man who seldom shared his inner reflections. He had never joined a church. So his religion was always in question. Even his closest friends were slow to accept that he "had any religion," as we have seen.

Complicating this may have been Lincoln's famed honesty, particularly in his later years, in matters of religion. He could easily have avoided all the rumors and attacks if he had simply joined a church. He could have affirmed a Christian faith he did not embrace, could have said he clung to the grace of Jesus Christ even if he did not. No one would have doubted him, and he would have taken the political high ground from his foes. It would have meant more votes and less political strife.

He wouldn't do it.

Whatever he was in his early years—when he famously lied about his religious views for political gain in his handbill—by most accounts he became a man who would not lie about religion for mere social acceptance. Herndon said that for Lincoln, "what was true, good and right, and just, he would never surrender; he would die before he would surrender his ideas of these."[5] Mary Lincoln agreed: "Poor Mr. Lincoln is almost a monomaniac on the subject of honesty."[6] Her husband, she insisted, "was truth itself."[7] Lincoln refused, at least in his more mature years, to play the usual religious games of politics, to appear to be what he was not. Many a man—many a politician in particular—has been able to attend a church that held doctrines he did not believe or to publicly avow what he privately denied. Lincoln could not bring himself to follow this example. He was always wrestling spiritually, always in transition, and was always equally unwilling to appear otherwise.

While president, he once turned to a visitor during a discussion of faith and asked, "What constitutes a true religious experience?"[8] By this time Lincoln had been attending church off and on for more than a decade, had surely heard enough preaching to fashion an answer of his own, and had no need to falsely present himself as a spiritual seeker. The likelihood is that he asked because he really wanted to know and he did not mind revealing that he was yet unsure. If this was the usual manner of the man, it did not serve him well in politics.

His political life was also complicated by his often-unorthodox religious views. He had moved in great strides toward Smith's Christianity but had not fully embraced all its doctrines. A friend who spoke with him about religion in the mid-1850s later recounted, "He did not nor could not believe in the endless punishment of any one of the human race. He understood punishment for sin to be a Bible doctrine; but that the punishment was parental in its object, aim and design and intended for the good of the offender; hence it must cease when justice is satisfied. He added all that was lost by the transgression of Adam was made good by the atonement, all that was lost by the fall was made good by the sacrifice." If this friend, Isaac Cogdal, remembered correctly, Lincoln was both moving toward Christian orthodoxy in affirming an atoning work of Christ and moving away from Christian orthodoxy by denying eternal punishment—all at the same time. This was consistent with a man in a process of religious change, which gave fodder to his critics and often confused his friends.

Finally, there was his distaste for the culture of the average church. Perhaps it was also a distaste for the manner of the average clergyman. Clearly, he had respect for men of God such as Smith and Miner, but the usual ways of church people and the usual brand of minister repelled him. This had been true ever since his first exposure to fiery preachers at frontier camp meetings. He could see that most of them were sincere, but even these were often uneducated, pushy, and proud. Others were worse. He found them much as he found Peter Cartwright:

spiritual bullies who tried to dominate a town or berate those slow to believe. Then, of course, there were the fakers and the immoral. As in all ages—and most all professions—there were those who feigned being men of faith for nothing more than gain. This disgusted him.

He likely found some of the demands of church people to be absurd. He had reasoned and studied and prayed himself toward God from the outside of church. He had not been shaped by church culture and the expectations of religious people. He had simply come in his earthiness and raw hunger to God. Once he became willing to attend church with Mary and his boys from time to time, he was almost certainly surprised at what some required, at what passed for holiness before a loving God.

An episode in the church he sometimes attended reveals the small-ness that often beset the religious people he knew. The records for a February 19, 1855, meeting of the Session—the ruling elders—of First Presbyterian Church show that Rev. Smith was instructed to investigate whether members of the congregation had been engaged in a grievous sin: dancing! Lincoln must have found this odd. Dancing had been a beloved part of the rowdy frontier celebrations he enjoyed as a young man and was part of his Springfield life as well. He had met Mary at a dance, been one of the sponsors of a "Cotillion Party" in 1839 where people danced, and was regularly at balls and parties in the capital, where the leading citizens danced away the night. Lincoln enjoyed the beauty and the gaiety. It likely helped to keep his inner darkness at bay. How could such a happy part of life be against the will of God?

It was a question lost on some of the city's Presbyterians. While Smith obediently tried to discover who at First Church was dancing, Reverend Albert Hale of Second Presbyterian decided to drive the offending practice from his flock. He was drawn into the battle by the wicked deeds of one of his church members—the Honorable Joel Aldrich Matteson, governor of Illinois. In January of 1856, Matteson hosted a reception at which dancing continued well past midnight. The next Sunday, Reverend Hale preached a "scorching sermon" against the vile practice. Governor Matteson was so enraged and humiliated by this public abuse from his own pastor that he left Second Presbyterian and never set foot inside a church of any denomination again. The governor did continue to dance, though, and often.[9] Lincoln must have watched such pettiness and reflected on how far the rules of men were from the laws of God.

He would have remembered this episode later in life when religious people criticized him for the smallest matter and did so certain of his sin. While commander in chief during a great and bloody war, he would receive letters assuring him of judgment because he approved the movement of troops on the Christian Sabbath. If an errant missile damaged a church, Abraham Lincoln was going to hell by the reasoning of some. If General Grant drank or General Hancock swore or General McClellan flirted with a woman, God opposed the Union.

It would continue even after Lincoln's death. After he had won a war, kept the Union together, and fallen at the hands of an assassin, the petty would not leave him alone. He was hounded—as he lay in his grave—for having died in a theater. The pastor of New York Avenue Presbyterian Church in Washington, D. C., said,

> Our lamented President fell in the theatre. Had he been murdered in his bed, or in his office, or on the street, or on the steps of the Capitol, the tidings of his death would not have struck the Christian heart of the country quite so painfully; for the feeling of that heart is that the theatre is one of the last places to which a good man should go.[10]

A Boston pastor lamented, "He was shot in a theatre. We are sorry for that. If ever any man had an excuse to attend a theatre, he had. This we will say: we are all sorry our best loved died there. But take the truth with its shadow." A Detroit pastor insisted, "Would that Mr. Lincoln had fallen elsewhere than at the very gates of Hell—in the theater to which, through persuasion, he reluctantly went."[11] It is fortunate

Lincoln did not know of these words. What he did know of churchy pettiness throughout his life kept him from joining a church or committing himself too unreservedly to a minister.

❦

His irritation with some ministers deepened as theological debates about slavery grew heated in the late 1850s. Horace Mann had written, "If the Bible has crossed the Atlantic to spread slavery over a continent where it was unknown before, then the Bible is a book of death and not a book of life."[12] Lincoln would have agreed. He knew that slavery existed in the Bible and that it had some sanction from God, but he also knew that the form of slavery practiced in the United States was not the form allowed in Scripture.

In the Bible, slavery was either voluntary, resulting from military conquest, or due to economic hardship. It was never based on race alone, and the kidnapping, rape, and murder of slaves was not allowed. In a speech he gave in Cincinnati in 1859, Lincoln mentioned those who were "trying to show that slavery existed in the Bible times by Divine ordinance." He insisted that the Bible could not be used to support American slavery. "When you establish that Slavery was right by the Bible, it will occur that that Slavery was the Slavery of the *white* man— of men without reference to color."[13]

Lincoln's most sarcastic and heated words against proslavery theology came after he had read the arguments of a famous Dr. Frederick A. Ross. In 1857, Ross's book *Slavery Ordained of God* had begun shaping the national debate by arguing a biblical case for slavery. Lincoln was incensed. To organize his thoughts and channel his intense feelings, he did something that had become a habit for him: he wrote his arguments on a scrap of paper, intending the exercise only for himself. Later, after his death, Lincoln's secretaries discovered the fragments and published them with his papers. It is Lincoln raw and caustic, but it allows us a sense of his inner dialogue as he confronted, once again, ministers who presumed to speak folly in the name of God.

The sum of pro-slavery theology seems to be this: "Slavery is not universally right, nor yet universally wrong; it is better for some people to be slaves; and, in such cases, it is the Will of God that they be such." Certainly there is no contending against the Will of God; but still there is some difficulty in ascertaining, and applying it, to particular cases. For instance we will suppose the Rev. Dr. Ross has a slave named Sambo, and the question is "Is it the Will of God that Sambo shall remain a slave, or be set free?" The Almighty gives no audible answer to the question, and his revelation—the Bible—gives none—or, at most, none but such as admits of a squabble, as to its meaning. No one thinks of asking Sambo's opinion on it. So, at last, it comes to this, that Dr. Ross is to decide the question. And while he considers it, he sits in the shade, with gloves on his hands, and subsists on the bread that Sambo is earning in the burning sun. If he decides that God Wills Sambo to continue a slave, he thereby retains his own comfortable position; but if he decides that God wills Sambo to be free, he thereby has to walk out of the shade, throw off his gloves, and delve for his own bread. Will Dr. Ross be actuated by that perfect impartiality, which has ever been considered most favorable to correct decisions?

As a good thing, slavery is strikingly peculiar in this, that it is the only good thing which no man ever seeks the good of, for himself. Nonsense! Wolves devouring lambs, not because it is good for their own greedy maws, but because it is good for the lambs!!![14]

We can feel Lincoln's seething frustration in these words, a river of resentment that surely had its source in his battles with Peter Cartwright, with the kind of Christians who even criticized his wife for political gain, with clergymen who aired their political opinions invoking the authority of heaven, and, yes, with ministers who sanctioned the vilest form of slavery with the pages of a Bible that proclaimed all men created in the image of God. It is little wonder Lincoln kept his distance from the typical church and embraced only exceptional men of God such as Reverend Smith as friends.

Clearly, he wanted a church, a spiritual home, but he found that the rules and dogmas of men got in the way. He had told Mrs. Rankin, during that bruising political race of 1846, he doubted "the possibility or propriety of settling the religion of Jesus Christ in the models of man-made creeds and dogmas." He said, too, that he could not "without mental reservations, assent to long and complicated creeds and catechisms. If the church would ask simply for assent to the Savior's statement of the substance of the law: 'Thou shalt love the Lord thy God with all thy heart, and with all thy soul, and with all thy mind, and thy neighbour as thyself,' that church would I gladly unite with."[15] Though he had traveled a great distance spiritually since those days, largely under Smith's ministry, he was still weary of the human complication of religion. It is no wonder he said not long after arriving in Washington, "I wish to find a church whose clergyman holds himself aloof from politics."[16]

⁓

We should not miss the point that upon arriving in Washington, D.C., Lincoln was eager to find a church. This would not always have been his way. The Lincoln of Indiana avoided church to avoid his father. The Lincoln of New Salem avoided church because he thought the whole matter of Christianity a hoax. The Lincoln of that first decade in Springfield had softened a bit toward God, toward the Bible, and toward the social good that religion might do, but he was still aloof from church and wounded by his Christian critics. Not until Smith's book entered his life—at his father-in-law's house in the fall of 1849—did

Lincoln begin the change that would prompt him to seek out a church as he began his presidency in the spring of 1861.

Yet what did Abraham Lincoln believe about religion as he left Springfield for Washington on the day he gave that tender farewell speech? Reverend Noyes W. Miner—the Baptist pastor to whom Lincoln lent his carriage and to whom Mary later confided her husband's final words—said,

> At the time Mr. Lincoln was elected President, I do not think he was what is termed an experimental Christian. But during my long and intimate acquaintance with him, and the many conversations I had with him from time to time, on numerous subjects, I never heard a word fall from his lips that gave me the remotest idea that his mind was ever tinctured with infidel sentiments; but on the contrary, the more intimate I became acquainted with him, the more deeply was I impressed with the conviction that he believed not only in the overriding Providence of God, but in the Divinity of the Sacred Scriptures, and had a profound reverence for everything true, and noble, and good.[17]

Going a bit further, John Wickizer, a friend and fellow lawyer who knew the Lincoln of the late 1850s, wrote, "I think he was naturally religious, but very liberal in his views, I think he believed in 'Jesus Christ, and him crucified.'"[18]

If we put these words together with Lincoln's own statements and the observations of his closest friends, we can conclude that he was, in the broadest possible sense, a theologically liberal Christian. He believed in God, in the rule of divine providence, in the Bible as divinely inspired in part if not as a whole, in heaven, in the resurrection of the dead, in the value of righteous churches, in the role of holy clergy, in the importance of prayer, and in Christian character and generosity. He also believed in Jesus Christ in some sense, too, and, though it may seem odd to speak of Christ peripherally when describing Lincoln's faith, this is exactly how we must understand what Lincoln believed of the Christian Savior.

It is true that he rarely mentioned Jesus Christ and that his friends from his early years doubted Lincoln believed what Christians usually believe about their Savior. Herndon insisted that Lincoln definitely did not "believe that Jesus was God."[19] Lincoln's close friend and later body-guard, Ward Hill Lamon, asserted that Lincoln "never told any one that he accepted Jesus as the Christ, or performed a single one of the acts which necessarily follow upon such a conviction. . . . Never . . . did he let fall from his lips or pen an expression which remotely implied the slightest faith in Jesus as the Son of God and the Savior of men."[20] Both men overstated, but they certainly had reason for their views. Lincoln seldom spoke of Christ publicly, and when he did it was in sweeping "the Savior" or "our Redeemer" language.

Regardless, we cannot let this fact alone keep us from considering the possibility that Lincoln was an orthodox Christian in his view of Jesus Christ at this time. He had identified for years with what today would be called "conservative Presbyterianism." Christ, his divinity, his atoning sacrifice, and his resurrection were at the center of this theology. Lincoln certainly had the option of other, more theologically liberal churches to choose from. In addition, many who knew him thought he had come to believe in the traditional Christian view of Jesus. Dr. James Smith did. James Matheny did. John Wickizer did. Ninian Edwards did. There were others. Lincoln also attended prayer meetings—as we shall see—and supported churches and ministries that taught of a divine, resurrected Jesus Christ, and extolled a Bible that proclaims Jesus Christ as God.

We should remember, also, that it was the rhetorical style of the times not to speak of divinity in familiar terms. A president would never have spoken publicly of "my Lord and Savior," even if he believed the words were true. This had also been the manner of America's founding fathers, who spoke often of "the Great Author of the Universe" or, as in the Declaration of Independence, the "Supreme Judge of the world." It did not mean that the majority of the founders were not deeply committed Christians. They were. Lincoln may have been as well. We simply cannot know with certainty. That he was "almost Christian"—that he was as near to being a Christian as a man can be who has not fully resolved the matter of Christ's divinity—is without question. He believed everything a Christian believed, with the possible exception—and this is far from a proven fact—that he may have been hesitant about the traditional view that Jesus Christ was both man and God.

Oddly, a tailor in Springfield may have had the final word on the matter. The man's name was James W. Keyes. He was Lincoln's tailor, and the two often spoke about the world of ideas, religion in particular.

In my intercourse with Mr. Lincoln I learned that he believed in a Creator of all things, who had neither beginning nor end, who possessing all power and wisdom, established a principle, in Obedience to which, Worlds move and are upheld and animal and vegetable life came into existence.

A reason he gave for his belief was, that in view of the Order and harmony of all nature which all beheld, it would have been more miraculous to have come about by chance than to have been created and arranged by some great thinking power—

As to the Christian theory, that, Christ is God, or equal to the Creator he said [it] had better be taken for granted—for by the test of reason all might become infidels on that subject, for evidence of Christ's divinity came to us in somewhat doubtful Shape—but that the system of Christianity was an ingenious one at least—and perhaps was calculated to do good.

As to the Ordinances adopted by the different denominations of Christians, I never heard him express any preference for one over the other.[21]

✑

And so Lincoln arrived in Washington. Along the route from Springfield—and after the farewell speech in which he said he was trusting in the same "Divine Being" who aided George Washington—he had continued to speak openly of religion. In Lafayette, Indiana, he told those who gathered around his train, "I trust in Christianity, civilization, patriotism."[22] At Cincinnati he spoke of "the Providence of God, who has never deserted us."[23] In Columbus, Ohio, he said he was turning "to the American people and to that God who has never forsaken them."[24] In Buffalo, New York, he confessed, "I must trust in that Supreme Being who has never forsaken this favored land, through the instrumentality of this great and intelligent people. Without that assistance I shall surely fail. With it I cannot fail."[25] And to the New Jersey state senate he famously said he would be "most happy indeed if I shall be an humble instrument in the hands of the Almighty, and of this, his almost chosen people."[26]

He was right to recognize his need for help beyond his own ability. The nation he was about to lead was remaking itself into something fearsome and new even while he rode the rails to Washington. In 1860, the country's population had risen to 31 million, 2 million more than that of Great Britain. The pace of immigration alone was staggering. In the decade before he entered office, 2.6 million people had arrived from overseas. In the year he took office, more than 400,000 arrived. The cities were also exploding. St. Louis had boasted only 5,000 citizens some twenty years before. When Lincoln took office, it numbered 74,000. Even Springfield had grown from 700 to nearly 7,000. In the *Blackwood's Magazine* that Lincoln enjoyed reading, he would have learned that America's population was expected to double in thirty years and then break 300 million by 1940.[27] Somehow, it was not hard to believe. The population in 1940 actually turned out to be far less than this number, but the prediction itself shows what many Americans living in 1860 expected of their future.

The pace of change must have been staggering for those of Lincoln's generation. In 150 years, colonists had settled a region that reached only one hundred miles inland from the Atlantic Ocean. During the first 50 years of the nineteenth century, Americans stretched their empire three thousand miles to the Pacific Ocean. Nearly five hundred wagons a day passed by Fort Kearney, Nebraska, heading west in pursuit of dreams fashioned further east. Stagecoaches took passengers from St. Louis to San Francisco in twenty-three days. The pony express ran mail from St. Joseph, Missouri, to San Francisco in eleven days.

Machines doubled and then tripled the crops one man could tend. The steam locomotive, the iron oceangoing steamship, and the power-driven factory had all begun promising a new world. While Lincoln was practicing law, burying a son, debating Senator Douglas, and making the speeches that brought him to national attention during the 1850s—the Peoria speech of 1854, the House Divided speech of 1858, both of which led to the defining Cooper Union address of 1860—others were reinventing how men lived. In 1851, Isaac Singer invented the sewing machine. In 1852, Foucault gave the world the gyroscope. Cayley invented the manned glider the next year, and by mid-decade Louis Pasteur was explaining pasteurization. From then until the day Lincoln arrived in Washington, the Pullman sleeping car, the washing machine, the internal combustion engine, the cylinder lock, the bicycle, and the modern elevator with safety brakes were born. Over the next year, the lightbulb, linoleum, the repeating rifle, the self-propelled torpedo, and the vacuum cleaner all began reshaping the world.

The most terrible change of all was the dissolution of the Union. Six weeks after Lincoln's election to the presidency, South Carolina seceded. In time, Alabama, Florida, Georgia, Louisiana, Mississippi, and Texas followed, all of which formed the Confederate States of America on February 4, 1861. Like many others, Lincoln had seen this coming years before in a dissolution of a different kind—when America's churches failed to maintain unity in the face of slavery. Lincoln's hero, Henry Clay, had warned of it as early as 1852. In an interview with the *Presbyterian Herald* of Louisville, Kentucky, given just weeks before his death, Clay chastised the churches of America for failing to rise above the partisan fray. "I tell you this sundering of the religious ties which have hitherto bound our people together, I consider the greatest source of danger to our country," he said. "If our religious men cannot live together in peace, what can be expected of us politicians, very few of whom profess to be governed by the subject of slavery. When the people of these states become thoroughly alienated from each other, and get their passions aroused, they are not apt to stop and consider what is to their interest." If the preachers would only keep the churches from "running into excesses and fanaticism," Clay thought the politicians could control the masses. But he admonished the reverend gentlemen, "Yours is the harder task; and if you do not perform it, we will not be able to do our part." Then he concluded: "That I consider to be the greater source of danger to our country."[28] The words were prophetic of events to come, and Lincoln's own Presbyterians led the way. They were the first to split, with the Baptists and Methodists dividing into pro-slavery and antislavery factions not long after. As the churches went, so went the nation, with despair filling the land.

An informed observer at the time might have been able to antici-pate the slaughter to come. There were three factors that told the tale. First, the partition of the states into North and South left the greater industrial strength in the North. The Union was comprised of twenty-three states with a population of more than 22 million people, 100,000 factories, 1.1 million workers, and 96 percent of all railroad equipment in the United States. The South, by contrast, was composed of only eleven states with a population of 9 million people, 20,000 factories, 101,000 workers, and only 9,000 miles of railroad. None of the South's factories produced munitions. What the South had in abundance was anger, religion, and warrior skill. At the beginning, this seemed enough.

The second factor was the gap between technology and strategy. In the decades prior to hostilities, the technology of war had advanced without much corresponding progress in tactics. The manuals carried by officers in the Civil War were based on the same theories employed by commanders in the American Revolution and the Napoleonic Wars. Little in martial thinking had changed. The tools of war, though, had changed dramatically. Men now used rifles—with spiraling grooves cut in the barrels that spun a conical bullet—rather than the simple muskets of their grandfathers. This meant that it was possible for a marksman to kill at hundreds of yards rather than dozens. Tennessee riflemen on the walls of the Alamo had killed Mexican officers at a distance of more than four hundred yards in 1836. Even more was possible by 1861. One Civil War general died from a shot fired from eight hundred yards away. Cannons were also improved. During the American Revolution, a cannon firing a three-pound ball was expected to reach no further than eight hundred yards. The guns that fired upon Fort Sumter on April 12, 1861, could reach a range of three miles. By Gettysburg, in 1863, this had grown to nearly five miles. The battlefield had broadened, but the strategies had not. Men died in staggeringly large numbers as a result.

Many died horribly. The state of medical science was not equal to the demands of this new kind of war. The standard field doctor's equipment was crude, resembling a modern household tool kit, and surgical techniques were similarly rough. More men died from the medical care they received after being wounded than they did from the wounds themselves. The many photographs of medical stations surrounded by piles of amputated arms and legs attest to these horrors. One such set of photographs from the vicious Battle of Franklin in Tennessee shows arms and legs stacked to the height of a second-story window. Men marched into battle past such scenes, and it often sucked the courage from their souls.

This was the kind of war—and the kind of nation—that Lincoln inherited. Like other presidents, he would have preferred different challenges. He likely dreamt as a younger man of being president and transforming the nation with railroads, bridges, canals, and roads. This had been his platform when he first went into politics. He could see himself in this cause, the presidential son of Henry Clay. He might also have hoped to transform the plight of the poor. A dismal frontier cabin and the faces of hungry children never left his memory; he would have felt his life well spent if he could help fashion a society in which the poor could rise. Then, too, there was his love of learning and the power of knowledge that had redirected his life. What might he have done in the cause of education, perhaps inspiring great future institutions of learning to train minds yet unborn? Instead, it was his fate—he understood it as his divine purpose—to lead the United States through the bloodiest of her wars, a titanic struggle over the meaning of the nation's founding and the definition of her most honored words. It would mean the deaths of hundreds of thousands and the mutilation of thousands more before it was done. It would mean brother killing brother and wounds that would not begin to heal for more than a century after. And it meant that Lincoln would be despised and deified, worshipped and branded an enemy of freedom for all history to see. And in time it would cost him, as we now know, his life.

It was fitting that he called upon his God as he entered Washington, D.C., in February of 1861.

꧁

Lincoln's first full day in the nation's capital was a Sunday—February 24—and he already had an invitation to church. Senator William Seward, newly named as secretary of state, had invited the president elect to attend St. John's Episcopal Church, which sat just across Lafayette Square from the White House. Designed by Benjamin Latrobe, the same architect who designed the city itself, St. John's was already gaining a reputation as the "church of the presidents." It lay so close to the White

St. John's Episcopal Church, Washington, D.C.

House that the two men were able to walk the distance in a few minutes that morning to attend the eleven o'clock service.

Lincoln sat in Seward's pew, just near the altar. Though the two men were nearly opposites, Lincoln liked Seward. He was a loud, fiery, heavy-drinking, hard-smoking man who swore so as to make an impression. His cussing was so legendary that Lincoln made sport of it weeks later in a tale that circulated throughout Washington. The new president had decided to review the Army of the Potomac and for some reason found himself soon after riding in an old ambulance pulled by six mules over the roughest of roads. The military driver grew angrier with each violent jolt of his vehicle and "occasionally let fly a volley of suppressed oaths." Playfully, Lincoln leaned forward and tapped the driver on the shoulder.

"Excuse me, my friend, are you an Episcopalian?"

"No, Mr. President; I am a Methodist."

"Well, I thought you must be an Episcopalian, because you swear just like Governor Seward, who is a churchwarden."[29]

Lincoln's position at the front of the church that day gave some of Washington's leading citizens their first glimpse of him. A campaign book from the time tells us what they might have seen. The six-foot, four-inch-tall president was described as "not muscular, but gaunt and wiry. In walking, his gait, though firm, is never brisk. He steps slowly and deliberately, almost always with his head inclined forward, and his hands clasped behind his back." He was, admittedly, not handsome, "but when his fine, dark-grey eyes are lighted up by any emotion, and his features begin their play, he would be chosen from among a crowd as one who had in him not only the kindly sentiments which women love, but the heavier metal of which full-grown men and Presidents are made."[30] His appearance aside, the congregation of St. John's would have been pleased to see, as a correspondent for New York's *Herald* did, that the president "read the service with the regular worshippers."[31]

Two days later, when the Committee of Congress reported the results of the Electoral College to him, Lincoln replied that he intended to rely on an "unspoken faith in the Supreme Ruler of nations."[32] It is the word *unspoken* that is revealing. It was descriptive of the manner of the upper class in Lincoln's time. Religion was not to be overt, was not thought elevated by being expressed. Instead, a man's faith drew wider respect if he never spoke of it but lived its values. This could sometimes make religion and behavior nearly the same thing, so that later generations had to reemphasize the matter of believing and trusting with the heart. Nonetheless, this was Lincoln trying to assure that his faith would always be there, acknowledged or not, quietly but powerfully shaping his actions in office.

That this statement comes just days before his First Inaugural Address may help to answer the critic's charge that the speech contains almost no meaningful religious content. He had worked on it for weeks and stayed home from church his second Sunday in Washington to add the finishing touches. His family could hear him pacing his rooms at the Willard Hotel, testing out versions and inflections. The next day, March 4, he read the final product to his family and then asked them all to leave the room so he could be alone. Mary later recalled that she could hear her husband praying aloud, asking God to give him grace in this first presidential act.[33]

Later that morning, Lincoln offered the address to the nation. He knew the task before him, and it was not preaching, even if he had been inclined. The need of the moment was to identify the events which had brought the country to this precipice, explain the position of the Union, appeal to the now-departed sister states in the South, and invoke the sacred memory of the nation's founding as a trumpet call of unity. He did mention "the Almighty Ruler of nations, with his eternal truth and justice," and he did appeal to "Christianity, and a firm reliance on Him who has never yet forsaken this favored land." These were more than obligatory nods to religion, but they were not the central message of the speech. The urgent need was to rescue the nation from war if possible and to make a case for war if necessary.

Toward the end came the paragraph that was nearly the sum of the whole:

> In your hands, my dissatisfied fellow countrymen, and not in mine, is the momentous issue of civil war. The government will not assail you. You can have no conflict, without being yourselves the aggressors. You have no oath registered in Heaven to destroy the government, while I shall have the most solemn one to "preserve, protect and defend" it.

It is touching to see Lincoln's belief that his presidential oath is "registered in Heaven," that the presidency is a sacred obligation he must fulfill. Though all presidents take the same oath, we suspect that Lincoln pondered the words and offered them on a more eternal altar than most.

What is striking also—given the horrors to come and what they would work into his being—is how he understands the matters before the nation to be under human control. Perhaps this was his "doctrine of necessity" returning or perhaps it is the natural worldview of a new president: *our decisions decide our fate.* This is understandable. Urging this view is how a candidate wins voters: *events are under our control, and I am the best man to exercise that control for you; vote for me.* By the time the candidate steps into office, he has even convinced himself: *Let us make a new world. Let us have a new beginning. Let us fashion a new history.* In Lincoln's case, whatever optimism loomed behind his words would soon depart. He would endure such horrors, such folly, and feel himself so powerless to shape events that he would come in time to a different view. This he would express in his Second Inaugural Address, as we shall see. The important point for now is how he gives his First Inaugural Address from a stronghold of certainty about the power of the human will. It is a stronghold that will eventually cave in around him and from which he will ultimately be forced to flee.

The conclusion of his speech is among the most poetic in the English language. Upon reading the harsh ending of an earlier draft, Seward had urged "some words of affection, some of calm and cheerful confidence."[34] Some scholars have suggested that Seward wrote the original version of the last paragraph himself with the final version reflecting Lincoln's edits. It is unlikely. Though Seward suggested the change, Lincoln was possessed of such a fine poetic sense and speechwriting was such a personal art for him that it is certain he would not leave the all-important last paragraph of a historic speech entirely in the hands of another man. Even if that man was a better writer—and

Seward was not—a speaker's script has to be customized, wrapped gently around the individual's unique rhetorical style. Lincoln understood this. Some combination of the two men's work—perhaps along with light suggestions from others—gave us among the gentlest and most lyrical appeals in history:

> I am loath to close. We are not enemies, but friends. We must not be enemies. Though passion may have strained it must not break our bonds of affections. The mystic chords of memory, stretching from every battlefield and patriot grave to every living heart and hearth-stone all over this broad land, will yet swell the chorus of the Union, when again touched, as surely they will be, by the better angels of our nature.

The response of the nation's newspapers was tepid at best. It says much about the literary and rhetorical level of Lincoln's time as distinct from our own that the Boston *Transcript* complained, "The language is level to the popular mind, the plain, homespun language of a man accustomed to talk with the 'folks' and the 'neighbors,' whose words fit his facts and thoughts." The *New York Herald* whined, "It would have been almost as instructive if President Lincoln had contented himself with telling his audience yesterday a funny story and letting them go"; however, the inaugural was "not a crude performance," for "it abounds with traits of craft and cunning." Southern newspapers heard the speech as the South's call to arms. The Montgomery *Advertiser* called Lincoln "the abolition chief." The Richmond *Enquirer* heard Lincoln's words as "the cool unimpassioned, deliberate language of the fanatic" and assured that "sectional war awaits only the signal gun. The Charleston *Mercury* declared, "It is our wisest policy to accept it as a declaration of war."

Perhaps the *New York Tribune* captured the majority of Lincoln's intent: "To twenty millions of people it will carry tidings, good or not, as the case may be, that the federal government of the United States is still in existence, with a Man at the head of it."[35]

༄

The Lincoln presidency had begun. The nation was hopeful. Lincoln himself, though, was troubled.

His unease had begun on the evening of his election to the presidency. He had seen something, and it had left him apprehensive about his life. God or nature or spirits were trying to tell him something. He wasn't quite sure what it was, but he sensed that somehow a message was being pressed into his life from the unseen world. He had long felt this way, long believed his great destiny was attended in turn by great spiritual forces. He was surer of it now than ever.

He had always been sensitive to the unseen. He admitted openly that he was superstitious and once told John Hay, his childhood friend and later secretary, "I believe I feel trouble in the air before it comes."[36] He came by this naturally, having grown up among a frontier people who lived by dreams, omens, superstitions, and signs. Lincoln's father once told him of a recurring dream in which a woman sat by a fireside, paring an apple. The dream came so often and haunted him so persistently that finally Thomas set off to find the face that ruled his imagination. Once he did, he married the woman. Lincoln's mother was also spiritually attuned. Abraham once explained, "Visions are not uncommon to me. Nor were they uncommon to that blessed mother of mine. . . . She often spoke of things that would happen [and] even foretold her early death . . . just when she would die."[37]

To understand this influence in Lincoln's life, we should imagine that the woods of Indiana were as magical a place for those who settled there as the enchanted forests of central Europe were thought to be and were as spirit-infused as the jungles of the Amazon are in a shaman's mind. To the early settlers of the region, their land was where spirits of darkness and light wrestled. As John Nicolay, Lincoln's secretary, wrote in the 1880s, these frontier people were "full of strange superstitions. The belief in witchcraft had long ago passed away with the smoke of the fagots from old and New England, but it survived far into this century in Kentucky and the lower halves of Indiana and Illinois—touched with a peculiar tinge of African magic."[38] We see this influence in Lincoln's early years. Herndon tells us that when Lincoln "went down to New Orleans in '31 he consulted a Negress fortune teller, asking her to give him his history, his end and his fate."[39]

Superstitions reigned in Lincoln's frontier world. A man who thought himself bewitched should shoot an image of that witch with a bullet fashioned from a melted half dollar. If a dog crossed a hunter's path, only hooking the fingers together and pulling until the animal moved out of view avoided immediate bad luck. Death announced itself in the form of a bird landing on a windowsill, a dog baying at specific hours, the cough of a horse near a child, or the touch of a snake's head. A wagon loaded with baskets passing a house warned those inside of bad weather. An occult view of time also ruled lives. Trees intended as fence rails had to be felled before noon and before a waxing moon. Build a fence when there was no moon and the fence would soon give way. In this and a thousand matters, the state of the moon reigned supreme.[40]

Inspired by the certainty that spirits ruled all things, superstitions influenced even medicine. Much of what passed for veterinary care was no more than folk magic. Human beings were treated in much the same way. Even the well educated accepted mystical nonsense without much critical thought. Late in the 1840s, a dog bit Robert Lincoln. Abraham and Mary shared their generation's dread of rabies and feared for his life. The solution, everyone knew, was a "mad stone." Also called a *bezoar,* a mad stone was a stony concretion usually taken from the stomach of a deer or cow. It was not unlike a very tight, hardened hair ball. They grew to about three inches in length, were cherished once discovered, and were never bought or sold lest they lose their power. Only mad stones that passed from father to son retained their healing abilities. The people of Lincoln's frontier communities believed that the mad stone could "draw out" poisons from a snakebite or a rabid dog. Over time, various rituals evolved in the use of mad stones, but their mystical properties were seldom questioned. Certainly not by the Lincolns. To treat Robert with only the most powerful stone, the Lincolns put Robert in a carriage and rode all the way to Terre Haute, Indiana, finding peace only when the stony object surrendered by a deer was rubbed on their son's wound.[41]

This helps us remember how removed Lincoln's time was from our own. Men still agreed to meet at a time of day called "candlelight," doctors still bled patients to remove bad "humors," and entire races were thought to have no souls. It was a more religious age, too, one where the supernatural was always near and every event had mystical meaning. The spiritual spoke through the natural. The natural was the gateway to the spiritual. This was the worldview of the ancient druids transplanted onto the American frontier. It was all taken with utmost seriousness. Only at risk of peril did one ignore dreams in the night or a squirrel at a morning window or the shape of smoke or the pattern of sticks on the ground. Curses, potions, and spells were real and were thwarted only through a dizzying array of rituals. With death and horror ever present and with disease so terrifyingly inexplicable, it is no surprise that these beleaguered settlers turned to the assurances of the occult.

The impressions of the spirit were not lost on Lincoln either, whose sensitive nature, eager mind, and depression-ravaged psyche made him tender to—even eager for—invisible realities. All his life he experienced dreams, omens, visions, and revelatory occurrences of nearly every kind, and they did not decrease with age. In 1858, during his series of debates with Senator Douglas, Lincoln told Herndon, "I feel as if I should meet with some terrible end."[42] The meaning of this premonition did not leave him. As he departed for Washington in 1861 and said his farewells to friends, Herndon recalled "the sorrow of parting from his old associations was deeper than most persons would imagine, but it was more marked in his case because of the feeling which had become irrepressible that he would never return alive."[43]

His foreboding had risen on the strength of a recent vision. As he recounted to Noah Brooks years later, on the day after his election, he "was well tired out and went home to rest, throwing myself down on a huge lounge in my chamber." He went on:

Opposite where I lay was a bureau with a swinging glass upon it, and looking in that glass I saw myself reflected nearly at full length; but my face, I noticed, had two separate and distinct images, the tip of the nose of one being about three inches from the tip of the other. I was a little bothered, perhaps started, and got up and looked in the glass, but the illusion vanished. On lying down again, I saw it a second time, plainer, if possible, than before; and then I noticed that one of the faces was a little paler—say five shades, than the other. I got up, and the thing melted away, and I went off, and in the excitement of the hour forgot all about it—nearly, but not quite, for the thing would once in a while come up, and give me a little pang as if something uncomfortable had happened. When I went home again that night I told my wife about it, and a few days afterward I made the experiment again, when sure enough the thing came again but I never succeeded in bringing the ghost back after that, though I once tried very industriously to show it to my wife, who was somewhat worried about it. She thought it was a "sign" that I was to be elected to a second term of office, and that the paleness of one of the faces was an omen that I should not see life through the last term.[44]

Another man might have seen this simply as one among the tricks that mirrors can play. Not Lincoln, who had been schooled—by his father, his mother, his superstitious frontier culture, and his own inner yearnings—to see such "visions" as windows into the spiritual world. He was haunted by this particular specter. He mentioned it to friends repeatedly during his White House years and saw still other signs as confirmation. Though he joked about his death with those who feared for him—when the widow of an old friend worried about his safety, he told her, "Hannah, if they do kill me I shall never die again"—he lived under the certainty that an early, violent death was his fate.

⸎

The images in his Springfield mirror troubled him as he settled in Washington and may have made him particularly eager to find a church home. He had attended St. John's Episcopal within hours of arriving in his new city. The next week he worked through the Sabbath on his first inaugural speech. Many of the city's churches hoped he would worship with them. First Presbyterian Church thought Lincoln might choose them as his congregation since Mary had worshipped there the day Lincoln went with Seward to St. John's. They sent the new president a note saying that they had reserved a pew that they were eager to put at his disposal "should it be your pleasure to attend public worship with us."[45] Lincoln ignored the invitation and on his third week in Washington took his family to New York Avenue Presbyterian Church to hear Dr. Phineas Gurley preach.

This church had much to commend it to a new president. It sat at the intersection of New York Avenue and Thirteenth and H streets, which was just three blocks from the White House. Though the congregation met in a new structure that had been dedicated only a year before, it had a venerable history. A Presbyterian church had met on or near this site since 1807 and had included among its members through the years eminent men like John Quincy Adams, Andrew Jackson, and James Buchanan. Lincoln was likely pleased to know of this heritage.

President Abraham Lincoln's pew in the original New York Avenue Presbyterian Church, Washington, D.C.

Still, it was almost certainly the engaging manner of the pastor that held his attention. Reverend Gurley was one of the most visible ministers in the nation, since he had already served as the chaplain of the U.S. Senate. He had attended Princeton and Union College and had led a successful church in Ohio before coming to Washington. He was a handsome man whose energy and intelligence made him a thrilling preacher. He was also fiery and forceful when he preached. Lincoln liked this. Perhaps he had absorbed more of the manner of the camp meeting than he liked to admit. He once said, "The fact is, I don't like to hear cut and dried sermons. No, when I hear a man preach, I like to see him act as if he were fighting bees!"[46]

Lincoln would visit other churches, some more than once. The week after he first attended New York Avenue Presbyterian, for example, he returned to St. John's Episcopal as the guest of Winfield Scott, general in chief of the army. In time, though, he and Mary settled on New York

Avenue and Reverend Gurley. Once they sent word of their choice, they then settled the all-important matter of renting a pew—deciding upon B-14, where President Buchanan worshipped for many years—and settled in.[47] By all accounts, they were devoted to their church home. They attended regularly, gave generously, and saw that their children were involved as well. Both Willie and Tad attended Sunday school, and Willie even participated in the Youth's Missionary Society, which raised funds to support missionaries to China.

It is significant that the New York Avenue congregation contained both supporters of the Union and those who sympathized with the Southern cause. Lincoln surely knew this when he began attending and must have endured heated lectures and cold stares from fellow worshippers more than once. It did not drive him off, and this is testimony to his tolerance, his respect for views other than his own. Nevertheless, his patience had a limit. Not long after he began attending, some secessionist members began noisily walking out of the service when Reverend Gurley prayed aloud for the president of the United States. The stomping, the grunting, and the slamming of pew gates created a huge and pointed distraction. This went on for weeks. Lincoln was likely grieved that his presence led to these weekly disruptions and may also have felt some anger at those who refused to pray for their leaders as Scripture commanded.

Finally, a lieutenant leading a squad of soldiers appeared at one of the Sunday services. Marching to the front of the sanctuary and turning in smart, drill-order fashion to the congregation, the young officer announced, "It is the order of the Provost Marshal that any one disturbing this service or leaving it before it is out will be arrested and taken to the guardhouse." The effect was immediate. The demonstrations ceased. Young Tad, a rowdy child who probably enjoyed the weekly chaos, famously said, "If I was Secesh, I wouldn't let him stop me banging pew doors." When his brother warned him that he would be put in jail if he did, Tad said, "Well, I guess Pa could get me out."[48]

Some historians have seen Lincoln's regular attendance in church as crass political theater. They believe the lifelong religious skeptic was merely posturing, appealing to the religious sentiments of a Christian nation at war without having any genuine religion of his own. The facts are against this. The truth is Lincoln continued the religious journey he had been on for some fifteen years. It was typical of him, for example, that he not only attended Sunday services at the New York Avenue church, but he also enjoyed its Thursday evening prayer meetings. Since the church was only three blocks from the White House, Lincoln often walked alone to the gatherings and joined in the prayers as he could. This, in time, presented a problem. As a doctor who attended the church later recalled, "It having become known that he was an attendant at the prayer meeting, many persons would gather in or near the church at the close of the service in order to have access to him for various purposes." This bothered Reverend Gurley, who wanted Lincoln to attend undisturbed. Since the meetings were in the church's basement, Gurley suggested to Lincoln that he enjoy the service from the pastor's office, which was nearby. Lincoln did and on many a week sat on a small sofa in Gurley's office and listened to the prayer service through an open door. The president later told Gurley "he had received great comfort from the meetings."[49]

❦

This does not fit the traditional image of a religiously skeptical Lincoln. Nor does much of what we know about him during the White House years. We know, for example, that a Bible commonly lay on his desk, that he kept another on a table at the end of a sofa, and that he routinely pulled out a pocket New Testament to quote a relevant verse. If he could not find the verses he needed, he consulted the helpful *A Complete Concordance to the Holy Scriptures of the Old and New Testament* that Alexander Cruden had compiled a hundred years before. He kept a copy in his library. He told a Treasury Department official, "If we had a witness on the stand whose general story we knew was true, we would believe him when he asserted facts of which we had no other evidence. . . . I decided [a] long time ago that it was less difficult to believe that the Bible was what it claimed to be than to disbelieve it."[50] A clergyman who knew Lincoln during these years was hesitant to be specific about the president's religious views but did say,

> This I know, however: he read the Bible frequently, loved it for its great truths, and profound teachings and he tried to be guided by its precepts. He believed in Christ, the Savior of sinners, and I think he was sincerely trying to bring his life into the principles of revealed religion.[51]

Lincoln was no longer the Springfield politician for whom few ministers would vote.

During the war years he supported Christian ministries, including some outside his own denomination. He called for and funded military chaplains, supported the work of the Young Men's Christian Association among the troops, and approved a bill that placed, for the first time, the slogan "In God We Trust" on a coin of the United States.[52]

As fierce as he was in matters of faith, he was no religious bigot. Though he was a Protestant, he enlisted a Roman Catholic archbishop in the cause of military chaplains. When General Grant inexplicably expelled all the Jews from his department, Lincoln reversed him and reminded the general that many Jews fought valiantly for the Union.[53] Rabbis around the country cheered the president for this, one celebrating that Lincoln's "mind was not subject to the vulgar clamor against Jews."[54] The president also met with a large gathering of Native Americans who crammed into the East Room of the executive mansion to hear him answer their questions. Though he spoke forcefully of the importance of faith in God, he also told them that he did not know

White House "Blue Room" in a double-image stereograph, around 1875

"whether, in the providence of the Great Spirit, who is the great Father of us all, it is best for you to maintain the habits and customs of your race, or adopt a new mode of life."[55]

Yet he also thought nothing of employing the moral judgments of Scripture to rebuke supporters of slavery. Two Confederate wives so angered him once that he described the experience in an article which he then had distributed to the nation's newspapers. It was entitled "The President's Last, Shortest and Best Speech."

On Thursday of last week two ladies from Tennessee came before the President asking the release of their husbands held as prisoners of war at Johnson's Island. . . . At each of the interviews one of the ladies urged that her husband was a religious man. On Saturday the President ordered the release of the prisoners, and then said to this lady, "You say your husband is a religious man; tell him when you meet him, that I say I am not much of a judge of religion, but that, in my opinion, the religion that sets men to rebel and fight against their government, because, as they think, that government does not sufficiently help some men to eat their bread on the sweat of other men's faces, is not the sort of religion upon which people can get to heaven![56]

As stern as he could be in such matters, it did not keep him from allowing his faith to work itself into his humor. He enjoyed the story of the two Quaker women discussing the end of the war. "I think," one said, "that Jefferson Davis will succeed." "Why does thee think so?" asked the other. "Because Jefferson is a praying man," replied the first. "And so is Abraham a praying man," the second answered. "Yes," came the reply, "but the Lord will think Abraham is joking."[57]

He was also moved by the symbolic accidents of war. At the battle of Cold Harbor, a soldier of the Fourth Maine Volunteers was hit by a bullet that ricocheted off his suspenders and penetrated his pocket New Testament until it stopped exactly upon Mark 12:36: "Sit thou on my right hand, till I make thine enemies thy footstool." When a Massachusetts soldier was saved from a rifle ball by the Bible he carried over his heart, Lincoln heard of it and sent the man another Bible.

Sandburg wrote, "A distinct trend toward a deeper religious note, a piety more assured of itself because more definitely derived from inner and private growths of Lincoln himself, this could be seen as the President from year to year fitted himself more deeply and awarely into the mantle and authorities of Chief Magistrate."[58] Joshua Speed, who had become Lincoln's friend decades before in Springfield, visited the White House during this time and concluded, "I think that when I knew Mr. L. he was skeptical as to the great truths of the Christian religion. I think that after he was elected President, he sought to become a believer—and to make the Bible a preceptor to his faith and a guide for his conduct."[59] Speed was wrong about Lincoln trying to become a believer only after he reached the White House. However, it is what he witnessed in the life of his friend that is important. He saw, during those terrible years, a man striving for righteousness.

❧

It should come as no surprise, then—nor should it be treated with the scholarly skepticism it has received—that when Congress suggested in August of 1861 "a day of Public humiliation, prayer and fasting," Lincoln eagerly complied. Only the month before, Union forces had been defeated at the Battle of Bull Run (Manassas). The death tolls had been mounting, and some of those who had died were Lincoln's friends. Already he sensed the devastations created in the fog of war, that events were not as much under human control as he had suggested those months before in his inaugural address. Yes, a call to prayer was needed. The proclamation he issued, probably with input from Seward and others, is one of the great American statements of faith.

> Whereas a joint Committee of both Houses of Congress has waited on the President of the United States, and requested him to "recommend a day of public humiliation, prayer and fasting, to be observed by the people of the United States with religious solemnities, and the offering of fervent supplications to Almighty God for the safety and welfare of these States, His blessings on their arms, and a speedy restoration of peace":
>
> And whereas it is fit and becoming in all people at all times, to acknowledge and revere the Supreme Government of God; to bow in humble submission to his chastisements; to confess and deplore their sins and transgressions in the full conviction that the fear of the Lord is the beginning of wisdom; and to pray, with all fervency and contrition, for the pardon of their past offenses, and for a blessing upon their present and prospective action:
>
> And whereas, when our own beloved Country, once, by the blessing of God, united, prosperous and happy, is now affiliate with faction and civil war, it is peculiarly fit for us to recognize the hand of God in this terrible visitation, and in sorrowful remembrance of

our own faults and crimes as a nation and as individuals, to humble ourselves before Him, and to pray for His mercy, to pray that we may be spared further punishment, though most justly deserved; that our arms may be blessed and made effectual for the re-establishment of law, order and peace, throughout the wide extent of our Country; and that the inestimable boon of civil and religious liberty, earned under His guidance and blessing, by the labors and sufferings of our fathers, may be restored in all its original excellence:

Therefore, I, Abraham Lincoln, President of the United States, do appoint the last Thursday in September next, as a day of humiliation, prayer and fasting for all the people of the nation. And I do earnestly recommend to all the People, and especially to all ministers and teachers of religion of all denominations, and to all heads of families, to observe and keep that day according to their several creeds and modes of worship, in all humility and with all religious solemnity, to the end that the united prayer of the nation may ascend to the throne of Grace and bring down plentiful blessing upon our Country.

FIVE

THE HAUNTING
OF GRAVES

S HE WAS A DIFFICULT WOMAN. SHE WAS CHARMING enough to skirt by nearly any misdeed she committed but fragile enough to collapse at the slightest rebuke. She was also vain. During the White House years, she insisted on being called Mrs. President Lincoln. She came to see herself as an American Queen Victoria. Anyone who impinged on her sense of station, who dared be too familiar with her husband, or who treated her as less than Abraham Lincoln's equal, risked the blowtorch of her rage. She was jealous of nearly every woman and resentful of any man who did not defer to her. She once told an acquaintance, "I understand that you forgive me, for all past offenses. Yet I am not Christian enough, to feel the same towards you."[1] She spent vast sums she did not have and humiliated her husband with her ostentatious displays when the nation was at war. She ended up almost friendless in Washington and lived her latter years complaining of impoverishment, haunted and alone.

The most that could be said of her by most Americans was that Abraham Lincoln loved her.

In the winter of 1861, Mary Lincoln was not at her best. It was the season of her first Christmas in Washington, and it had been a dreary, damp, uninspiring affair. Adding to the general gloom was the darkness enveloping her husband. With every visitor who brought news from the front, with every new cable from the War Office, his shoulders sagged; his gaze became unfocused and distant. The pain etched in her husband's face was almost more than Mary could take. The man sat alone in his office or paced with an agonized step that could be heard in the rooms below. The poet Walt Whitman had written of the prevailing mood: "awful consternation, uncertainty, rage, shame, helplessness and stupefying disappointment."[2] If he had added fear and unutterable frustration, he would have described the spirit that occupied the White House.

Mary Lincoln could not let this continue. She decided that what the city and her husband needed—perhaps even the nation, as well—was a party. This was something she knew well. Parties. She had been raised in a family addicted to the excitement of dances and balls, to the intrigue and elegance of "the season" among the elite. It was just what this humdrum city of Washington needed, she thought. And it would be good for her husband. She had often seen him happy at the big social events in Springfield. Yes, this was how she could help.

Having made her decision, she did not waste time. By the end of January 1862, more than five hundred invitations had been sent. Many of Washington's powerful were delighted to know they were included. Others felt the intended slight. Mary was never above dealing the vengeful blow.

She spared nothing. Despite objections, she hired Maillard's of New York, the country's most expensive caterer. She arranged for the best wine and champagne, had the White House staff dressed in new mulberry-colored uniforms, and made sure that her husband's black swallowtail coat was brushed. She chose to wear what the *New York*

Herald later described as "a magnificent white satin robe, with a black flounce half a yard wide, looped with black and white bows, a low corsage trimmed with black lace and a bouquet of crape myrtle on her bosom."[3]

The night of the ball, February 5, the Lincolns received in the East Room while the Marine Band played in a nearby hall. It was a dazzling affair. There were distinguished ambassadors and grandly attired generals and women who surpassed the finery of Europe in what they wore. The guests arrived at nine o'clock that evening. Dinner was served at eleven thirty. The hearty were still excitedly chatting at two o'clock the next morning.

Years later, Mary would remember the evening with regret: "I had become so wrapped up in the world, so devoted to our own political advancement that I thought of little else besides." She had come to believe that the tragedy unfolding even as she welcomed her guests to

The White House as it appeared during the Lincoln administration

the White House was divine intervention: "Our Heavenly Father sees fit, oftentimes to visit us, at such times for our worldliness; how small & insignificant all worldly honors are, when we are thus so severely tried."[4]

⁓

What blackened the party in Mary's memory was that all through the evening her son Willie lay upstairs in bed with fever. Mary and Abraham had taken turns leaving their guests to check on him. They likely felt some guilt. Willie had been sick for several days, and there was talk of canceling the grand ball. The boy's father was in favor of it. Mary probably objected and talked him out of it. Sandburg quotes a woman who attended the party as recalling, "A sadder face than that of the President I have rarely seen. He was receiving at the large door of the East Room, speaking to the people as they came, but feeling so deeply that he spoke of what he felt and thought, instead of welcoming the guests. To General Fremont he at once said that his son was very ill and he feared for the result . . . The ball was becoming a ghastly failure."[5]

Those who knew Lincoln knew the wild affection he had for his sons. He had once explained, "It is my pleasure that my children are free—happy, and unrestrained by paternal tyranny. Love is the chain whereby to lock a child to its parent."[6] In an age in which children were often worked endlessly or shoved to the periphery of life, Lincoln was an exception. A shoemaker who lived near the Lincolns remembered that Abraham would "take his Children and would walk out on the Rail way out in the Country—would talk to them—Explain things Carefully—particularly. He was Kind—tender and affectionate to his children."[7]

He was almost certainly trying to rise above the harsh methods of his own father. He may have taken this to extremes. He and Mary fought over the discipline of their children constantly, and one friend remembered, "He was the most indulgent parent I ever knew. . . . His children literally ran over him and he was powerless to withstand their importunities."[8] Others put the matter more bluntly: the Lincoln boys were like a destructive tornado wherever they went. Lincoln's long-suffering law partner, Herndon, remembered all his life the dreadful occasions when Lincoln took his sons to work:

> These children would take down the books, empty ash buckets, coal ashes, inkstand, papers, gold pens, letters, etc, etc, in a pile and then dance on the pile. Lincoln would say nothing, so abstracted was he and so blinded to his children's faults. Had they s—t in Lincoln's hat and rubbed it on his boot, he would have laughed and thought it smart. Lincoln was a fool in this line. . . . He worshiped his children and what they worshipped; he loved what they loved and hated what they hated . . . which was everything that did not bend to their freaks, whims, follies and the like.[9]

Protected by their father's weakness for them, the boys—Willie in particular—terrorized the White House staff. The two little terrors drove goat carts through the West Wing's halls, bypassed protocol by taking visitors unannounced to see their father in exchange for candy, and interrupted cabinet meetings with their antics. No matter was too small to take to their father. With two playmates they once fashioned a doll out of rags. They named the doll Jack, clothed him, and inducted him into the army. Then, found sleeping on guard duty, Jack was sentenced to be shot. A White House gardener suggested they pardon Jack. This meant only one thing: appeal to the president of the United States. Moments later, they burst into a weary Lincoln's office and had his full attention as they made their case. Lincoln soberly wrote on official stationery:

> The doll Jack is pardoned.
> By order of the President.
> A. Lincoln[10]

Yet there was more to Willie than boyish pranks. He was clearly brilliant. He loved trains and could call out all the stations from New York to Chicago in perfect order by memory. He spent hours inventing an imaginary railroad with exacting timetables and would play conductor with flair and precision. He was imaginative, bookish, and smart. His mentor reported that Willie "had only to con over once or twice a page of his speller and definer, and the impression became so fixed that he went though without hesitation or blundering, and his other studies in proportion."[11]

It is not hard to understand how Lincoln adored him. It was often said that Willie cocked his head slightly to the left the way his father did. The two even thought alike. Once when his younger brother was troubled, Willie determined to think himself to a solution. A visitor to the White House recalled that Willie "lapsed into a profound, absorbed silence, which Mr. Lincoln would not allow to be disturbed. This lasted for ten or fifteen minutes, then he clasped both hands together, shut his teeth firmly over the under lip, and looked up smilingly into his father's face, who exclaimed, 'There! You have it now, my boy, have you not?' Turning to his guest, Lincoln said, 'I know every step of the process by which that boy arrived at his satisfactory solution of the question before him, as it is by just such slow methods I attain results.'"[12]

William Wallace "Willie" Lincoln (1848)

The sweetness of the child and the closeness he shared with his father are reflected in a letter he wrote during a trip to Chicago when he was eight.

This town is a very beautiful place. Me and father went to two theatres the other night. Me and father have a nice little room to ourselves. We have two little pitchers on a washstand. The smallest one for me, the largest one for father. We have two little towels on a top of both pitchers. The smallest one for me, the largest one for father. We have two little beds in the room, the smallest one for me, the largest one for father.[13]

⁓⧸⦚◡⧹⁓

It was the affection that Lincoln and others felt for Willie that led to the boy being given a pony. Rowdy as he was, it was Willie's habit to ride the animal no matter the weather, imagining himself a Napoleon or Washington leading troops in battle. While out challenging invisible foes on one chilly, wet day, Willie caught a cold that quickly transformed into a fever. He had suffered with it only a short while when the grand ball took place at the White House. Even during the course of that evening he grew worse. His mother never left his side afterward. Within a few days of the party, the Washington press was reporting that the president's son suffered from "bilious fever." The White House staff began canceling events in deference to the child's anxious parents. Then, gratefully, a few days later, doctors informed the press he was "out of danger."

This was false hope. Another two days and the public heard that both boys, Tad and Willie, were ill and that there was serious worry over the younger. By February 16, eleven days after the party, doctors announced that both children had improved and their full recovery was expected soon. Horribly, the very next day, a bulletin declared Willie "past all hope of recovery." On the evening of February 20, he died. Doctors said Willie was the victim of varioloid, a form of small-pox. This fact was kept from the public to prevent the panic that came at mere mention of the disease. In later years, scholars determined the boy actually died of typhoid. Whatever the cause, Abraham and Mary Lincoln had lost another son.

One of Lincoln's secretaries recorded in his journal, "At about 5 o'clock this afternoon, I was lying half asleep on the sofa in my office, when his entrance aroused me. 'Well, Nicolay,' said he choking with emotion, 'my boy is gone—he is actually gone!' and bursting into tears, turned and went into his own office."[14] Later Lincoln was seen pacing, repeating over and again, "This is the hardest trial of my life! Why is it? Why is it?"[15] Mary, fractured by her loss, retreated to bed. The haunting of graves had returned.

Elizabeth Keckly, former slave who had become Mary Lincoln's seamstress, helped wash and dress Willie's body before it was placed in the casket and taken to the White House Green Room. Soon after, Lincoln arrived. Taking the cloth from his child's face, he murmured, "My poor boy, he was too good for this earth. God has called him home. I know that he is much better off in heaven, but then we loved him so. It is hard, hard to have him die!"[16]

When Lincoln arose on February 24, the day of his son's funeral, he must have thought the weather was somehow a reflection of his own stormy heart. An early morning fog gave way to winds so strong newspapers compared them to tornadoes. Roofs blew off houses, church buildings collapsed, and the skylights in the Library of Congress were destroyed. Waves from the Potomac River pummeled the shore and washed over bridges.

When the service began that afternoon at two o'clock, Mary was too grieved and Tad was too ill to attend. Lincoln and his son Robert joined a hundred other mourners in the East Room for a service that stabbed the heart with grief. Dr. Gurley, the Lincolns' pastor at New York Presbyterian, gave the oration. It was tender and wise, thoroughly rooted in the ancient wisdom of Scripture. Gurley's last paragraph lived in the memory of those who mourned with him that day.

Only let us bow in His presence with an humble and teachable spirit; only let us be still and know that He is God; only let us acknowledge His hand, and hear His voice, and inquire after His will, and seek His holy spirit as our counselor and guide, and all, in the end, will be well. In His light shall we see light; by His grace our sorrows will be sanctified—they will be made a blessing to our souls—and by and by we shall have occasion to say, with blended gratitude and rejoicing, "It is good for us that we have been afflicted."[17]

Lincoln was so moved by the sermon that he asked Gurley for a printed copy. Both Abraham and Mary read the transcript in the following months and gave it to grief-stricken friends. The Lincolns found such comfort in the words that they sent Gurley the gift of a gold-headed cane to express their appreciation.

Then came the most heart-wrenching scene of all. When the service was done, children from Willie's Sunday school class followed their dead friend's casket to the hearse. It was too much. Mourners wiped away tears. General McClellan, commander in chief of the Union army, wept openly. Then friends watched as once again Abraham Lincoln placed his hand on the casket of a son. Once again he joined the bleak procession carrying his child to a cemetery. Once again he heard the eternal words that sent his flesh and blood into the earth.

❧

In the months that followed, Lincoln somehow kept from collapsing under the burden of his mourning, his wife's decline, and the worsening war. A moment recalled by a senior officer at Fort Monroe reveals how the president sometimes could not keep his anguish from spilling over.

The day after Mr. Lincoln came to us he said to me: "I suppose you have neither a Bible nor a copy of Shakespeare here?" I replied that I had a Bible, and the General had Shakespeare, and that the latter never missed a night without reading it. "Won't he lend it to me?" inquired the President. I answered, "Yes," and, of course, obtained it for him.

The day following he read by himself in one of my offices, two hours or more, entirely alone. I being engaged in a connecting room on duty. He finally interrupted me, inviting me to rest while he would read to me. He read from *Macbeth, Lear,* and finally, *King John.* In reading the passage where Constance bewails to the King the loss of her child, I noticed that his voice trembled and he was deeply moved.[18]

The words Lincoln read were words he had revisited often since the death of Eddie more than a decade before. Now, they inspired deeper feelings in him than ever.

> *Father cardinal, I have heard you say*
> *That we shall see and know our friends in heaven.*
> *If that be true, I shall see my boy again; . . .*
> *Grief fills the room up of my absent child.*
> *Lies in his bed, walks up and down with me,*
> *Puts on his pretty looks, repeats his words,*
> *Remembers me of all his gracious parts,*
> *Stuffs out his vacant garments with his form;*
> *Then, have I reason to be fond of grief?*
> *O Lord! my boy, my Arthur, my fair son!*
> *My life, my joy, my food, my all the world!*
> *My widow-comfort, and my sorrows' cure!*[19]

Once Lincoln had finished reading to the Fort Monroe officer, he laid his volume of Shakespeare aside.

"Did you ever dream of a lost friend and feel that you were having a sweet communion with that friend, and yet a consciousness that it was not a reality?"

"Yes," I replied, "I think almost anyone may have had such an experience."

"So do I," he mused: "I dream of my dead boy, Willie, again and again."

I shall never forget the sigh nor the look of sorrow that accompanied this expression. He was utterly overcome; his great frame shook, and, bowing down on the table he wept as only such a man in the breaking down of a great sorrow could weep. It is needless to say that I wept in sympathy, and quietly left the room that he might recover without restraint.[20]

Grief took its toll upon Lincoln. He told friends Willie's death was a blow that nearly became his undoing. The public could see the effects of the president's suffering in his appearance. To a visitor at church one Sunday, Lincoln looked aged and almost broken by sadness, with his "gait more stooping, his countenance sallow, and there is a sunken, deathly look about the large cavernous eyes, which is saddening to those who see there the marks of care and anxiety, such as no President of the United States has ever before known." Still, he was gracious: "Recognizing with a cheerful nod, his friends on either side, his homely face lighted with a smile." Yet the congregation saw the president as a mournful, tragedy-stricken figure. "God bless him," the visitor concluded.[21]

There was a time when overwhelming sorrow might have sent Lincoln into one of his hypos. He couldn't afford it now, but he had help he had not known in his earlier life. His friendships with Christian ministers became lifelines for him. His pastor, Dr. Gurley, met with him often. One morning a member of New York Avenue Presbyterian saw Gurley leaving the White House. As Gurley later remembered the conversation, the man said,

"Why doctor it is not nine o'clock. What are you doing at the Executive Mansion?"

To this I replied, "Mr. Lincoln and I have been having a morning chat."

"On the war, I suppose?"

"Far from it," I said. "We have been talking of the state of the soul after death. That is a subject of which Mr. Lincoln never tires. I have had a great many conversations with him on the subject. . . . This morning, however, I was a listener, as Mr. Lincoln did all the talking."[22]

Willie's death had obviously forced the familiar theme of lost loved ones into Lincoln's mind. Now, though, he had a different view of death from when he had told the mother of a friend, "It isn't a pleasant thing to think that when we die that is the last of us."[23] He had said this in the late 1830s, when he had followed Paine, Volney, and Burns away from Christian beliefs, far from the certainty of an afterlife. Then had come Reverend Smith, membership in two Presbyterian churches, and a recovered belief in God that began to permeate his life. Under these influences and from his own reading of Scripture, he had come to believe that Willie was in heaven, and he took comfort in this certainty, much as he had encouraged his dying father in 1851 to find comfort in the idea that he would soon be joined with lost family and friends. The meetings with Dr. Gurley would only have deepened his faith in the resurrection and helped him see Willie's death—in fact, all the deaths he had known—in the light of Christian theology.

In April of 1862, Reverend Noyes Miner, Lincoln's Baptist pastor friend from Springfield, also visited the White House. Miner later made notes on his conversation with the president and recalled him saying, "If I were not sustained by the prayers of God's people, I could not endure this constant pressure. . . . It has pleased Almighty God to place me in my present position and looking up to Him for wisdom and divine guidance I must work my destiny as best I can." Miner added years later, "If Mr. Lincoln was not a Christian, he was acting like one."[24]

⌒꙰꙰⌒

Lincoln visited as well with a Dr. Francis Vinton, another of the nation's famous ministers, and the meeting of the two has become one of the most controversial among scholars of Lincoln's faith. Dr. Vinton was a cadet at West Point and a student at Harvard Law School before he gave up his career in law to become an Episcopal priest in 1838. He quickly gained a reputation as the eloquent preacher at Trinity Episcopal Church on Broadway in New York City. His visit with Lincoln came only weeks after Willie's death, when the president's tortured mourning nearly debilitated him. In fact, it was news of this grief that moved Vinton to see Lincoln.

The meeting was recounted in a memoir by the noted painter F. B. Carpenter, who spent six months in the White House in 1864 to paint the dramatic scene later titled *The First Reading of the Emancipation Proclamation of President Lincoln*. Carpenter's work would become one of the great American historical paintings, often compared with the works of John Trumbull, who gave us our enduring image of the signing of the Declaration of Independence, and those of Emmanuel Leutze, who embedded in our national memory his vision of Washington crossing the Delaware. Not long after Carpenter completed his masterpiece, he wrote a book that eventually acquired the ambitious title *The Inner Life of Abraham Lincoln: Six Months at the White House*. Scholars respect much of the book, though some suspect that Carpenter's evangelical Christianity may have led him to exaggerate episodes pertaining to Lincoln's faith.

This is what leads to the controversy surrounding Reverend Vinton's meeting with Lincoln. According to Carpenter, during each of the two Thursdays after Willie died, Lincoln had locked himself away to mourn the loss of his son. Mrs. Lincoln had become concerned. She thought that this "indulgence of grief" was an unhealthy extreme. Dr. Vinton thought so too.

Lincoln received Vinton in the White House parlor, which gave the minister "opportunity . . . to chide him [the president] for showing so rebellious a disposition to the decrees of Providence":

> He told him plainly that the indulgence of such feelings, though natural, was sinful. It was unworthy of one who believed in the Christian religion. He had duties to the living, greater than those of any other man, as the chosen father, and leader of the people, and he was unfitting himself for his responsibilities by thus giving way to his grief. To mourn the departed as *lost* belonged to heathenism—not to Christianity. "Your son," said Dr. Vinton, "is alive, in Paradise. Do you remember that passage in the Gospels: 'God is not the God of the dead but of the living, for all live unto him'?"
>
> The President had listened as one in a stupor, until his ear caught the words, "Your son is alive." Starting from the sofa, he exclaimed, "Alive! *alive!* Surely you mock me." "No, sir, believe me," replied Dr. Vinton; "it is a most comforting doctrine of the church founded upon the words of Christ himself."
>
> Mr. Lincoln looked at him a moment, then, stepping forward, he threw his arm around the clergyman's neck, and, laying his head upon his breast, sobbed aloud. "Alive? alive?" he repeated. "My dear sir," said Dr. Vinton, greatly moved, as he twined his own arm around the weeping father, "believe this, for it is God's most precious truth. Seek not your son among the dead; he is not there; he lives to-day in Paradise."

Vinton then proceeded to cite Scripture in support of his message, and after referring particularly to the words of Jesus and Jacob, he said:

"And so God has called your son into his upper kingdom—a kingdom and an existence as real, more real, than your own. It may be that he too, like Joseph, has gone, in God's good providence, to be the salvation of his father's household."

Finally, Vinton offered, "I have a sermon upon this subject, which I think might interest you." Mr. Lincoln begged him to send it at an early day—thanking him repeatedly for his cheering and hopeful words. The sermon was sent, and read over and over by the President, who caused a copy to be made for his own private use before it was returned. Through a member of the family, I [Carpenter] have been informed that Mr. Lincoln's views in relation to spiritual things seemed changed from that hour.[25]

The story is endearing, and something like it may indeed have happened. Dr. Vinton was indeed this bold. What he is supposed to have told Lincoln about undue grieving is consistent with the Episcopal theology of the day. Even the detail of Lincoln asking for a copy of Vinton's sermon rings true, for Lincoln loved to read speeches and sermons in print.

Nonetheless, as is often the case in accounts of Lincoln's faith, there is disturbing inconsistency. First, it is nearly impossible that Mary Lincoln had concerns about her husband's unhealthy grief. Two weeks after Willie died, Mary was barely cognizant of anything but her own agony. Each day she wailed her pain so loudly that the sound haunted the White House staff for years afterward. Even if she had been aware of Abraham's mourning, she could not have been concerned about his emotional imbalance without having greater concerns about her own. She was famous both for her emotional extremes and for her wild behavior when in grief. The idea that she would contact friends to help her husband because he sat quietly and gloomily in a darkened room for two Thursdays in a row brings that part of this account into question.

More critically, Carpenter indicates that the idea of Willie being alive in heaven or paradise was new to Lincoln. Yet Lincoln already had a belief in an afterlife and had said to Elizabeth Keckly, Mary's seamstress, that his son was in heaven. This doctrine was nothing new to him, as we have seen. Lincoln had affirmed a faith in the resurrection of the dead and in heaven in his 1851 note to his father. He affirmed it in the reciting of the creed each Sunday he went to his Presbyterian church. Even where he struggled with Christian doctrine, as in his resistance to the idea of eternal punishment, he had no disagreement with the idea of eternal life. In short, there was nothing so new in Vinton's words to expect that "spiritual things seemed changed from that hour" in Lincoln's life. If the episode Carpenter reports is true, then the most that Vinton's words did was to remind a distraught man of truths he already knew but had lost in his heartache. Perhaps this was enough.

Some scholars have objected to Lincoln's tears and emotional embrace of Vinton as depicted in this story, yet these are perfectly consistent with the Lincoln we know. Nicolay, the president's secretary, said Lincoln wept on the day Willie died. It should come as no surprise. The senior army officer at Fort Monroe also recalled Lincoln weeping at the memory of his son. Tears were not that odd for him, nor would a manly embrace have been that foreign either, particularly if the one he embraced had just delivered life-changing news about his son. None of this is too strange to believe—if the rest of the story is true.

As with much that pertains to Lincoln's faith, we cannot know with certainty if Carpenter's account is even partially true. We should give the man his due, though. He was a respected painter whose account of his months in the White House tells us much we would never have known otherwise and much that we heard for the first time from his pen but which scholars were able afterward to affirm. We should also remember that Carpenter being an evangelical does not automatically mean that he exaggerated to serve his religious views. He was a credible witness to events in the Lincoln White House for a time, and we should be slow to discount his testimony.

Nevertheless, it is frustrating to deal with such contradictory information. It is the way of things in the study of Lincoln's faith, particularly in testimony regarding the period following Willie's death. Consider, for example, the memory of Mary Lincoln from this time. Following Lincoln's death, she told William Herndon her husband "was a religious man always, as I think. He first thought—to say think—about his subject was when Willie died—never before."[26] Clearly, this wasn't true. Lincoln had been giving serious thought to the subject of religion since he was in his twenties. To say he pondered themes of faith only after Willie's death was silly. Lincoln scholar David Herbert Donald has written, "That statement perhaps told more about the lack of intimacy in the Lincoln marriage than it did about the President's state of mind."[27]

But Mary Lincoln could be forgiven her sometimes flawed memory. She had endured more than most are called to endure in this life. Even after she had buried yet another son, she was forced to read this taunt from a Washington merchant: "I suppose Mrs. Lincoln will be providentially deterred from giving any more parties which scandalized so many good persons who did not get invitations."[28] The city's elite prattled about invitations and social slights. Mary spent unending nights haunted by visions of her sons decaying in the grave.

⁂

As he had following Eddie's death, Lincoln mined his faith for its riches after Willie died. He yearned for comfort in his grief. He also needed strength to lead the country. He read. He took counsel with his minister friends. He prayed. From this season came a greater moral certainty, a broader embrace of Christian truth, a more personal connection to the very God he had long believed cursed him and kept him at bay. These new realities shaped his latter years in the presidency.

The terms he used for explaining to a friend how God guided him were surprising and showed that a new spiritual dynamic was at work in his life.

That the Almighty does make use of human agencies, and directly intervenes in human affairs, is one of the plainest statements of the Bible. I have had so many evidences of His direction, so many instances when I have been controlled by some other power than my own will, that I cannot doubt that this power comes from above. I frequently see my way clear to a decision when I am conscious that I have no sufficient facts upon which to found it. But I cannot recall one instance in which I have followed my own judgment, founded upon such a decision, where the results were unsatisfactory; whereas, in almost every instance where I have yielded to the views of others, I have had occasion to regret it. I am satisfied that when the Almighty wants me to do or not do a particular thing, He finds a way of letting me know it. I am confident that it is His design to restore the Union. He will do it in His own good time. We should obey and not oppose his will.[29]

There is a new intimacy in these words, a new confidence that God is near. Lincoln's public pronouncements usually lead scholars to conclude that he was almost a deist, that he saw God as the creator of the world but also as a distant deity who seldom involved himself in the daily affairs of mankind. These words show otherwise. Clearly, at this point in his life, Lincoln understood God not only as loving and concerned, but also as faithful, intimate, and good. He was certain God would always find a way of letting him know what he needed to know. For Lincoln, God had become more father than demanding dictator, more New Testament shepherd than Old Testament offended king.

This may have inspired a more traditional view of Jesus Christ. When the "Loyal Colored People of Baltimore" honored him with an expensive Bible, he thanked them and said, "In regard to this Great Book, I have but to say, it is the best gift God has given to man. All the good the Savior gave to the world was communicated through this book. But for it we could not know right from wrong. All things most desirable for man's welfare, here and hereafter, are to be found portrayed in it."[30] This reference alone does not make Lincoln an orthodox Christian, but it does show that he had broadened in his view of Jesus Christ and felt no hesitation in identifying with the Christian gospel.

Equally revealing is a conversation Joshua Speed had with Lincoln at the Soldier's Home cottage, the Lincolns' cherished summer retreat. The two had known each other mainly during Lincoln's New Salem and early Springfield years, and so Speed still thought of Lincoln as an unrepentant religious skeptic. During his visit, he was surprised to discover his old friend reading his Bible and said so, explaining that he himself was still a skeptic, particularly regarding the Bible. "You are wrong, Speed," Lincoln responded, putting his hand gently on Speed's shoulder. "Take all of this book upon reason that you can, and the balance on faith, and you will live and die a happier and better man."[31] It is likely this is exactly what Lincoln had chosen to do. Clearly, it changed him, both as a man and as president.

In later years, a clergyman tried to capture Lincoln's religious views by stitching together his public statements on faith, changing them as little as possible, and adding the words "I believe." Because Carl Sandburg included a portion of this "creed" in his much-loved book, the words have framed the popular view of Abraham Lincoln's religion.

> I believe in national humiliation, fasting, and prayer, in keeping a day holy to the Lord, devoted to the humble discharge of the religious duties proper to such a solemn occasion.
>
> . . . I believe in Him whose will, not ours, should be done.
>
> I believe the people of the United States, in the forms approved by

their own consciences, should render the homage due to the Divine Majesty for the wonderful things He has done in the nation's behalf, and invoke the influence of His Holy Spirit to subdue anger.

. . . I believe in His eternal truth and justice. I believe the will of God prevails; without Him all human reliance is vain; without the assistance of that Divine Being I cannot succeed; with that assistance I cannot fail.

I believe I am a humble instrument in the hands of our Heavenly Father; I desire that all my works and acts may be according to his will; and that it may be so, I give thanks to the Almighty and seek his Aid.

I believe in praise to Almighty God, the beneficent Creator and Ruler of the Universe.[32]

This "creed" certainly captures much of what Lincoln said publicly about his faith. Yet this is Lincoln's political faith, what later scholars might have called his "civil religion." It is what he urged of God and religion upon his fellow citizens, what he understood to be the spiritual responsibilities of those blessed to be Americans. It is certainly not all that he believed, and it is unfortunate that it has come to be taken as such by generations of Sandburg's readers.

It is obvious from what we have seen that Lincoln believed much more. He believed in God as Creator, as ruler of the world, Judge, Comforter, the author of justice, the author also of much if not all of the Bible, and, increasingly, as benevolent guide. He believed in the Holy Spirit and in Jesus Christ as teacher, Savior of the world, and model for mankind. He believed in heaven, in the resurrection of the dead, and in what Christians call eternal life. He believed in the value of Christian ministry, in the duty of generosity, in fasting and prayer as a means of urging God to change human affairs, in repentance from sins, in observing the Sabbath, in reading Scripture, and in the religious training of the young. And, yes, he also believed in the citizens of the United States being a "Christian people," in her military forces being "Christian soldiers and sailors," in American history as the carefully woven tapestry of a sovereign God, and in the nation possessing a divine destiny yet to fulfill.

Against all of this the most often repeated objection is that Lincoln never joined a church. It was true. He had found church culture too petty, most clergymen too weak, and, certainly, most creeds too far afield from the simplicity of Christ, so he said. Later Americans, with their emphasis on "spirituality" over "organized religion," would certainly understand.

Yet if Lincoln was doubtful of churches, he came to revel in the Bible, and we must conclude that the hours he spent in its pages became the essential source of what he believed. A close friend, Noah Brooks, reported that "prayer and the reading of Scripture was his constant habit." Brooks claimed Lincoln could quote whole chapters of Isaiah, the New Testament, and the Psalms. He could tell when someone misquoted the Bible and usually offered chapter and verse for where the correct words were to be found. He worked phrases from Scripture into his daily conversations with such ease that often his listeners did not realize until later he had mentioned a dozen verses from the Bible in a single visit with friends. He would speak of getting older and refer to the phrase "his eye was not dim, nor his natural force abated" (Deut. 34:7). He would speak of the Union's enemies and add "the stars in their courses fought against Sisera" (Judges 5:20).[33] Usually only the clergy or those trained in biblical history knew exactly what he meant.

Despite this, scholars rarely grant religion its due honor when writing of Lincoln's latter years. This cannot be for lack of evidence or for reticence on Lincoln's part to speak openly of what he believed. Perhaps historians need Lincoln to act as a transitional figure between an age of faith and an age of incredulity. Perhaps it is because he had once been an outspoken critic of religion but then slowly, hesitantly, came to embrace a broad Christianity without the dramatic conversion experience we are schooled to expect. Perhaps, too, it was the effect of his self-depre-cating manner. He once told a gathering of Presbyterian ministers, "I have often wished that I was a more devout man than I am."[34] Was this because some sinful temptation conspired against him or because he had a natural insecurity about spiritual things? Was this the demon of his mother's illegitimacy rearing its head and making Lincoln feel once again he had been cursed? Or was this simply a rare expression of the very humility that being devoted to a holy God ought to inspire? It is hard to know with certainty, but we can be sure that Lincoln did not intend statements such as this to betray the truths upon which he had come to base his life and presidency.

❧

Fortunately, both for Lincoln and for us, there was always his sense of humor and his delight in teasing about religion. When an official once spewed a stream of "intemperate language" in anger over some imag-ined slight, Lincoln needled the man about his faith in a disarming manner that friends had seen often.

"You are an Episcopalian aren't you, Senator?"

"Yes, sir. I belong to that church."

"I thought so. You Episcopalians all swear alike. Seward is an Episcopalian. But Stanton is a Presbyterian. You ought to hear him swear."[35]

Lincoln then proceeded to survey the varieties of swearing he had heard and to categorize each according to church affiliation. Before long both men were laughing, the angry mood was broken, and Lincoln had issued what amounted to a religious rebuke without the other man having a chance to take offense.

This was indicative of Lincoln's approach to both men and reli-gion. Indirect. Principled. Cautious. Unemotional. Well-considered. Heartfelt. And wise.

Tragically, Mary Lincoln did not choose the same path as her husband. Though she attended her Presbyterian church and sought the help of God in her grief, she was so desperate for some connection to her dead sons that she attended séances, welcomed the counsel of mediums, and turned to practices her church labeled occult. She would continue in this for the rest of her life. It did not serve her or her husband's reputation well, but it was part of a larger movement of spiritualism that had been sweeping the nation for decades.

A friend of the Lincolns later attributed Mary's involvement in spiritualism to Elizabeth Keckly, the freed slave who served the First Lady as seamstress and confidante. There may have been some racism in this. While African religious practices and superstitions were understandably common among slaves, it was white people who had made spiritualism a fashionable craze in America. Nor was this movement unique to the lower classes who worked more closely with Africans and were more likely to be influenced by them. Instead, spiritualism was a trend encouraged by the elite, by the educated, by the famous, and by the fashionable set in every American city—Boston and Washington in particular. Elizabeth Keckly could have done no more than encourage Mary Lincoln in what she already experienced with her white, upper-class friends.

There had always been an undercurrent of spiritualism, the occult, and witchcraft in American history, of course. Whites may have brought their Christianity from Europe, but their African slaves and the natives of the New World cherished practices that the Europeans thought satanic. This created tensions even in the earliest English settlements. The famous Salem, Massachusetts, witch trials, in which a slave named Tituba allegedly taught occult practices to the children of white settlers, is the most famous early example.

In the decades following the birth of the nation, what was once thought

Mary Lincoln in 1860

occult gained new respect-ability. Novel movements and figures such as Shakers under Mother Ann Lee, Jemima "The Friend" Wilkinson, the early Mormons, the "seer" Andrew Jackson Davis, some utopian efforts, and even extreme Freemasons kept practices designed to connect with the "spirit world" alive. These were isolated and dis-connected efforts, though the Shakers had prophesied that spirits "would visit every city and hamlet, every palace and cottage in the land."[36]

Many spiritualists believe this greater movement began in 1848. Sir Arthur Conan Doyle, author of the famous Sherlock Holmes stories and an ardent spokesman for spiritualism in his latter years, was so confident this was true that he later wrote, "Fancy a new spiritual departure in a frame house in an American hamlet."[37] He was referring to the happenings in the home of the Fox family in Hydesville, New York.

At the beginning of the year, loud noises began to occur in the Foxes' house. On March 31, these intensified. The two Fox girls, Kate and Margaret, told their Methodist parents that these noises were "spirit raps" and demonstrated how they had worked out a language with whatever was making the noise. They could ask questions and receive answers. The girls were convinced that the spirit behind the raps belonged to a peddler who was rumored to be buried in the basement. The girls called him Mr. Splitfoot. Their parents doubted at first but then, confronted with the obvious truth of the happenings in their home, began to believe. So did the local authorities, clergy, and newspapermen. News of these strange events spread. In time Horace Greeley, a justice on the New York Supreme Court, and a number of scientists all agreed: spirits were communicating with humans in Hydesville, New York.

The idea that spirits wished to speak was nothing new. This had long been the province of palm readers, mediums, seers, and necromancers of every kind. What Hydesville taught the watching world in 1848 was, as Mitch Horowitz has written in his valuable *Occult America*, "Spirit communication was open to anyone, anytime. If two teenage girls could reach the other world, it stood to reason that *everyone* could. It was a completely egalitarian take on the supernatural, with newspapers and publicity-hungry investigators ready to spread the word."[38]

These events occurred in an age already eager to reach the dead. Most deaths were among children under five, as we have seen. Mothers longed for any sign of a departed child's well-being and defied the prohibitions of their traditional faith to peer "beyond the veil." Harriet Beecher Stowe, the author of *Uncle Tom's Cabin*, was a famous example. She lost a son to cholera in 1849 and began consulting mediums to reach him in death. She spoke openly about this, which helped move spiritualism toward greater social acceptance. Later, she lost another son, but this time did not need help communicating with him. She reported that he contacted her five times after he died.

In *Uncle Tom's Cabin*, one of the most influential books in history, she wrote of an experience reported by thousands: "Oh! mother that reads this, has there never been in your house a drawer, or a closet, the opening of which has been to you like the opening again of a little grave? Ah! Happy mother that you are, if it has not been so." Themes like this in popular literature focused the attention of the nation upon the possibility of contact with the dead and did so just before a raging civil war took 620,000 lives from this world. Séances, tarot cards, and anything mediums required became the rage.

Kate and Margaret Fox became famous mediums and inspired thousands of others to make a profession of reaching the dead as well. Among these was Henrietta Colburn, known simply as Nettie, born in Bolton, Connecticut, in 1841. Caught up in the flood of spiritualism that swept through New England after the Hydesville phenomenon, Nettie gained an early and widespread reputation as a "trance medium," someone who spoke for the dead while fixed in a trance. She was joined by Parthenia Hannum, whom she introduced as her "controlling spirit." The two women arrived in Washington in November of 1862 with a letter of introduction from Thomas Gales Foster, one of the nation's most prominent spiritualists. The very next month, Nettie was summoned to perform a séance for an elite gathering in Georgetown. In attendance were two congressmen, the U. S. Commissioner of Agriculture, and the wife of the president of the United States, Mary Lincoln.

Spiritualism was nothing new to Mary. She was aware of the times and the spiritual trends that flowed through fashionable society. One biographer believes her introduction to spiritualism "had probably taken place first in Lexington from the household slaves and then in Springfield from the white prophets who appeared in the Midwest during the early 1850s."[39] By then, spirits had become entertainment. Mary likely attended the performance of a "spirit conveyer" on the stage of Springfield's Masonic Hall and would have been fascinated with the device a visiting mesmerist used to cure a facial tic shortly after the Lincolns married. Indeed, in the 1850s, a clairvoyant offered services from a building on Fifth Street, just three blocks south of the Springfield courthouse square. None of this would have escaped Mary Lincoln's notice. Once the Lincolns moved to Washington, spiritualism had become such the rage that Mary would have known dozens of practitioners. Congressmen, senators, judges, White House staffers, and even presidential advisers were among those claiming special powers. The city's parlors crackled with the doings of the dead.

The Georgetown meeting at which Nettie, Parthenia, and Mary Lincoln met for the first time took place on the last day of 1862. As usual, Nettie went into a trance; and not surprisingly she focused her attention on the needs of the First Lady. Soon, the spirit of Willie Lincoln spoke. By the time the dramatic experience concluded, Mary was won by Nettie's gifts. She asked friends to provide Parthenia and Nettie with jobs and helped the mediums make the rounds in the upper tier of Washington society.

Now contacting the dead was more in style, more what the fashionable people did, than ever. The president's wife was involved, after all, and Nettie knew how to put on a show. She often summoned an Indian spirit named Pinkie. This thrilled the wives of the powerful, who were delighted that the spirits chose to grace their elegant parlors. When Pinkie did not appear and Willie was nowhere to be found, Nettie and her fellow mediums—for there were dozens of others—gave political advice. A spiritualist in Georgetown told the nervous and eager First Lady that the entire cabinet was against her husband and they should all be dismissed. Others gave the poor woman military strategies guaranteed to end the war if she would but run to her husband and tell them what the spirits had to say. She often did.

The president was distracted and uninterested in his wife's new passion until he realized what it might mean. Not only did Mary take the slightest statement of a medium as equal with divine revelation but Lincoln was also concerned she was being manipulated—that she was being duped by hucksters or that political opponents were laying a trap. His decision to judge for himself may have led to the famous séance in the Crimson Room of the White House in April of 1863. It was no hidden affair. A reporter from the *Boston Gazette* was present, as were two of Lincoln's cabinet secretaries and a trance medium named Charles E.

Shockle. When the "spirit visitors" came, Lincoln threw questions at Shockle to see for himself if what Mary said was true.

Lincoln seemed in good humor, enjoying the séance as a novel parlor game. When Shockle—who was under such strain he passed out twice during the evening—told the president that an Indian spirit had a message for him, Lincoln replied, "Well, sir, I should be happy to hear what his Indian Majesty has to say. We have recently had a visitation from our red brethren, and it was the only delegation—black, white or blue—which did not volunteer some advice about the conduct of the war."

Shockle next announced he had a message of great import from none other than Henry Knox, the secretary of war to George Washington, dead for more than half a century. Lincoln listened but seemed unimpressed: "Well, opinions differ among the saints as well as the sinners. They don't seem to understand running the machine among the celestials much better than we do. Their talk and advice sounds very much like the talk of my Cabinet."[40] The evening passed with little gained for spiritualism. Lincoln fared much better. Many of the nation's papers picked up the story from the *Boston Gazette* and readers seemed to find the president's lightheartedness endearing, particularly with war raging just miles from the White House. Newspapers in the South also ran the story and it only served the Union cause for the commander in chief to appear relaxed, glib, and in command before her enemies.

Nevertheless, Lincoln was concerned about the impact of these experiences upon Mary. He particularly mistrusted a medium named Charles J. Colchester, who had taken to calling himself Lord Colchester. Mary had invited the man to perform séances in the White House, as she had numerous other spiritualists, and the president sensed something was amiss. He asked his friend Dr. Joseph Henry, the secretary of the Smithsonian Institution, to consult with him on the matter. The two had sat up many a night discussing the latest scientific ideas, and Lincoln knew Henry to be an impartial, wise, and learned man.

Dr. Henry allowed Colchester to conduct a séance in his office. He quickly concluded that Colchester was a fake, but he could not figure out how the medium created the seemingly convincing sounds and brushes of air without examining Colchester's body. Noah Brooks, the journalist who became a dear friend to the Lincolns, also began to suspect Colchester. During one White House session, Brooks waited in the dark with the other attendees as a séance unfolded. At just the right moment, he grabbed Colchester's arm and called for a friend to light a match. This exposed the charlatan, and Brooks angrily ran him out of the White House. Lincoln's suspicions were confirmed. Not long after, Dr. Henry found the man who manufactured the device Colchester wore on his arm that allowed him to create the illusion of spirits moving about the room.

It would be pleasant to think that Mary Lincoln's fascination with spiritualists ended with the Colchester affair. It did not. Though her husband remained unimpressed with spiritualism—he told a concerned Dr. Gurley he had no interest in the practice—Mary grew ever more captivated.[41] With each tragedy, each death that marred her life, she turned more eagerly to the guidance of the mediums. This continued late into her life, when both Nettie and Margaret Fox met with her often and drew her more deeply into fascination with spirits. Nettie Colburn eventually married a man named Maynard and under that name—Nettie Colburn Maynard—wrote an article in 1891 entitled "Was Abraham Lincoln a Spiritualist?" published in the nation's leading spiritualist journal at a time when spiritualism was still widely popular. Nettie claimed she was "constantly consulted" by Lincoln and that her pronouncements were of "momentous consequence" to the course of the war. Her article would eventually be fashioned into a book, take on the subtitle *Curious Revelations from the Life of a Trance Medium*, and be republished until as late as 1956.[42] The entire episode stained Lincoln's reputation and confused the issue of his religious beliefs for generations after, and it had all come from Mary's tortured grieving and her insistence upon pushing beyond the boundaries of her Presbyterian faith.

⁊

Newspaper accounts of the White House séance gave the impression that Lincoln was untroubled, lighthearted, and at peace on that April night in 1862. If true, he may have been posturing to ease the public's concerns. He knew a reporter was present. In reality, he was devastated by how badly the war was going and was daily wrestling with questions about the will of God. When Union forces were defeated at the Second Battle of Bull Run on August 30, Lincoln agonized about why God would allow the Union, which to his mind represented a righteous stand against slavery, to suffer such losses. It was his nature to sort out his thoughts pen in hand, and sometime in the first week of September, he wrote down the debate that was playing out in his mind.

> The will of God prevails. In great contests each party claims to act in accordance with the will of God. Both *may* be, and one *must* be wrong. God can not be *for* and *against* the same thing at the same time. In the present civil war it is quite possible that God's purpose is something different from the purpose of either party—and yet the human instrumentalities, working just as they do, are of the best adaptation to effect His purpose. I am almost ready to say this is probably true—that God wills this contest, and wills that it shall not end yet. By his mere quiet power, on the minds of the now contestants, He could have either saved or destroyed the Union without a human contest. Yet the contest began. And having begun He could give the final victory to either side any day. Yet the contest proceeds.[43]

This has come to be known as Lincoln's "Meditation on the Divine Will," and from it we learn how far he had come. He had moved beyond his youthful confidence in a mechanical, impersonal "doctrine of necessity." He had moved beyond belief in a world God oversees but only through laws and principles set in motion long ago. He had also discarded a belief in what some call "occasional providence," or the idea that God may exercise his sovereignty from time to time, but he largely leaves history to unfold through human will. Now, Lincoln's view was that God orchestrates all things according to his will, that "the will of God prevails"—the first line of his note.

History, then, is personal. A perfect, Divine Being does as he wills with the people of the earth, certainly with the outcome of battles and the course of nations. This Being is all-powerful. He can determine any outcome. His will is inescapable. All that happens is according to a purpose, God's purpose, whether men know it or not. Lincoln had absorbed this from his reading of Scripture and from the preaching in his Presbyterian church—perhaps even to some extent from the hyper-Calvinism of his parents' frontier religion.

He might easily have concluded this also from his own observation of the war. Abraham Lincoln's experience in the early years of the Civil War was one of near-complete frustration. What should have worked easily did not. Generals who ought to have been brilliant and victorious instead failed. The simplest order suddenly seemed impossible for the most capable of troops. Lincoln was left to shake his head and wonder if he was fighting God *and* the Confederacy. He put one of the most capable generals in America in charge of his Army and then had to beg the man to fight, famously saying, "If General McClellan is not going to use the Army, I would like to borrow it." His pleading tone with McClellan at one point was nearly that of a parent with a child: "I beg to assure you that I've never written you, or spoken to you, in greater kindness of feeling than now, nor with a fuller purpose to sustain you, so far as is in my most anxious judgment, I consistently can. *But you must act.*"[44]

Even when Lincoln's officers did eventually achieve stunning victories, they often squandered their advantage. After the Union victory at Gettysburg, for example, General Mead allowed the defeated Confederate General Robert E. Lee to slip back into the safety of the South. A note Lincoln wrote Meade but did not send captured the frustration of these years: "Again, my dear general, I do not believe you appreciate the magnitude of the misfortune involved in Lee's escape. He was within your easy grasp. . . . as it is, the war will be prolonged indefinitely. . . . As you have learned that I was dissatisfied, I have thought it best to kindly tell you why."[45] It was not the first or the last time Lincoln was stunned by the utter incompetence of his commanders.

∾

It is no wonder, then, that in the fall of 1862 Lincoln was baffled by the odd course of the war and by the reason an all-powerful God did not grant victory to one side or the other. Indeed, why had God allowed the war at all? These questions were the start of a broader understanding of the conflict in Lincoln's mind. We can see this just surfacing in his "Meditation" from phrases like "God's purpose is something different from the purpose of either party" and "God wills this contest, and wills that it shall not end yet." Lincoln was beginning to conclude that God was about something else. But what was it? It certainly was beyond mere victory for North or South. Perhaps, he was beginning to believe, God was about removing the scourge of slavery from the land and pouring out judgment on both sides for the nation's sinful treatment of Africans.

Obviously, he drew his conclusions quickly. He had written his "Meditation on the Divine Will" the first week of September. Two weeks later, when Union troops drove Lee's army into retreat at Antietam Creek on September 17, Lincoln had already begun a plan to appease what he was just beginning to understand as God's will for the war. In fact, the victory at Antietam was the signal from God he had been waiting for, the sign that it was time to begin. At a cabinet meeting on the twenty-second, he explained what he was about to do. Salmon Chase, secretary of the Treasury, recorded the moment in his diary.

> Gentlemen, I have, as you are aware, thought a great deal about the relation of this war to Slavery; and you all remember that, several weeks ago, I read to you an Order I had prepared on this subject, which, on account of objections made by some of you, was not issued. Ever since then, my mind has been much occupied with this subject, and I have thought all along that the time for acting on it might very probably come. I think the time has come now. I wish it were a better time. I wish that we were in a better condition. The action of the army against the rebels has not been quite what I should have liked. But they have been driven out of Maryland, and Pennsylvania is no longer in danger of invasion. When the rebel army was at Frederick, I determined, as soon as it should be driven out of Maryland, to issue a Proclamation of Emancipation such as I thought most likely to be useful. I said nothing to any one; *but I made the promise to myself, and (hesitating a little)—to my Maker. The rebel army is now driven out, and I am going to fulfill that promise.*[46]

According to F. B. Carpenter, the artist commissioned to paint Lincoln deliberating with his cabinet over the proclamation, Chase told him that the president had dropped his voice just at the moment he mentioned his promise to God. Chase asked if he had heard correctly. Lincoln replied, *"I made a solemn vow before God, that if General Lee was driven back from Pennsylvania, I would crown the result by the declaration of freedom to the slaves."*[47]

Gideon Welles was also at this meeting and, like Chase, wrote of it in his diary.

> In the course of the discussion on this paper, which was long, earnest, and on the general principle involved, harmonious, *he remarked*

that he had made a vow, a covenant, that if God gave us the victory in
the approaching battle he would consider it an indication of Divine
will, and that it was his duty to move forward in the cause of eman-
cipation. It might be thought strange, he said, that he had in this way
submitted the disposal of matters when the way was not clear to his
mind what he should do. God had decided this question in favor of
the slaves. He was satisfied it was right, was confirmed and strengthened in his action by the vow and the results.[48]

It would be easy to make too much of this, but perhaps it is just:
historians have long made too little of it. While declaring Lincoln a
lifelong religious skeptic, they have ignored dramatic moments such
as this one, in which Lincoln's ever-deepening faith decisively shaped
the course of the nation. It is not going too far to simply say what
Lincoln did: that he issued his Emancipation Proclamation—an act he
considered one of the crowning achievements of his life—inspired by
a covenant he made with God. That covenant, in turn, was possible
only because Lincoln had moved from believing in God as angry
father to rejecting God as myth, and then had progressed from thinking of God as the kind of being who cursed a man for his parentage,
to accepting God as ruler of the world, and finally to honoring God
as a good and covenant-keeping Father of all men. None of this made
him arrogant about his decision, though. Two days after that historic
cabinet meeting, he told an audience, "I can only trust in God I have
made no mistake."[49]

The Emancipation Proclamation would have its critics. Through
the years, some would claim it had not freed a single slave. It became
a standard complaint that Lincoln had cleverly declared slaves free
where he did not have the authority to do so but had not freed them
in the Northern states where he had the authority. It was not true.
First, Lincoln had no authority to take slaves from owners who were
not enemies of the Union, owners who were still loyal to the United

States. That would come in time, but had not come by January 1, 1863, when the Emancipation Proclamation became law. Since it was a war measure, it could apply only to states and territories then in rebellion. Second, tens of thousands of slaves and "contrabands" lived in Union-controlled portions of North and South Carolina, Georgia, Florida, Mississippi, and Arkansas. The Proclamation did apply to these slaves, did liberate them, and therefore it is untrue that Lincoln's act freed not a slave. There were also many slaves who simply freed themselves, taking their leave of masters on the basis of "Father Abraham's word." Finally, the Proclamation transformed the purpose of the war. Prior to January 1, 1863, the war was about preserving the union. Afterward, Union armies became armies of liberation.

Yet the Emancipation Proclamation signaled something even more profound in Lincoln's life. He had come to understand history as orchestrated by God, nations as accountable to him, and men as the means by which God fulfills his will. In this light, Lincoln no longer thought of the war as a contest between North and South alone. He began to accept that this war was the result of a controversy between God and the United States. Righteousness—right standing with the Ruler of Nations, with God the Father not just military victory, was the need of the hour. Lincoln told one minister during the war, "God only knows the issue of this business. He has destroyed nations from the map of history for their sins. Nevertheless, my hopes prevail generally above my fears for our Republic. The times are dark, the spirits of ruin are abroad in all their power, and the mercy of God alone can save us."[50] This is why, soon after that, he famously said that his concern was not whether God was on the side of the Union, but rather whether "this nation should be on the Lord's side."[51] For Lincoln, the Civil War had ceased being just a war: it was an act of judgment by an offended God—an act of judgment on the nation as a whole.

Given what we have seen of Lincoln's ever-deepening faith, it is not difficult to accept the testimony of Major General Daniel Edgar Sickles, commander of the Third Corps of the Union army, about a conversation he had with the president following the battle of Gettysburg.

The battlefield at Gettysburg (1863)

Sickles lost his right leg on the second day of that great battle and was immediately moved to Washington to recuperate. At three o'clock on Sunday afternoon, July 5, Sickles was smoking a cigar and battling the pain in his stump at a house on F Street across from Ebbitt House when a member of his staff, Lieutenant Colonel James Rusling, dropped by for a visit. The two had just greeted each other when Abraham Lincoln walked in.

The president tenderly asked about Sickles's wounds and then questioned the general about the fighting at Gettysburg. When Lincoln was satisfied, Sickles asked his commander in chief how he felt during the three days of fighting in Pennsylvania. Sickles had heard

there was great fear in Washington and wondered if Lincoln had experienced it too. The answer was not what Sickles had expected, and we should be grateful that Lieutenant Colonel Rusling was there to write down what followed.

The devastation of war: Canal Basin in Richmond, VA (1863)

> In the pinch of your campaign up there, when everybody seemed panic-stricken, and nobody could tell what was going to happen, oppressed by the gravity of our affairs, I went into my room one day and locked the door and got down on my knees before Almighty God and prayed to him mightily for victory at Gettysburg. I told him this was his war and our cause, his cause, but that we couldn't stand another Fredericksburg or Chancellorsville. And I then and there made a solemn vow to Almighty God that if he would stand by our boys at Gettysburg, I would stand by him. And he did, and I will. And after that, I don't know how it was and I can't explain it, but soon a sweet comfort crept into my soul that things would go all right at Gettysburg, and this is why I had no fears about you.[52]

Sickles was surprised by Lincoln's response and wanted to probe further. A battle loomed at Vicksburg, Mississippi, and Sickles decided to see if the president had the same sense of victory about it that he'd had before Gettysburg. The president replied, "I've been praying over

Vicksburg also and believe our Heavenly Father is going to give us victory there too because we need it in order to bisect the Confederacy and have the Mississippi flow unvexed to the sea."[53]

Lincoln knew how he sounded and concluded the interview with a bit of encouraging humor. "General, you will get well." Sickles objected and waved Lincoln off with a grunt. The president wouldn't back down: "I'm a prophet today and I say you will get well, and that we will have glorious news from Vicksburg." With this, Lincoln departed.

Neither man knew that Vicksburg had already fallen to General Grant the day before.[54] And Lincoln was right: Sickles got well—and lived until 1914.

It is in these documented, confirmable deeds that Lincoln's faith is best revealed. He had become a man who prayed in secret that the God of Battles would grant victory to the beleaguered Union and one who knew the matter was settled when "sweet comfort crept into" his heart. He had become a man who made covenants with God and trusted that divine confirmation of these covenants should signal events even as momentous as the signing of the Emancipation Proclamation. He had become a man who instinctively grasped for deeper faith in God during seasons of suffocating grief, as he did in the tortured season following Willie's death. These deeds speak of the man and they reveal in an unarguable manner how Lincoln's ever-evolving faith shaped the course of America.

It is unfortunate, then, that discussion of Lincoln's faith usually descends into a battle of quotes. This is what has long made studies of Lincoln's faith so unsatisfying, such poor literature. The graceful drama is lost in the graceless war between conflicting sources, some of which even contradict themselves. Journalist Noah Brooks might report, as he did to a friend in 1872, that Lincoln had "a hope of blessed immortality through Jesus Christ."[55] William O. Stoddard, one of Lincoln's secretaries, could counter, "I cannot at this moment recall any distinct assertions made by Mr. Lincoln, relating to matters of his religious belief." Yet, in the maddening manner of many witnesses to Lincoln's life of faith, Stoddard also said, "I am convinced this day that, in the best and truest sense, Abraham Lincoln was a Christian."[56] How could he know this if Lincoln made no "distinct assertions?" Another Lincoln secretary, John Nicolay, famously reported, "Mr. Lincoln did not, to my knowledge, in any way change his religious views, opinions, or beliefs, from the time he left Springfield to the day of his death." The words became nearly a slogan to advocates of Lincoln the lifelong religious skeptic. Yet Nicolay also wrote, "Benevolence and forgiveness were the very basis of his character. His nature was deeply religious, but he belonged to no denomination: he had faith in the eternal justice and boundless mercy of Providence, and made the Golden Rule of Christ his practical creed."[57] Equally confusing, one White House regular during the Civil War wrote, "I would scarcely call Mr. Lincoln a religious man,—and yet I believe him to have been a sincere Christian."[58]

And so this "battle of quotes" has continued through the years, shedding more ink than light. Always standing apart from it is Lincoln the man. Perhaps he is the one to blame for the fog of uncertainty that envelops students of his religious life. One of Lincoln's earliest and most frustrated biographers wrote that he had

conversed with multitudes of men who claimed to know Mr. Lincoln intimately; yet there are not two of the whole number who agree in their estimate of him. The fact was that he rarely showed more than one aspect of himself to one man. He opened himself to men in different directions. It was rare that he exhibited what was religious in him; and he never did this at all, except when he found just the nature and character that were sympathetic with that aspect and element of his nature. A great deal of his best, deepest, largest life he kept almost constantly from view, because he would not expose it to the eyes and apprehension of the careless multitude. . . . Thus not two men among his intimate friends will agree concerning him.[59]

⁓∾

It is this never-reconciled testimony that leaves us a Lincoln who is always a surprise, who is seldom what we have been taught, and who is ever saying or doing the unexpected. His religious life was often over-shadowed, usually thought insignificant, criticized, and esteemed of value only with the passage of time. This is why Lincoln's faith is very much typified by his speech at Gettysburg.

He had been asked to appear at the dedication of the battlefield cemetery and "formally set apart these grounds to their Sacred use by a few appropriate remarks." Folklore portrays him preparing these remarks in a bouncing train and on the back of an envelope. It isn't true. Lincoln was known for carefully planning his speeches, and this one was no different. He had begun days before with his writing, editing, rehearsing, and whispered prayers. He arrived at Gettysburg on November 18 and spent the night in the home of a family named Wills. He slept unusually well, he later said, having received a telegram informing him that

Lincoln with his son Tad

his son Tad was "slightly better." We can imagine the fear that must have followed him north from Washington, given his memories of sick and dying sons.

The next day he joined the fifteen-minute march to the cemetery, riding on a large, chestnut horse. When all the notables were assembled upon the makeshift stage looking out over the crowd of five thousand or more, someone realized that the other speaker for the day, Edward Everett, had not arrived. The military band played for more than an hour until the eminent Everett arrived.

This gave Lincoln a chance to look out over the grounds, which must have made him feel uneasy. There were still Confederate bones bleaching in the sun. Graves were often little more than loosely piled rocks, and large mounds of mud marked where entire units had fallen during those bloody days in July. Lincoln surely thought of his friends who had died and of others who had left arms, legs, and perhaps sons on the field of battle.

The way Lincoln's words that day compared with the verbose and airy offerings of the other speakers reminds us of his story of faith. A Reverend Dr. Thomas Hewlings Stockton, chaplain of the United States Senate, had been asked to open the ceremony with prayer. Dr. Stockton read his prayer as though it were an oratorical exhibition intended to impress. The prayer was so long and so involved that Lincoln's secretary, John Hay, wrote in his diary that Stockton had "made a prayer which thought it was an oration."[60]

Then came Edward Everett—a noted scholar, the former president of Harvard, and a U.S. senator. Classically trained, Everett gave an oration filled with accounts of battle, religious sentiment, Latin phrasing, and patriotic pleading. It lasted two hours. Lincoln listened respectfully. When Everett died on January 15, 1865, Lincoln asked a friend, "What great work of Everett do you remember?" His companion could not recall even one. Lincoln somberly replied, "Now, do you know, I think Edward Everett was very much overrated. He hasn't left any enduring monument."[61] Clearly, the matter of legacy was on the president's mind.

Finally it was Lincoln's turn. He stood, pulled two sheets of paper from his pocket, and pressed his spectacles on his nose. An officer in attendance recalled, "He looked so very sad and deep in thought like his mind was somewhere else." Lincoln glanced at his notes, put the papers back in his pocket, and began to give his speech. He had prepared so thoroughly that what he wanted to say was embedded in his memory.

It was all over in three minutes. Lincoln had spoken 272 words—ten sentences—against Everett's two hours. Few applauded. A witness said, "Mr. Lincoln's sad face and the solemnity of the occasion, seemed to forbid any excessive demonstration." Lincoln returned to his seat, turned to his friend Lamon Hill, and said, "Lamon, that speech won't scour! It is a flat failure, and the people are disappointed."[62]

Some of the nation's press agreed. The Chicago *Times* called the speech "silly, flat, and dish-watery." The Harrisburg *Patriot and Union* insisted that the "silly remarks" should have the "veil of oblivion . . . dropped over them so that they shall no more be repeated or thought of."

The *Chicago Tribune*, however, captured the counsel of generations: "The dedicatory remarks of President Lincoln will live among the annals of man."[63] The finest tribute, perhaps, came the next day from Edward Everett himself. "I should be glad if I could flatter myself," he wrote in a letter to Lincoln, "that I came as near to the central idea of the occasion in two hours as you did in two minutes." Lincoln's reply was gracious: "In our respective parts yesterday, you could not have been excused to make a short address, nor I a long one. I am pleased to know that, in your judgement, the little I did say was not entirely a failure."[64]

Everett knew what Lincoln had done. He had distilled. He had cut away the excess, the unnecessary. He had wrestled for years with the meaning of America and had honed this meaning and the language required to express it in a thousand torch-lit speeches. At Gettysburg, Lincoln incarnated the spirit of the nation into the poetic expressions of his early reading, of the American tradition, and of his own sensitive, reflective soul. He had given himself to the struggle—for the founders' purpose, for the ways of righteousness, even for his own sanity in a troubled world. Once he emerged, he did not need two hours to articulate the meaning of death in a desperate war. Three minutes would do. Brevity was possible for the man already familiar with the meaning of graves.

This distilling and refining of meaning into the lyrical essential was as much true of Lincoln's approach to religion as it was of Lincoln's speech at Gettysburg. He could draw men to holy vision more effectively than the performing preacher and inspire men to greatness more thoroughly than the overheated scholar because he called his listeners only to the place where he had—at long last—arrived himself. It was not hard to describe to others a journey he had already completed.

Lincoln must have been gratified by the honor his words received. Walt Whitman, Edward Everett, the historian George Bancroft, and dozens of other luminaries asked for handwritten copies. Perhaps he began to have some sense of what the speech might mean to future generations.

He may, too, have smiled at his final bit of struggle over the language of the speech. It had come in the Wills' house late on the night before the dedication ceremony. He had retired earlier than usual to reflect and rehearse. That is when he realized something wasn't quite right, that an important point was missing. He thought; he prayed; he read. For a time, he couldn't quite see what was needed. Then, it came to him. The text of this third draft read, "That the nation shall have a new birth of freedom; and that Government of the people, by the people and for the people, shall not perish from the earth." Lincoln took his pen and wrote the words that would make it complete.

Now, it read, "That this nation, *under God*, shall have a new birth of freedom . . ." It was not a change the Lincoln of New Salem or perhaps even of Springfield might have made. But it was consistent with the Lincoln at Gettysburg: he could not leave God out of this matter of the nation's "new birth."

The Lincoln Tomb and War Memorial in Springfield, Illinois

EPILOGUE

※※※※

PURPOSES OF
THE ALMIGHTY

THE DATE WAS MARCH 4, 1865, THE DAY ON WHICH Abraham Lincoln was sworn to a second term as president of the United States. All of Washington was astir. The ceremony was not scheduled to begin until noon, but by first light, the city of just over sixty thousand people had swelled to tens of thousands more. The streets teemed with the eager and the curious, the thoughtful excitement of a historic moment almost tangible in the air.

It would be easy to romanticize this day, but we should try to picture it as it was, beginning with the city of Washington itself. One historian described her as the "almost-city," a city perpetually incomplete—symbolized until not too long before inauguration day by the scaffolding around the Capitol that workers used to replace the old wooden dome with another made of iron. Lincoln often looked upon the unfinished work and saw it as a sign of the unfinished Union. Indeed, there was much yet undone in Washington, as there was in the nation. Two decades before, Charles Dickens had called the American capital "the City of Magnificent Intentions." He had discovered "spacious avenues, that begin in nothing and lead to nowhere; streets, mile-long, that only want houses, roads, and inhabitants; public buildings that need but a public to be complete."[1] He might have been describing the Washington of 1865.

Except for the soldiers. Their tents now filled those empty spaces Dickens had written about, their wounded claiming nearly

The last photograph ever taken of Abraham Lincoln

every house and makeshift shelter available. They roamed in bands from tent to drill to saloon and back again. Their campfires smoked the city just as their songs and homesick eyes charmed the heart. They endured as they could, and they had much to brave. Typhoid raged through camps not far from the White House, and this joined with malaria—the gift of Washington's swampy setting by the Potomac—to decimate the ranks. There was also the enemy, which for most of the war was but a few miles away. Indeed, so close were Confederate troops that on many a night Mary Lincoln fell asleep chilled by the sound of cannon fire.

Making matters worse on this inaugural day was the heavy rain that had fallen all through the morning. It had turned the usual smelly bog of Washington into a slimy pool of mud. Lincoln's journalist friend, Noah Brooks, described how "flocks of women streamed around the Capitol, in most wretched plight; crinoline was smashed, skirts bedaubed, and moiré antique, velvet, laces and such dry good were streaked with mud from end to end."[2] In the ten inches of mud that coated the unpaved streets, buggies stalled, men cursed the brown splattering of their finest clothes, and children had to be carried for fear of being trampled and lost.

Despite all of this, the *New York Herald* could report, "The crowd was good-natured."[3] Why shouldn't it be? The war that had cost more than six hundred thousand lives was largely over. It had not been easy to believe that such a day might come. Just the previous summer, the Union cause had appeared lost. Offensives failed and carnage spread. Many in the North wanted Lincoln to sue for peace. Horace Greeley had editorialized in the *New-York Tribune*, "Our bleeding, bankrupt, almost dying country longs for peace—shudders at the prospect of fresh conscriptions, of further wholesale devastations, and of new rivers of human blood."[4] This was on July 7. In August, Lincoln wrote a memo to his cabinet admitting it was "exceedingly probable that this Administration will not be re-elected." The Union cause and Lincoln's presidency appeared near an end. Then, on September 3, a telegram arrived at the White House. It was from General William T. Sherman: "Atlanta is ours, and fairly won." The news shot through the Union and lifted the gloom. Then came word of General Philip Sheridan's victories in the Shenandoah Valley. Grant was on the move, too, and had the Confederate capital of Richmond in his sights. And Lincoln was reelected.

By March of 1865, no mud or crowding or stench could drive off the joy. Victory was drawing near, and Father Abraham still governed from the White House.

The surest symbols of the nation's changing fortunes were the thousands of black faces that graced the day. Some had estimated the crowd at nearly thirty thousand, others at twenty. Whatever the number, most agreed that half the crowd was black. It was arguably the largest gathering of African Americans in the country's history to that time. During the parade that began the day's celebrations, the Forty-Fifth

Regiment of United States Colored Troops marched four companies strong. Then came a lodge of African-American Odd Fellows. Knowing what this meant, the crowd went wild in applause. Some remembered that a black man had already been permitted to argue before the U.S. Supreme Court. Certainly, President Lincoln's "new birth of freedom" had begun.

The rain forced the inaugural ceremony indoors. It would prove to be a gift that the early portions of the inaugural ceremony were held in the Senate chamber, far from public view. None of it went well. There was a speech by Hannibal Hamlin, the retiring vice president, which was dry and frequently interrupted by giggling women, late-coming senators, and the great ordeal of seating Mrs. Lincoln in the gallery. Andrew Johnson was next, and he did not speak long before everyone in the room realized he was drunk; he had been suffering an illness and had medicated himself with whiskey. It was an embarrassment that ended with a boozy kiss of the Bible on which he had just taken the oath of office. A humiliated Lincoln turned to a marshall and whispered, "Do not let Johnson speak outside."[5]

Mercifully, the rain stopped, and this allowed the rest of the ceremony to continue on the Capitol grounds, where an eager public awaited. The officials made their way from the Senate chamber to a temporary wooden platform accompanied by dozens of soldiers. Hundreds of other soldiers had already spread out into the crowd. It was a precaution required by what came next: a speech by the president himself. The nation was still at war, and the president's life was under constant threat. The generals were determined there would be no rebel disruption this day.

When Lincoln was introduced, the crowd roared its gratitude and refused to be quieted. Though they had come close to denying him reelection just months before, now he was their victorious commander in chief. They were just beginning to understand what they owed him. The moment Lincoln took the podium was remembered with awe for years after because of what occurred just then in the heavens. As one journalist reported, "At that moment the sun, which had been obscured all day, burst forth in its unclouded meridian splendor, and flooded the spectacle with glory and with light."[6]

We should freeze this moment to consider the scene. A weary, somehow ancient president stood before an eager crowd just as a murderous Civil War neared its end. It was his task to define the historical context, to explain what they had all been through, and to point to the new day ahead. What must his listeners have expected? Perhaps they hoped he would excoriate the South for having caused the war and then declare that the Confederates must now feel the Union's wrath. Perhaps they thought Lincoln might raise the bloody sword and declare vindication in victory. Or maybe some hoped he would simply describe what was to come and how the country might heal and begin to thrive.

The crowd may also have had expectations about the form of the speech. They had only Lincoln's first inaugural to use as a guide. Those four years before, in his First Inaugural Address, he had used more than thirty-six hundred words. It had taken him just about half an hour. He had summarized events, used sophisticated terms, and addressed himself to the great matters yet to be decided by human will.

Though the crowd could not have known it, this second inaugural speech would be shocking by comparison. It consisted of a mere 703 words; most of those words—505, to be exact—were of one syllable. This meant there were only twenty-five sentences in the four-paragraph speech and that it would not last—despite the fact that Lincoln was notoriously slow in delivery—more than seven minutes.

Our frozen moment—before the president has spoken a word—is almost violent with the clash of expectations, and it is made historic by the misalignment of what had been with what was to come.

Lincoln began. His first paragraph was nothing unusual. He admitted there was no need for a long address, that he had already said much of what should be said, and that he was taking comfort in how the war was concluding although he would venture no predictions.

The second paragraph surely gave some in the audience the impression that he was going to chastise the South. He mentioned the insurgents who were in Washington during his first inauguration. It was a bitter memory. Then he reminded his listeners that while both North and South did not want war, "one of them would make war rather than let the nation survive; and the other would accept war rather than let it perish."

The next four words signaled his thesis: *And the war came.* Neither North nor South wanted it to, but it came anyway. Events take on a life of their own. Human intention does not rule all. "And the war came"—despite our will.

Though most in the audience did not initially perceive it, this was the start of a turn in Lincoln's speech, the fruit of a revolution in his life. He had said to the South in his first inaugural, "Into your hands, my dissatisfied fellow countrymen, and not in mine, is the momentous issue of civil war." He could not say such a thing on this day. He had seen too much, had control wrenched too violently from his hands. He knew there was another will that determines the path of history. He had already said elsewhere, "I claim not to have controlled events, but confess plainly that events have controlled me."[7]

Not just events, though, but God—as we shall see.

His third paragraph reminded his audience of the specter of slavery that hovered over the land four years before. All knew then, he insisted, that however it was framed, slavery was the cause of the looming conflict. No one knew, though, what would come—how hideous and vile it all would be—or even if slavery would still exist when the war was over. In those still-innocent days, each side naively hoped for "an easier triumph, and a result less fundamental and astounding."

Then came the moral case that had long burned in Lincoln's mind. Though both North and South were rooted in the Christian faith—"both read the same Bible, and pray to the same God"—it was hard for a righteous man to understand how anyone could ask God to help him profit from another man's enslavement. Still, Lincoln would not allow himself to say more: "but let us judge not that we be not judged."

He ceased making this case because it was not the one he was eager to plead on that day. The theme of the next sentence is the heart of his message: "The Almighty has His own purposes." This is what Lincoln believed now, and why he thought the war had taken the course it had. Events were not ruled by North or South—even their prayers were not fully answered, he admitted—but the war had unfolded according to the purposes of God. This because men do not contend with myth or principle or an absent sovereign, as Lincoln once believed. Instead, there was a God, a divine person, who ruled nations—and he was, as the preachers said, offended with America. We should not be surprised. Indeed,

> If we shall suppose that American Slavery is one of those offences, which, in the providence of God, must needs come, but which having continued through His appointed time, He now wills to remove, and that He gives to both North and South, this terrible war, as the woe due to those by whom the offence came, shall we discern any departure from those divine attributes which believers in a Living God always ascribe to Him?

Many in the crowd were stunned, almost refusing to believe they had heard correctly. Lincoln had come close to prosecuting the South but had turned, instead, to prosecuting the nation. The president insisted the war was no accident and was not caused by either North or South alone. Instead, God gave the war. Yes, God, and he did so as payment for sin—the sin of American slavery. And isn't this just what we know of God's justice and righteous judgments?

Nonetheless, Lincoln said, Americans should pray the season of judgment passed quickly—"that this mighty scourge of war may speedily pass away." Yet if God did not choose to do so, to soon take the country's punishment away, it was his business. He could not be thought unjust, so great was the offense of the United States: for "if God wills that it [the war] continue, until all the wealth piled up by the bond-man's two hundred and fifty years of unrequited toil shall be sunk, and until every drop of blood drawn with the lash, shall be paid by another drawn with the sword, as was said three thousand years ago, so still it must be said 'the judgments of the LORD are true and righteous altogether'" (Ps. 19:9).

We must leave these matters to God, Lincoln said. He is Lord. We are not. His will be done. We can only do what is in our power to do: "With malice toward none; with charity for all; with firmness in the right, as God gives us to see the right, let us strive on to finish the work we are in; to bind up the nation's wounds; to care for him who shall have borne the battle, and for his widow, and his orphan—to do all which may achieve and cherish a just, and a lasting peace, among ourselves, and with all nations."[8]

This Second Inaugural Address was more than a speech. It was Lincoln as prophet pleading the case of God. It was Lincoln as Jeremiah or Isaiah or Daniel. And it had taken courage to do it. Before he had even begun speaking, he already expected that many of his listeners would be disappointed. As he moved through the day's parties and receptions, he could feel the mystification, the questioning manner in a receiving line handshake. He understood it, for as he later wrote in explaining the address to a friend, "Men are not flattered by being shown that there has been a difference of purpose between the Almighty and them."[9]

This "difference of purpose" was what Lincoln hoped America

might see. Men had experienced the Civil War as a battle of brothers over issues of union, rights, and property. God saw it differently and would punish until satisfied if he so chose. Men, to be righteous, must honor this sovereign prerogative, turn from their national sin, and work to heal what had been torn.

This was where Abraham Lincoln had finally arrived in his understanding of God. He had once hated God, had felt tortured and rejected by him, like Job of old. Ultimately and through a process of years, Lincoln came to see God as good and just. He learned to rely on his comfort, trust in his guidance, and stand in awe of his perfect judgments. He may even have learned to love God as a heavenly Father far beyond any earthly father he had known.

⁓

Forty-one days after this inauguration, Abraham Lincoln was dead. He lived to see General Lee surrender, to walk the streets of Richmond while freed slaves cheered his name, and to dream with Mary of their lives after the war. He did not live but hours beyond the moment John Wilkes Booth's Derringer ball entered his brain.

He ceased being conscious of this world with plans to walk in the footsteps of "the Savior" on his lips. This is, at least, what Mary Lincoln told us. It may well have been true. Many who knew him thought Lincoln had become a Christian at some point, though perhaps only in the broadest sense. Dr. Gurley, his pastor, certainly thought so and expected that Lincoln intended to make his faith public. The minister said that the slain president had been

> sound not only on the truth of the Christian religion but on all its fundamental doctrines and teaching. . . . After the death of his son Willie, and his visit to the battlefield of Gettysburg, he said . . . that he had lost confidence in everything but God, and that he now believed

his heart was changed, and that he loved the Savior, and if he was not deceived in himself, it was his intention soon to make a profession of religion.[10]

Gurley's words led to speculation that Lincoln had intended to be baptized, perhaps even during that next Easter Sunday service, the one that came two days after his journey of faith was tragically interrupted. For those who want a Christian Lincoln, it would be nice to believe. We simply have no evidence it was true.

What is, perhaps, more important is that the possibility of Lincoln agreeing to be baptized is not inconsistent with the Lincoln we now know. He had once been the village atheist in New Salem and Springfield, but he had grown beyond those days and become the kind of man who could valiantly declare his Second Inaugural Address—what must surely be the greatest American political sermon—to a wounded, angry, self-righteous nation. That he died a prophetic figure, determined to show his countrymen the difference between "the Almighty's" purposes and their own, is perhaps all the statement of Lincoln's religion we need.

In the end, the most vital concern may not be what Lincoln believed of God, but rather how God chose to use Lincoln. The president had come to trust that a heavenly Father rules history for the good of mankind. If he was right, then his own life was part of that providential history, a vibrant strand in the divinely woven tapestry of time. We can give Lincoln no greater tribute than to declare what he himself came to believe: that his magnificent life was a life destined by God. We do both Lincoln and his God honor by simply being grateful this was so.

THOUGHTS ON
LINCOLN, RELIGION,
AND SOURCES

I T WAS WINSTON CHURCHILL WHO SAID, "WE WANT ENGI-
neers in the world, but we do not want a world of engineers."
The same is true of historians. We want the cautious, fastidious
historian with his statistics, his quantitative analysis, and his constant
fussing over the accuracy of sources. Yet we also want the historian as
poet, as prophet, and as bard. These two types of scholars have long
been at war in the field of Lincoln studies. They likely always will be.

It must be a maddening experience for the technically minded
Lincoln scholar. Myths abound. Popular lore exaggerates. Public speakers distort, from religious leaders to overheated politicians. Even the
esteemed poet/author Carl Sandburg contributed to the crisis. In writing his *Abraham Lincoln: The Prairie Years* and *Abraham Lincoln:
The War Years*, Sandburg routinely invented dialogue, reported events
Lincoln scholars have yet to confirm, and never cited a single source for
his work. For his inventions, he received the Pulitzer Prize. Meanwhile,
Lincoln experts who have dutifully stayed within the traditional boundaries of scholarship labor on in obscurity.

The problem is that so much of what we know of Lincoln comes from sources the professional historian has reason to doubt. The causes for this are many. Lincoln rose from obscurity to prominence relatively quickly. When he did, the nation was in crisis. He disclosed little of himself in writing, and what others wrote about him often came long after his death and as a weapon in the ongoing war over his legacy, his religious legacy in particular. Entire episodes of Lincoln's life, dear to the hearts of schoolchildren, have a single person—often recalling events decades old—as their source. It is no wonder that Lincoln historians squabble.

A favorite cause of skirmishes is the work of William H. Herndon. As we have seen in the previous pages, Herndon was Lincoln's junior law partner and friend. After Lincoln was killed, Herndon felt an obligation to tell his story accurately. He was also offended by the deification of his earthy, skeptical, troubled friend. He spent decades conducting interviews and carefully following up on correspondence with witnesses to Lincoln's life. Herndon was a skilled researcher, but he had his biases. He had also never held much affection for Mary Lincoln. The two had only tolerated each other while Lincoln lived, and this may be one of the reasons that Herndon lent so much credence to the Ann Rutledge story. Mary Lincoln was naturally offended by the intimation that Rutledge was the true love of her husband's life, and she fought with Herndon publicly for years over this and other such matters. Herndon also despised depictions of Lincoln as a Christian, the version many pious Victorians seemed to prefer. Herndon himself was a religious skeptic who identified with the Lincoln of the New Salem and early Springfield years and did not want to surrender his beloved friend to the revisionism of the pulpit.

Though Herndon's work has proven invaluable to historians, they nevertheless grumble about the skimpy external support for many of Herndon's tales. A typical Herndon story might have one elderly man as its source, and Herndon's interview with the man might have occurred decades after the events the man recounted. All other witnesses had likely passed away, forcing reliance on one aging man's memory. It is how some of the most treasured Lincoln stories have come to us, and yet it is no wonder that Lincoln specialists have been driven to distraction by questions of evidence.

This problem becomes no easier in the study of Lincoln's religion. Not only do recollections of the man's faith suffer the same evidentiary suspicions that other Lincoln remembrances do, but they also endure both biases like Herndon's as well as those of professional historians—a tribe renowned for undervaluing the role of religion as a motive force in past events.

A brief example reveals the problem. In a unique work eventually entitled *The Inner Life of Abraham Lincoln*, a man commissioned to paint Lincoln's portrait in 1864 later provided what amounted to an insider's look at the Lincoln White House. Historians are cautious about this source, finding in its early pages a fascinating window into Lincoln's war years but also complaining that the book eventually descends into a weary recitation of Lincoln wit and wisdom. There are gems, though, and one of them might be the tale of a minister's visit to a grieving Lincoln in the months after Willie's death. The story has already been recounted in this book. Though the minister was indeed a friend of the president and though he might very well have said exactly what the author, F. B. Carpenter, recalled, historians have usually discounted the episode. One reason has been Carpenter's account of Lincoln dissolving into tears and then embracing the clergyman. A critic has written, "No one who has read many books about Lincoln can easily picture him putting his arms around a Protestant minister previously unknown to him and blubbering." Then there is the fact that Carpenter claims Lincoln would sit in Willie's bedroom one day a week and grieve for his lost son. It does not fit some records of how Lincoln spent his time in those grief-filled months.

We can be sure that had this same eyewitness testified to Lincoln's atheism, historians would have taken the recollection as a certainty. Since the memory is an affirmation of some version of faith on Lincoln's part, the story must, of course, be false. The fact that an otherwise credible witness is the source of the tale does not seem to matter. Moreover, the idea that a grieving father might conduct himself with uncommon emotion in the presence of his pastor is apparently too outlandish a notion to be believed. And so this episode in the president's life is rarely included in Lincoln biographies, nor are other faith-oriented events and quotations from the life of one of our most religious presidents.

The solution is not for sketchy recollections from unattributed sources to be mindlessly treated as fact in the study of Lincoln's religion. Rather, the solution is for the rich texture of Lincoln's spirituality to emerge without being burdened by demands for certainty greater than those imposed in any other arena of Lincoln studies. If during our Civil War a White House dressmaker finds Lincoln reading the book of Job, and a congressman recalls a discussion of divine destiny with the president, and Lincoln's own written reflections reveal a man wrestling with God's purposes, and a clergyman confirms that Lincoln sat in on prayer meetings, and if Lincoln's Second Inaugural Address is more sermon than a political speech—then certainly there is room to consider that Lincoln in the White House was not the Lincoln of New Salem or Springfield. The evidence—not the myth—demands this conclusion, and historians must follow the evidence where it leads.

Similarly, those who insist upon a more religious Lincoln than the evidence allows also err. Christian ministers have long assumed Lincoln was a devoted Christian merely because he often spoke of God. Yet Lincoln rarely spoke publicly of Jesus Christ, and his distaste for the average clergyman and prickly church culture never left him. The problem seems to be that we want conclusions rather than processes, and we want conversions rather than religious journeys. The search for Abraham Lincoln's faith disappoints only if we begin that journey assuming there will be a dramatic resolution, that at some point in the story Abraham Lincoln will kneel at an altar and satisfy us with a veri-fiable spiritual experience. It does not happen. The journey is all the revelation we receive. Perhaps the most that can be said is what has already been written in these pages: John Wilkes Booth's derringer ball interrupted a life in spiritual pursuit. What might have crowned that pursuit, had Lincoln lived, will long be the stuff of academic seminars and debate among the faithful.

We must try to let the evidence speak for itself without bias, human though we are. There is no greater evidence for a young Lincoln reading by firelight than there is for Lincoln weeping in the arms of a clergy-man over the death of his son. There is no greater evidence for Lincoln seeing slaves in New Orleans and determining then and there to strike at the vile institution of slavery than there is for Lincoln rethinking his opposition to Christianity because of a book he found in his father-in-law's home. Let us allow all the voices to speak. The silencing of Lincoln's faith by the secular and the exaggerating of Lincoln's faith by the religious have given us a less accurate and a less engaging Lincoln. We are poorer for the distortions.

Let us not allow the technical historian to choke the poet and bard as he recounts the past. Let us also not allow the poet to despise the cau-tions of the specialist or to mistake his own imaginings for confirmed events of the past. An accurately portrayed past—taken as the record of man alone in the universe, as the nonreligious believe, or taken as the unfolding providence of God, as the faithful believe—is its own reward.

APPENDIX

ABRAHAM LINCOLN'S FIRST
INAUGURAL ADDRESS

MARCH 4, 1861

Fellow-Citizens of the United States: In compliance with a custom as old as the Government itself, I appear before you to address you briefly and to take in your presence the oath prescribed by the Constitution of the United States to be taken by the President "before he enters on the execution of this office."

I do not consider it necessary at present for me to discuss those matters of administration about which there is no special anxiety or excitement.

Apprehension seems to exist among the people of the Southern States that by the accession of a Republican Administration their property and their peace and personal security are to be endangered. There has never been any reasonable cause for such apprehension. Indeed, the most ample evidence to the contrary has all the while existed and been open to their inspection. It is found in nearly all the published speeches of him who now addresses you. I do but quote from one of those speeches when I declare that—

I have no purpose, directly or indirectly, to interfere with the institution of slavery in the States where it exists. I believe I have no lawful right to do so, and I have no inclination to do so.

Those who nominated and elected me did so with full knowledge that I had made this and many similar declarations and had never recanted them; and more than this, they placed in the platform for my acceptance, and as a law to themselves and to me, the clear and emphatic resolution which I now read:

Resolved, That the maintenance inviolate of the rights of the States, and especially the right of each State to order and control its own domestic institutions according to its own judgment exclusively, is essential to that balance of power on which the perfection and endurance of our political fabric depend; and we denounce the lawless invasion by armed force of the soil of any State or Territory, no matter what pretext, as among the gravest of crimes.

I now reiterate these sentiments, and in doing so I only press upon the public attention the most conclusive evidence of which the case is susceptible that the property, peace, and security of no section are to be in any wise endangered by the now incoming Administration. I add, too, that all the protection which, consistently with the Constitution and the laws, can be given will be cheerfully given to all the States when lawfully demanded, for whatever cause—as cheerfully to one section as to another.

There is much controversy about the delivering up of fugitives from service or labor. The clause I now read is as plainly written in the Constitution as any other of its provisions: No person held to service or labor in one State, under the laws thereof, escaping into another, shall in consequence of any law or regulation therein be discharged from such service or labor, but shall be delivered up on claim of the party to whom such service or labor may be due.

It is scarcely questioned that this provision was intended by those who made it for the reclaiming of what we call fugitive slaves; and the intention of the lawgiver is the law. All members of Congress swear their support to the whole Constitution—to this provision as much as to any other. To the proposition, then, that slaves whose cases come within the terms of this clause "shall be delivered up" their oaths are unanimous. Now, if they would make the effort in good temper, could they not with nearly equal unanimity frame and pass a law by means of which to keep good that unanimous oath?

There is some difference of opinion whether this clause should be enforced by national or by State authority, but surely that difference is not a very material one. If the slave is to be surrendered, it can be of but little consequence to him or to others by which authority it is done. And should anyone in any case be content that his oath shall go unkept on a merely unsubstantial controversy as to how it shall be kept?

Again: In any law upon this subject ought not all the safeguards of liberty known in civilized and humane jurisprudence to be introduced, so that a free man be not in any case surrendered as a slave? And might it not be well at the same time to provide by law for the enforcement of that clause in the Constitution which guarantees that "the citizens of each State shall be entitled to all privileges and immunities of citizens in the several States"?

I take the official oath to-day with no mental reservations and with no purpose to construe the Constitution or laws by any hypercritical rules; and while I do not choose now to specify particular acts of Congress as proper to be enforced, I do suggest that it will be much safer for all, both in official and private stations, to conform to and abide by all those acts which stand unrepealed than to violate any of them trusting to find impunity in having them held to be unconstitutional.

It is seventy-two years since the first inauguration of a President under our National Constitution. During that period fifteen different and greatly distinguished citizens have in succession administered the executive branch of the Government. They have conducted it through many perils, and generally with great success. Yet, with all this scope of precedent, I now enter upon the same task for the brief constitutional term of four years under great and peculiar difficulty. A disruption of the Federal Union, heretofore only menaced, is now formidably attempted.

I hold that in contemplation of universal law and of the Constitution the Union of these States is perpetual. Perpetuity is implied, if not expressed, in the fundamental law of all national governments. It is safe to assert that no government proper ever had a provision in its organic law for its own termination. Continue to execute all the express provisions of our National Constitution, and the Union will endure forever, it being impossible to destroy it except by some action not provided for in the instrument itself.

Again: If the United States be not a government proper, but an association of States in the nature of contract merely, can it, as a contract, be peaceably unmade by less than all the parties who made it? One party to a contract may violate it—break it, so to speak—but does it not require all to lawfully rescind it?

Descending from these general principles, we find the proposition that in legal contemplation the Union is perpetual confirmed by the history of the Union itself. The Union is much older than the Constitution. It was formed, in fact, by the Articles of Association in 1774. It was matured and continued by the Declaration of Independence in 1776. It was further matured, and the faith of all the then thirteen States expressly plighted and engaged that it should be perpetual, by the Articles of Confederation in 1778. And finally, in 1787, one of the declared objects for ordaining and establishing the Constitution was "to form a more perfect Union."

But if destruction of the Union by one or by a part only of the States be lawfully possible, the Union is less perfect than before the Constitution, having lost the vital element of perpetuity. It follows from these views that no State upon its own mere motion can lawfully get out of the Union; that resolves and ordinances to that effect are legally void, and that acts of violence within any State or States against the authority of the United States are insurrectionary or revolutionary, according to circumstances.

I therefore consider that in view of the Constitution and the laws the Union is unbroken, and to the extent of my ability, I shall take care, as the Constitution itself expressly enjoins upon me, that the laws of the Union be faithfully executed in all the States. Doing this I deem to be only a simple duty on my part, and I shall perform it so far as practicable unless my rightful masters, the American people, shall withhold the requisite means or in some authoritative manner direct the contrary. I trust this will not be regarded as a menace, but only as the declared purpose of the Union that it will constitutionally defend and maintain itself.

In doing this there needs to be no bloodshed or violence, and there shall be none unless it be forced upon the national authority. The power confided to me will be used to hold, occupy, and possess the property and places belonging to the Government and to collect the duties and imposts; but beyond what may be necessary for these objects, there will be no invasion, no using of force against or among the people anywhere. Where hostility to the United States in any interior locality shall be so great and universal as to prevent competent resident citizens from holding the Federal offices, there will be no attempt to force obnoxious strangers among the people for that object. While the strict legal right may exist in the Government to enforce the exercise of these offices, the attempt to do so would be so irritating and so nearly impractica-ble withal that I deem it better to forego for the time the uses of such offices.

The mails, unless repelled, will continue to be furnished in all parts of the Union. So far as possible the people everywhere shall have that sense of perfect security which is most favorable to calm thought and reflection. The course here indicated will be followed unless current events and experience shall show a modification or change to be proper, and in every case and exigency my best discretion will be exercised, according to circumstances actually existing and with a view and a hope of a peaceful solution of the national troubles and the restoration of fraternal sympathies and affections.

That there are persons in one section or another who seek to destroy the Union at all events and are glad of any pretext to do it I will neither affirm nor deny; but if there be such, I need address no word to them. To those, however, who really love the Union may I not speak?

Before entering upon so grave a matter as the destruction of our national fabric, with all its benefits, its memories, and its hopes, would it not be wise to ascertain precisely why we do it? Will you hazard so desperate a step while there is any possibility that any portion of the ills you fly from have no real existence? Will you, while the certain ills you fly to are greater than all the real ones you fly from, will you risk the commission of so fearful a mistake?

All profess to be content in the Union if all constitutional rights can be maintained. Is it true, then, that any right plainly written in the Constitution has been denied? I think not. Happily, the human mind is so constituted that no party can reach to the audacity of doing this. Think, if you can, of a single instance in which a plainly written provision of the Constitution has ever been denied. If by the mere force of numbers a majority should deprive a minority of any clearly written constitutional right, it might in a moral point of view justify revolution; certainly would if such right were a vital one. But such is not our case. All the vital rights of minorities and of individuals are so plainly assured to them by affirmations and negations, guaranties and prohibitions, in the Constitution that controversies never arise concerning them. But no organic law can ever be framed with a provision specifically applicable to every question which may occur in practical administration. No foresight can anticipate nor any document of reasonable length contain express provisions for all possible questions. Shall fugitives from labor be surrendered by national or by State authority? The Constitution does not expressly say. May Congress prohibit slavery in the Territories? The Constitution does not expressly say. Must Congress protect slavery in the Territories? The Constitution does not expressly say.

From questions of this class spring all our constitutional controversies, and we divide upon them into majorities and minorities. If the minority will not acquiesce, the majority must, or the Government must cease. There is no other alternative, for continuing the Government is acquiescence on one side or the other. If a minority in such case will secede rather than acquiesce, they make a precedent which in turn will divide and ruin them, for a minority of their own will secede from them whenever a majority refuses to be controlled by such minority. For instance, why may not any portion of a new confederacy a year or two hence arbitrarily secede again, precisely as portions of the present Union now claim to secede from it? All who cherish disunion sentiments are now being educated to the exact temper of doing this.

Is there such perfect identity of interests among the States to compose a new union as to produce harmony only and prevent renewed secession?

Plainly the central idea of secession is the essence of anarchy. A majority held in restraint by constitutional checks and limitations, and always changing easily with deliberate changes of popular opinions and sentiments, is the only true sovereign of a free people. Whoever rejects it does of necessity fly to anarchy or to despotism. Unanimity is impossible. The rule of a minority, as a permanent arrangement, is wholly inadmissible; so that, rejecting the majority principle, anarchy or despotism in some form is all that is left.

I do not forget the position assumed by some that constitutional questions are to be decided by the Supreme Court, nor do I deny that such decisions must be binding in any case upon the parties to a suit as to the object of that suit, while they are also entitled to very high respect and consideration in all parallel cases by all other departments of the Government. And while it is obviously possible that such decision may be erroneous in any given case, still the evil effect following it, being limited to that particular case, with the chance that it may be overruled and never become a precedent for other cases, can better be borne than could the evils of a different practice. At the same time, the candid citizen must confess that if the policy of the Government upon vital questions affecting the whole people is to be irrevocably fixed by decisions of the Supreme Court, the instant they are made in ordinary litigation between parties in personal actions the people will have ceased to be their own rulers, having to that extent practically resigned their Government into the hands of that eminent tribunal. Nor is there in this view any assault upon the court or the judges. It is a duty from which they may not shrink to decide cases properly brought before them, and it is no fault of theirs if others seek to turn their decisions to political purposes.

One section of our country believes slavery is right and ought to be extended, while the other believes it is wrong and ought not to be extended. This is the only substantial dispute. The fugitive-slave clause of the Constitution and the law for the suppression of the foreign slave trade are each as well enforced, perhaps, as any law can ever be in a community where the moral sense of the people imperfectly supports the law itself. The great body of the people abide by the dry legal obligation in both cases, and a few break over in each. This, I think, can not be perfectly cured, and it would be worse in both cases after the separation of the sections than before. The foreign slave trade, now imperfectly suppressed, would be ultimately revived without restriction in one section, while fugitive slaves, now only partially surrendered, would not be surrendered at all by the other.

Physically speaking, we can not separate. We can not remove our respective sections from each other nor build an impassable wall between them. A husband and wife may be divorced and go out of the presence and beyond the reach of each other, but the different parts of our country can not do this. They can not but remain face to face, and intercourse, either amicable or hostile, must continue between them. Is it possible, then, to make that intercourse more advantageous or more satisfactory after separation than before? Can aliens make treaties easier than friends can make laws? Can treaties be more faithfully enforced between aliens than laws can among friends? Suppose you go to war, you can not fight always; and when, after much loss on both sides and no gain on either, you cease fighting, the identical old questions, as to terms of intercourse, are again upon you.

This country, with its institutions, belongs to the people who inhabit it. Whenever they shall grow weary of the existing Government, they can exercise their constitutional right of amending it or their revolutionary right to dismember or overthrow it. I can not be ignorant of the fact that many worthy and patriotic citizens are desirous of having the National Constitution amended. While I make no recommendation of amendments, I fully recognize the rightful authority of the people over the whole subject, to be exercised in either of the modes prescribed in the instrument itself; and I should, under existing circumstances, favor rather than oppose a fair opportunity being afforded the people to act upon it. I will venture to add that to me the convention mode seems preferable, in that it allows amendments to originate with the people themselves, instead of only permitting them to take or reject propositions originated by others, not especially chosen for the purpose, and which might not be precisely such as they would wish to either accept or refuse. I understand a proposed amendment to the Constitution—which amendment, however, I have not seen—has passed Congress, to the effect that the Federal Government shall never interfere with the domestic institutions of the States, including that of persons held to service. To avoid misconstruction of what I have said, I depart from my purpose not to speak of particular amendments so far as to say that, holding such a provision to now be implied constitutional law, I have no objection to its being made express and irrevocable.

The Chief Magistrate derives all his authority from the people, and they have referred none upon him to fix terms for the separation of the States. The people themselves can do this if also they choose, but the Executive as such has nothing to do with it. His duty is to administer the present Government as it came to his hands and to transmit it unimpaired by him to his successor.

Why should there not be a patient confidence in the ultimate justice of the people? Is there any better or equal hope in the world? In our present differences, is either party without faith of being in the right? If the Almighty Ruler of Nations, with His eternal truth and justice, be on your side of the North, or on yours of the South, that truth and that justice will surely prevail by the judgment of this great tribunal of the American people.

By the frame of the Government under which we live this same people have wisely given their public servants but little power for mischief, and have with equal wisdom provided for the return of that little to their own hands at very short intervals. While the people retain their virtue and vigilance no Administration by any extreme of wickedness or folly can very seriously injure the Government in the short space of four years.

My countrymen, one and all, think calmly and well upon this whole subject. Nothing valuable can be lost by taking time. If there be an object to hurry any of you in hot haste to a step which you would never take deliberately, that object will be frustrated by taking time; but no good object can be frustrated by it. Such of you as are now dissatisfied still have the old Constitution unimpaired, and, on the sensitive point, the laws of your own framing under it; while the new Administration will have no immediate power, if it would, to change either. If it were admitted that you who are dissatisfied hold the right side in the dispute, there still is no single good reason for precipitate action. Intelligence, patriotism, Christianity, and a firm reliance on Him who has never yet forsaken this favored land are still competent to adjust in the best way all our present difficulty.

In your hands, my dissatisfied fellow-countrymen, and not in mine, is the momentous issue of civil war. The Government will not assail you. You can have no conflict without being yourselves the aggressors. You have no oath registered in heaven to destroy the Government, while I shall have the most solemn one to "preserve, protect, and defend it."

I am loath to close. We are not enemies, but friends. We must not be enemies. Though passion may have strained it must not break our bonds of affection. The mystic chords of memory, stretching from every battlefield and patriot grave to every living heart and hearthstone all over this broad land, will yet swell the chorus of the Union, when again touched, as surely they will be, by the better angels of our nature.

ABRAHAM LINCOLN'S SECOND
INAUGURAL ADDRESS

MARCH 4, 1865

Fellow Countrymen:

At this second appearing to take the oath of the presidential office, there is less occasion for an extended address than there was at the first. Then a statement, somewhat in detail, of a course to be pursued, seemed fitting and proper. Now, at the expiration of four years, during which public declarations have been constantly called forth on every point and phase of the great contest which still absorbs the attention, and engrosses the energies of the nation, little that is new could be presented. The progress of our arms, upon which all else chiefly depends, is as well known to the public as to myself; and it is, I trust, reasonably satisfactory and encouraging to all. With high hope for the future, no prediction in regard to it is ventured.

On the occasion corresponding to this four years ago, all thoughts were anxiously directed to an impending civil-war. All dreaded it—all sought to avert it. While the inaugural address was being delivered from this place, devoted altogether to saving the Union without war, insurgent agents were in the city seeking to destroy it without war— seeking to dissolve the Union, and divide effects, by negotiation. Both parties deprecated war; but one of them would make war rather than let the nation survive; and the other would accept war rather than let it perish. And the war came.

One eighth of the whole population were colored slaves, not distributed generally over the Union, but localized in the Southern part of it. These slaves constituted a peculiar and powerful interest. All knew that this interest was, somehow, the cause of the war. To strengthen, perpetuate, and extend this interest was the object for which the insurgents would rend the Union, even by war; while the Government claimed no right to do more than to restrict the territorial enlargement of it. Neither party expected for the war, the magnitude, or the duration, which it has already attained. Neither anticipated that the cause of the conflict might cease with, or even before, the conflict itself should cease. Each looked for an easier triumph, and a result less fundamental and astounding. Both read the same Bible, and pray to the same God; and each invokes His aid against the other. It may seem strange that any men should dare to ask a just God's assistance in wringing their bread from the sweat of other men's faces; but let us judge not that we be not judged. The prayers of both could not be answered; that of neither has been answered fully. The Almighty has His own purposes. "Woe unto the world because of offenses! for it must needs be that offenses come; but woe to that man by whom the offense cometh!" If we shall suppose that American Slavery is one of those offenses which, in the providence of God, must needs come, but which, having continued through His appointed time, He now wills to remove, and that He gives to both North and South, this terrible war, as the woe due to those by whom the offense came, shall we discern therein any departure from those divine attributes which the believers in a Living God always ascribe to Him? Fondly do we hope—fervently do we pray—that this mighty scourge of war may speedily pass away. Yet, if God wills that it continue, until all the wealth piled by the bond-man's two hundred and fifty years of unrequited toil shall be sunk, and until every drop of blood drawn with the lash, shall be paid by another drawn with the sword, as was said three thousand years ago, so still it must be said "the judgments of the Lord, are true and righteous altogether."

With malice toward none; with charity for all; with firmness in the right, as God gives us to see the right, let us strive on to finish the work we are in; to bind up the nation's wounds; to care for him who shall have borne the battle, and for his widow, and his orphan—to do all which may achieve and cherish a just, and a lasting peace, among our-selves, and with all nations.

THE EMANCIPATION
PROCLAMATION

JANUARY 1, 1863

Whereas on the 22nd day of September, A.D. 1862, a proclamation was issued by the President of the United States, containing, among other things, the following, to wit:

"That on the 1st day of January, A.D. 1863, all persons held as slaves within any State or designated part of a State the people whereof shall then be in rebellion against the United States shall be then, thence-forward, and forever free; and the executive government of the United States, including the military and naval authority thereof, will recog-nize and maintain the freedom of such persons and will do no act or acts to repress such persons, or any of them, in any efforts they may make for their actual freedom.

"That the executive will on the 1st day of January aforesaid, by proclamation, designate the States and parts of States, if any, in which the people thereof, respectively, shall then be in rebellion against the United States; and the fact that any State or the people thereof shall on that day be in good faith represented in the Congress of the United States by members chosen thereto at elections wherein a majority of the qualified voters of such States shall have participated shall, in the absence of strong countervailing testimony, be deemed conclusive evidence that such State and the people thereof are not then in rebellion against the United States."

Now, therefore, I, Abraham Lincoln, President of the United States, by virtue of the power in me vested as Commander-In-Chief of the Army and Navy of the United States in time of actual armed rebellion against the authority and government of the United States, and as a fit and necessary war measure for suppressing said rebellion, do, on this 1st day of January, A.D. 1863, and in accordance with my purpose so to do, publicly proclaimed for the full period of one hundred days from the first day above mentioned, order and designate as the States and parts of States wherein the people thereof, respectively, are this day in rebellion against the United States the following, to wit:

Arkansas, Texas, Louisiana (except the parishes of St. Bernard, Palquemines, Jefferson, St. John, St. Charles, St. James, Ascension, Assumption, Terrebone, Lafourche, St. Mary, St. Martin, and Orleans, including the city of New Orleans), Mississippi, Alabama, Florida, Georgia, South Carolina, North Carolina, and Virginia (except the forty-eight counties designated as West Virginia, and also the counties of Berkeley, Accomac, Northhampton, Elizabeth City, York, Princess Anne, and Norfolk, including the cities of Norfolk and Portsmouth), and which excepted parts are for the present left precisely as if this proclamation were not issued.

And by virtue of the power and for the purpose aforesaid, I do order and declare that all persons held as slaves within said designated States and parts of States are, and henceforward shall be, free; and that the Executive Government of the United States, including the military and naval authorities thereof, will recognize and maintain the freedom of said persons.

And I hereby enjoin upon the people so declared to be free to abstain from all violence, unless in necessary self-defense; and I recommend to them that, in all cases when allowed, they labor faithfully for reasonable wages.

And I further declare and make known that such persons of suitable condition will be received into the armed service of the United States to garrison forts, positions, stations, and other places, and to man vessels of all sorts in said service.

And upon this act, sincerely believed to be an act of justice, warranted by the Constitution upon military necessity, I invoke the considerate judgment of mankind and the gracious favor of Almighty God.

LINCOLN'S THANKSGIVING PROCLAMATION OF APRIL 10, 1862

Washington, D.C.

By the President of the United States

It has pleased Almighty God to vouchsafe signal victories to the land and naval forces engaged in suppressing an internal rebellion, and at the same time to avert from our country the dangers of foreign intervention and invasion.

It is therefore recommended to the people of the United States that at their next weekly assemblages in their accustomed places of public worship which shall occur after notice of this proclamation shall have been received they especially acknowledge and render thanks to our

Heavenly Father for these inestimable blessings, that they then and there implore spiritual consolation in behalf of all who have been brought into affliction by the casualties and calamities of sedition and civil war, and that they reverently invoke the divine guidance for our national counsels, to the end that they may speedily result in the restoration of peace, harmony, and unity throughout our borders and hasten the establishment of fraternal relations among all the countries of the earth.

In witness whereof I have hereunto set my hand and caused the seal of the United States to be affixed.

Done at the city of Washington, this 10th day of April A.D. 1862, and of the Independence of the United States the eighty-sixth.

By the President: Abraham Lincoln

LINCOLN'S PROCLAMATION APPOINTING A NATIONAL FAST DAY OF MARCH 30, 1863

By the President of the United States of America.
A Proclamation.

Whereas, the Senate of the United States, devoutly recognizing the Supreme Authority and just Government of Almighty God, in all the affairs of men and of nations, has, by a resolution, requested the President to designate and set apart a day for National prayer and humiliation.

And whereas it is the duty of nations as well as of men, to own their dependence upon the overruling power of God, to confess their sins and transgressions, in humble sorrow, yet with assured hope that genuine repentance will lead to mercy and pardon; and to recognize the sublime truth, announced in the Holy Scriptures and proven by all history, that those nations only are blessed whose God is the Lord.

And, insomuch as we know that, by His divine law, nations like individuals are subjected to punishments and chastisements in this world, may we not justly fear that the awful calamity of civil war, which now desolates the land, may be but a punishment, inflicted upon us, for our presumptuous sins, to the needful end of our national reformation as a whole People? We have been the recipients of the choicest bounties of Heaven. We have been preserved, these many years, in peace and prosperity. We have grown in numbers, wealth and power, as no other nation has ever grown. But we have forgotten God. We have forgotten the gracious hand which preserved us in peace, and multiplied and enriched and strengthened us; and we have vainly imagined, in the deceitfulness of our hearts, that all these blessings were produced by some superior wisdom and virtue of our own. Intoxicated with unbroken success, we have become too self-sufficient to feel the necessity of redeeming and preserving grace, too proud to pray to the God that made us!

It behooves us then, to humble ourselves before the offended Power, to confess our national sins, and to pray for clemency and forgiveness.

Now, therefore, in compliance with the request, and fully concurring in the views of the Senate, I do, by this my proclamation, designate and set apart Thursday, the 30th. day of April, 1863, as a day of national humiliation, fasting and prayer. And I do hereby request all the People to abstain, on that day, from their ordinary secular pursuits, and to unite, at their several places of public worship and their respective homes, in keeping the day holy to the Lord, and devoted to the humble discharge of the religious duties proper to that solemn occasion.

All this being done, in sincerity and truth, let us then rest humbly in the hope authorized by the Divine teachings, that the united cry of the Nation will be heard on high, and answered with blessings, no less than the pardon of our national sins, and the restoration of our now divided and suffering Country, to its former happy condition of unity and peace.

In witness whereof, I have hereunto set my hand and caused the seal of the United States to be affixed.

Done at the City of Washington, this thirtieth day of March, in the year of our Lord one thousand eight hundred and sixty-three, and of the Independence of the United States the eighty-seventh.

By the President: Abraham Lincoln

William H. Seward, Secretary of State.

LINCOLN'S PROCLAMATION OF THANKSGIVING OF JULY 15, 1863

BY THE PRESIDENT OF THE UNITED STATES OF AMERICA.

A Proclamation.

It has pleased Almighty God to hearken to the supplications and prayers of an afflicted people, and to vouchsafe to the army and the navy of the United States victories on land and on the sea so signal and so effective as to furnish reasonable grounds for augmented confidence that the Union of these States will be maintained, their constitution preserved, and their peace and prosperity permanently restored. But these victories have been accorded not without sacrifices of life, limb, health and liberty incurred by brave, loyal and patriotic citizens. Domestic affliction in every part of the country follows in the train of these fearful bereavements. It is meet and right to recognize and confess the presence of the Almighty Father and the power of His Hand equally in these triumphs and in these sorrows.

Now, therefore, be it known that I do set apart Thursday the 6th. day of August next, to be observed as a day for National Thanksgiving, Praise and Prayer, and I invite the People of the United States to assemble on that occasion in their customary places of worship, and in the forms approved by their own consciences, render the homage due to the Divine Majesty, for the wonderful things he has done in the Nation's behalf, and invoke the influence of His Holy Spirit to subdue the anger, which has produced, and so long sustained a needless and cruel rebellion, to change the hearts of the insurgents, to guide the counsels of the Government with wisdom adequate to so great a national emergency, and to visit with tender care and consolation throughout the length and breadth of our land all those who, through the vicissitudes of marches, voyages, battles and sieges, have been brought to suffer in mind, body or estate, and finally to lead the whole nation, through the paths of repentance and submission to the Divine Will, back to the perfect enjoyment of Union and fraternal peace.

In witness whereof, I have hereunto set my hand and caused the seal of the United States to be affixed.

Done at the city of Washington, this fifteenth day of July, in the year of our Lord one thousand eight hundred and sixty-three, and of the Independence of the United States of America the eighty-eighth.

By the President: Abraham Lincoln

William H. Seward, Secretary of State.

LINCOLN'S THANKSGIVING PROCLAMATION OF OCTOBER 3, 1863

The year that is drawing toward its close has been filled with the blessings of fruitful fields and healthful skies. To these bounties, which are so constantly enjoyed that we are prone to forget the source from which they come, others have been added which are of so extraordinary a nature that they can not fail to penetrate and soften even the heart which is habitually insensible to the ever-watchful providence of Almighty God.

In the midst of a civil war of unequaled magnitude and severity, which has sometimes seemed to foreign states to invite and to provoke their aggression, peace has been preserved with all nations, order has been maintained, the laws have been respected and obeyed, and harmony has prevailed everywhere, except in the theater of military conflict, while that theater has been greatly contracted by the advancing armies and navies of the Union. Needful diversions of wealth and of strength from the fields of peaceful industry to the national defense have not arrested the plow, the shuttle, or the ship; the ax has enlarged the borders of our settlements, and the mines, as well of iron and coal as of the precious metals, have yielded even more abundantly than heretofore. Population has steadily increased notwithstanding the waste that has been made in the camp, the siege, and the battlefield, and the country, rejoicing in the consciousness of augmented strength and vigor, is permitted to expect continuance of years with large increase of freedom.

No human counsel hath devised nor hath any mortal hand worked out these great things. They are the gracious gifts of the Most High God, who, while dealing with us in anger for our sins, hath nevertheless remembered mercy.

It has seemed to me fit and proper that they should be solemnly, reverently, and gratefully acknowledged, as with one heart and one voice, by the whole American people. I do therefore invite my fellow-citizens in every part of the United States, and also those who are at sea and those who are sojourning in foreign lands, to set apart and observe the last Thursday of November next as a day of thanksgiving and praise to our beneficent Father who dwelleth in the heavens. And I recommend to them that while offering up the ascriptions justly due to Him for such singular deliverances and blessings they do also, with humble penitence for our national perverseness and disobedience, commend to His tender care all those who have become widows, orphans, mourners, or sufferers in the lamentable civil strife in which we are unavoidably engaged, and fervently implore the interposition of the Almighty hand to heal the wounds of the nation and to restore it, as soon as may be consistent with the divine purpose, to the full enjoyment of peace, harmony, tranquility, and union.

In testimony whereof I have hereunto set my hand and caused the seal of the United States to be affixed.

Done at the city of Washington, this 3d day of October A.D. 1863, and of the Independence of the United States the eighty-eighth.

Abraham Lincoln

PROCLAMATION OF A
DAY OF PRAYER

JULY 7, 1864

By the President of the United States of America:

A Proclamation.

Whereas, the Senate and House of Representatives at their last Session adopted a Concurrent Resolution, which was approved on the second day of July instant, and which was in the words following, namely:

"That, the President of the United States be requested to appoint a day for humiliation and prayer by the people of the United States; that he request his constitutional advisers at the head of the executive departments to unite with him as Chief Magistrate of the Nation, at the City of Washington, and the members of Congress, and all magistrates, all civil, military and naval officers, all soldiers, sailors, and marines, with all loyal and law-abiding people, to convene at their usual places of worship, or wherever they may be, to confess and to repent of their manifold sins; to implore the compassion and forgiveness of the Almighty, that, if consistent with His will, the existing rebellion may be speedily suppressed, and the supremacy of the Constitution and laws of the United States may be established throughout all the States; to implore Him as the Supreme Ruler of the World, not to destroy us as a people, nor suffer us to be destroyed by the hostility or connivance of other Nations, or by obstinate adhesion to our own counsels, which may be in conflict with His eternal purposes, and to implore Him to enlighten the mind of the Nation to know and do His will; humbly believing that it is in accordance with His will that our place should be maintained as a united people among the family of nations; to implore Him to grant to our armed defenders and the masses of the people that courage, power of resistance and endurance necessary to secure that result; to implore Him in His infinite goodness to soften the hearts, enlighten the minds, and quicken the consciences of those in rebellion, that they may lay down their arms and speedily return to their allegiance to the United States, that they may not be utterly destroyed, that the effusion of blood may be stayed, and that unity and fraternity may be restored, and peace established throughout all our borders."

Now, therefore, I, Abraham Lincoln, President of the United States, cordially concurring with the Congress of the United States in the penitential and pious sentiments expressed in the aforesaid Resolution, and heartily approving of the devotional design and purpose thereof, do, hereby, appoint the first Thursday of August next, to be observed by the People of the United States as a day of national humiliation and prayer.

I do, hereby, further invite and request the Heads of the Executive Departments of this Government, together with all Legislators,—all Judges and Magistrates, and all other persons exercising authority in the land, whether civil, military or naval,—and all soldiers, seamen and marines in the national service,—and all the other loyal and law-abiding People of the United States, to assemble in their preferred places of public worship on that day, and there and then to render to the Almighty and Merciful Ruler of the Universe, such homages and such confessions, and to offer to Him such supplications, as the Congress of the United States have, in their aforesaid Resolution, so solemnly, so earnestly, and so earnestly, and so reverently recommended.

In testimony whereof, I have hereunto set my hand and caused the seal of the United States to be affixed.

Done at the City of Washington, this seventh day of July, in the year of our Lord, one thousand eight hundred and sixty-four, and of the Independence of the United States the eighty-ninth.

By the President: Abraham Lincoln

William H. Seward, Secretary of State.

SELECTED
BIBLIOGRAPHY

Ahlstrom, Sydney E. *A Religious History of the American People*. New Haven: Yale University Press, 1972.

Baker, Jean H. *Mary Todd Lincoln: A Biography*. New York: W. W. Norton & Co., 1987.

Barton, William E. *The Soul of Abraham Lincoln*. Chicago: The University of Illinois Press, 2005.

Basler, Roy P., Marin Dolores Pratt, and Lloyd A. Dunlap, eds. *The Collected Works of Abraham Lincoln*. 8 vols. New Brunswick: Rutgers University Press, 1953.

Bishop, Jim. *The Day Lincoln Was Shot*. New York: Gramercy, 1984.

Burkhimer, Michael. *Lincoln's Christianity*. Yardley, PA: Westholme Publishing, 2007.

Burlingame, Michael. *The Inner World of Abraham Lincoln*. Urbana and Chicago: University of Illinois Press, 1994.

Bush, Harold K., ed. *Lincoln in His Own Time*. Iowa City: University of Iowa Press, 2011.

Carnegie, Dale. *Lincoln the Unknown*. Garden City, NY: Dale Carnegie & Associates, 1970.

Carpenter, F. B. *The Inner Life of Abraham Lincoln: Six Months at the White House*. Lincoln: University of Nebraska Press, 1995.

Carwardine, Richard. *Lincoln: A Life of Purpose and Power*. New York: Vintage, 2007.

Donald, David Herbert. *Lincoln*. New York: Simon & Schuster, 1995.

Fehrenbacher, Don E., ed. and comp., and Virginia Fehrenbacher, ed. and comp. *Recollected Words of Abraham Lincoln*. Stanford: Stanford University Press, 1996.

Goodwin, Doris Kearns. *Team of Rivals: the Political Genius of Abraham Lincoln*. New York: Simon & Schuster, 2006.

Guelzo, Allen C. *Abraham Lincoln: Redeemer President*. Library of Religious Biography. Grand Rapids: William B. Eerdmans Publishing Company, 2003.

Herndon, William H., and Jesse W. Weik. *Herndon's Lincoln*. Knox College Lincoln Studies Center. Edited by Douglas L. Wilson and Rodney O. Davis. Urbana and Chicago: University of Illinois Press, 2006.

Hertz, Emanuel. *The Hidden Lincoln*. New York: Blue Ribbon Books, 1940.

Horowitz, Mitch. *Occult America: White House Séances, Ouija Circles, Masons, and the Secret Mystic History of Our Nation*. Repr. ed. New York: Bantam, 2010.

Johnson, Paul. *Civil War America: 1850–1870*. New York: Harper Perennial, 2011.

Keckley, Elizabeth. *Behind the Scenes: Or, Thirty Years a Slave, and Four Years in the White House*. Schomburg Library of Nineteenth-Century Black Women Writers. New York: Oxford University Press, 1989.

Keneally, Thomas. *Abraham Lincoln*. Penguin Lives. New York: Viking Adult, 2002.

Kennedy, Walter D., and Al Benson. *Red Republicans and Lincoln's Marxists: Marxism in the Civil War*. New York: iUniverse, Inc., 2007.

Lamb, Brian, and Susan Swain. *Abraham Lincoln: Great American Historians on Our Sixteenth President*. C-Span Books. New York: PublicAffairs, 2008.

Lincoln, Abraham, and Archer H. Shaw. *The Lincoln Encyclopedia: The Spoken and Written Words of A. Lincoln Arranged for Ready Reference*. New York: The MacMillan Company, 1950.

Marshall, Peter, and David Manuel. *From Sea to Shining Sea*. Old Tappan: Revell, 1985.

———. *Sounding Forth the Trumpet*. Grand Rapids: Revell, 1998.

Martinez, Susan B. *The Psychic Life of Abraham Lincoln*. Franklin Lakes: New Page Books, 2009.

McPherson, James M. *Abraham Lincoln: A Presidential Life*. New York: Oxford University Press, USA, 2008.

Minor, Charles L. C., and Lyon Gardiner Tyler. *The Real Lincoln*. 4th ed. Harrisonburg: Sprinkle Publications, 1992.

Noll, Mark A. *America's God: From Jonathan Edwards to Abraham Lincoln*. New York: Oxford University Press, 2005.

——— *The Civil War as a Theological Crisis*. Chapel Hill: The University of North Carolina Press, 2006.

Oates, Stephen B. *Abraham Lincoln: Man Behind the Myths*. New York: Harper Perennial, 1994.

Owen, G. Frederick. *Abraham Lincoln: The Man and His Faith*. Wheaton: Tyndale House Publishers, 1981.

Sandburg, Carl. *Abraham Lincoln: The Prairie Years and the War Years*. New York: Harcourt, Inc., 1982.

Shenk, Joshua Wolf. *Lincoln's Melancholy: How Depression Challenged a President and Fueled His Greatness*. Boston: Houghton Mifflin, 2005.

Temple, Wayne C. *Abraham Lincoln: From Skeptic to Prophet*. Mahomet, IL: Mayhaven Publishing, 1995.

White Jr., Ronald C. *Lincoln's Greatest Speech: The Second Inaugural*. New York: Simon & Schuster, 2006.

Wilson, Douglas L. *Honor's Voice: The Transformation of Abraham Lincoln*. New York: Vintage, 1999.

Wilson, Douglas L., ed., and Rodney O. Davis, ed. *Herndon's Informants: Letters, Interviews, and Statements About Abraham Lincoln*. Urbana and Chicago: University of Illinois Press, 1997.

NOTES

INTRODUCTION: FINAL WORDS

1. Don E. Fehrenbacher and Virginia Fehrenbacher, eds., *Recollected Words of Abraham Lincoln* (Stanford: Stanford University Press, 1996), 297.

2. Allen C. Guelzo, *Abraham Lincoln: Redeemer President* (Grand Rapids: William C. Eerdmans Publishing Company, 1999), 434–35; Wayne C. Temple, *Abraham Lincoln: From Skeptic to Prophet* (Mahomet, IL: Mayhaven Publishing, 1995), 305.

3. Doris Kearns Goodwin, *Team of Rivals: The Political Genius of Abraham Lincoln* (New York: Simon & Schuster, 2005), 733. Goodwin describes the Lincolns' Holy Land conversation as happening during the carriage ride on the afternoon of April 14. Some historians agree, concluding that Mary's recollection of Lincoln's hopes for a pilgrimage to walk in the steps of Jesus were blended into the tragic events of that evening but were actually from earlier in the day. This may well be true, but we cannot be certain, and it does not alter the religious implications of Lincoln's words.

4. Author interview with James M. Cornelius, PhD, August 16, 2011.

5. William H. Herndon and Jesse W. Weik, *Herndon's Lincoln*, eds. Douglas L. Wilson and Rodney O. Davis (Chicago: University of Illinois Press, 2006), 269.

6. Ibid.

7. An example is Susan B. Martinez's *The Psychic Life of Abraham Lincoln* (Franklin Lakes, NJ: New Page Books, 2009).

Chapter 1: A Mother's Legacy

1. Herndon to J. E. Remsberg, September 1887, quoted in Paul M. Angle, ed., *Herndon's Life of Lincoln* (New York: Fawcett Publications, 1965), xxxix.

2. John L. Scripps to William H. Herndon, June 24, 1865. Douglas L. Wilson and Rodney O. Davis, eds., *Herndon's Informants* (Chicago: University of Illinois Press, 1998), 57.

3. Don E. Fehrenbacher and Virginia Fehrenbacher, eds., *Recollected Words of Abraham Lincoln* (Stanford: Stanford University Press, 1996), 240.

4. Herndon and Weik, *Herndon's Lincoln*, 16.

5. Fehrenbacher and Fehrenbacher, *Recollected Words*, 240–41.

6. Ibid., 240.

7. Herndon and Weik, *Herndon's Lincoln*, 22.

8. Usher F. Linder, *Reminiscences of the Early Bench and Bar of Illinois* (Chicago: Chicago Legal News Co., 1879), 39.

9. Ibid.

10. Carl Sandburg, *Abraham Lincoln: The Prairie Years and the War Years* (New York: Harcourt, Brace and Company, 1954), 13.

11. Ibid.

12. Ibid., 14.

13. Herndon and Weik, *Herndon's Lincoln*, 22.

14. Ibid.

15. Sandburg, *Abraham Lincoln*, 11.

16. All descriptions quoted in Joshua Wolf Shenk, *Lincoln's Melancholy: How Depression Challenged a President and Fueled His Greatness* (New York: Houghton Mifflin Company, 2005), 12.

17. William Henry Herndon, "Analysis of the Character of Abraham Lincoln," lecture delivered in Springfield, 12 December 1865, *Abraham Lincoln Quarterly* 1 (September 1941), 359.

18. *Hypo* was Lincoln's shorthand for *hypochondriasis*, a form of melancholia. As a medical term, it refers to a disease of the lower organs.

19. Letter to John Stuart, 20 January 1841. From Roy P. Basler, Marion Dolores Pratt, and Lloyd A. Dunlap, eds., *The Collected Works of Abraham Lincoln* (New Brunswick: Rutgers University Press, 1953), 1:228.

20. Shenk, *Lincoln's Melancholy*, 98.

21. Isaiah 53:3.

22. Fawn Brodie, "Hidden Presidents," *Harpers* 254 (April 1977), 71.

23. "Significant factors" quote from Felix Brown, "Depression and Childhood Bereavement," *Journal of Mental Science* 107 (1962), 770. "Present loss" quote from E. S. Paykel, "Life Events and Early Environment," in *Handbook of Affective Disorders*, ed. E. S. Paykel (New York: Guilford Press, 1982), 146–61. Both cited in Michael Burlingame, *The Inner World of Abraham Lincoln* (Chicago: University of Illinois Press, 1994), 94.

24. Sandburg, *Abraham Lincoln*, 11.

25. Herndon and Weik, *Herndon's Lincoln*, 31.

26. Douglas L. Wilson and Rodney O. Davis, eds., *Herndon's Informants* (Chicago: University of Illinois Press, 1998), 557.

27. Shenk, *Lincoln's Melancholy*, 20.

28. Fehrenbacher and Fehrenbacher, *Recollected Words*, 372.

29. Thomas Paine, *The Age of Reason* (Lewes, UK: Vigo Books, 1795, 2010), 66.

30. Ibid., 243.

31. Ibid., 360.

32. Henry Adams, *The United States in 1800* (Ithaca: Cornell University Press, 1960), 24.

33. Bernard A. Weisberger, *They Gathered at the River* (Boston: Little, Brown & Co., 1958), 3.

34. Warren A. Candler, *Great Revivals and the Great Republic* (Nashville: Publishing House of the Methodist Episcopal Church, South, 1904), 172.

35. Catherine C. Cleveland, *The Great Revival in the West, 1797–1805* (Chicago: University of Chicago Press, 1916), 40.

36. Weisberger, *They Gathered at the River*, 24.

37. Charles A Johnson, *The Frontier Camp Meeting* (Dallas: Southern Methodist University Press, 1955), 35.

38. John Rogers, *The Biography of Elder Barton Warren Stone* (Joplin: College Press Publishing Co., Inc., 1986), 34.

39. Luther A. Weigle, *American Idealism* (New Haven: Yale University Press, 1928), 152.

40. Rogers, *Biography of Elder Barton Warren Stone*, 41–42.

41. Ibid., 69–72.

42. Weisberger, *They Gathered at the River*, 64–65.

43. Ibid., 41–42.

44. Herndon and Weik, *Herndon's Lincoln*, 23.

45. Sandburg, *Abraham Lincoln*, 8–9.

46. T. D. Jones, "Recollections of Mr. Lincoln," *Cincinnati Commercial*, October 18, 1959, 4.

47. Allen C. Guelzo, *Abraham Lincoln: Redeemer President* (Grand Rapids: William C. Eerdmans Publishing Company, 1999), 36.

48. Louis A. Warren, *Lincoln's Youth: Indiana Years, 1816–30* (Indianapolis: Indiana Historical Society, 2002), 28–32. Quoted in Guelzo, *Redeemer President*, 38.

CHAPTER 2: LINCOLN'S ALMA MATER

1. Quoted in William H. Herndon and Jesse W. Weik, *Herndon's Lincoln*, Douglas L. Wilson and Rodney O. Davis, eds. (Chicago: University of Illinois Press, 2006), 60.

2. Michael Burlingame, *The Inner World of Abraham Lincoln* (Chicago: University of Illinois Press, 1994), 237.

3. Emanuel Hertz, ed., *The Hidden Lincoln: From the Letters and Papers of William H. Herndon* (Garden City, NY: Blue Ribbon Books, 1938), 361.

4. Elizabeth Keckley, *Behind the Scenes; or, Thirty Years a Slave and Four Years in the White House* (New York: G. W. Carleton, 1868), 228–29; confirmed in Herndon and Weik, *Herndon's Lincoln*, 135. Note: Keckley's name was misspelled by the publisher. The correct spelling is "Keckly."

5. Quoted in Herndon and Weik, *Herndon's Lincoln*, 62.

6. Lawrence A. Cremin, *American Education: The Colonial Experience 1607–1783* (New York: Harper and Row Publishers, 1970), 543.

7. Douglas L. Wilson and Rodney O. Davis, eds., *Herndon's Informants* (Chicago: University of Illinois Press, 1998), 76.

8. Ibid., 577.

9. Robert Burns, "Holy Willie's Prayer," 1785, available at Robert Burns Country, www.robertburns.org/works/58.shtml (accessed 17 March 2012).

10. Herndon and Weik, *Herndon's Lincoln*, 266.

11. Volney's full name was Constantin-François Chasseboeuf, comte de Volney—thus his designation as simply "Volney" in this text.

12. Philip S. Foner, ed., *The Complete Writings of Thomas Paine, 2 Vols.* (New York: Citadel Press, 1945), 1:464.

13. Ibid.

14. Ibid.

15. Ibid.

16. Constantin de Volney, *Volney's Ruins; or, Meditation on the Revolutions of Empires and the Law of Nature* (Boston: Charles Baylord, 1833), 4.

17. Ibid., 99.

18. Ibid., 51.

19. Herndon and Weik, *Herndon's Informants*, 576.

20. Quoted in Douglas L. Wilson, *Honor's Voice: The Transformation of Abraham Lincoln* (New York: Random House, 1998), 84.

21. Herndon and Weik, *Herndon's Lincoln*, 266.

22. Quoted in Wilson, *Honor's Voice*, 81.

23. Abraham Lincoln, "For the Beardstown Chronicle, New Salem, September 7, 1834," in *Beardstown Chronicle, And Illinois Military Bounty Land Advertiser*, November 1, 1834, 1; Douglas L. Wilson, "A Most Abandoned Hypocrite," *American Heritage*, XLV, no. 1 (Feb.–Mar. 1994), 36–49.

24. Hertz, *The Hidden Lincoln*, 52.

25. Ibid., 36.

26. Walter B. Stevens, *A Reporter's Lincoln* (St. Louis: Missouri Historical Society, 1916), 11–12.

27. William Knox, "Mortality," 1847, available at Scottish Poetry Library, www.scottishpoetrylibrary.org.uk/poetry/poems/mortality (accessed 17 March 2012).

28. Interview with William Butler, 1875, in Michael Burlingame, ed., *An Oral History of Abraham Lincoln: John G. Nicolay's Interviews and Essays* (Carbondale: Southern Illinois University Press, 1996), 22.

29. Though we cannot know for certain that Lincoln contracted syphilis, the evidence that he frequented prostitutes is convincing. In a letter to Jesse W. Weik, William Herndon wrote, "About the year 1835–6 Mr. Lincoln went to Beardstown and during a devilish passion had Connection with a girl and Caught the disease." See WHH to Jesse W. Weik, January 1891, Herndon–Weik Collection, Library of Congress; printed in Hertz, *Hidden Lincoln*, 259. Also, in Herndon and Weik, *Herndon's Informants*, 719, Herndon records Joshua Speed's story of sending Lincoln to a prostitute.

30. Joshua Wolf Shenk, *Lincoln's Melancholy: How Depression Challenged a President and Fueled His Greatness* (New York: Houghton Mifflin Company, 2005), 56. See also Jean H. Baker, *Mary Todd Lincoln: A Biography* (New York: W. W. Norton & Company, 1987), 88.

31. Thomas Keneally, *Abraham Lincoln* (New York: Penguin Books, 2003), 29.

32. Harvey Wish, ed., "Confessions of Nat Turner," in *Slavery in the South* (New York: Farrar, Straus & Co., 1964), 8–10.

33. William Styron, "Nat Turner," *Encyclopedia Britannica* (1970), 22:413.

34. Sidney Ahlstrom, *A Religious History of the American People* (New Haven: Yale University Press, 1972), 651.

35. Louis Ruchames, *The Abolitionists: A Collection of Their Writings* (New York: G. P. Putnam's Sons, 1963), 31.

36. Ernest Trice Thompson, *Presbyterians in the South, Volume 1:1607–1861* (Richmond: John Knox Press, 1963), 535.

Chapter 3: The "Infidel"

1. Douglas L. Wilson and Rodney O. Davis, eds., *Herndon's Informants* (Chicago: University of Illinois Press, 1998), 588–90.

2. Roy P. Basler, Marin Dolores Pratt, and Lloyd A. Dunlap, eds., *The Collected Works of Abraham Lincoln* (New Brunswick: Rutgers University Press, 1953), 1:320.

3. For helpful discussion of this poem and Lincoln's psychology, see Joshua Wolf Shenk, *Lincoln's Melancholy: How Depression Challenged a President and Fueled His Greatness* (New York: Houghton Mifflin Company, 2005), 39.

4. Quoted in Richard Lawrence Miller, "Lincoln's Suicide Poem: Has It Been Found?" *For the People* 6, no. 1 (Spring 2004), 6.

5. Jean H. Baker, *Mary Todd Lincoln: A Biography* (New York: W. W. Norton & Company, 1987), 87.

6. Wilson and Davis, *Herndon's Informants*, 133, 475.

7. Shenk, *Lincoln's Melancholy*, 59.

8. Basler, Pratt, and Dunlap, *Collected Works*, 1:228.

9. William H. Herndon and Jesse W. Weik, *Herndon's Lincoln*, Douglas L. Wilson and Rodney O. Davis, eds. (Chicago: University of Illinois Press, 2006), 144.

10. Wilson and Davis, *Herndon's Informants*, 472.

11. Ibid., 576.

12. William C. Temple, *Abraham Lincoln: From Skeptic to Prophet* (Mahomet, IL: Mayhaven Publishing, 1995),25. Emphasis added.

13. Charles Hamilton and Lloyd Ostendorf, *Lincoln in Photographs* (Dayton: Morningside Press, 1985), 88.

14. Wilson and Davis, *Herndon's Informants*, 132.

15. Basler, Pratt, and Dunlap, *Collected Works*, 1:320.

16. Herman A. Norton, *Religion in Tennessee, 1777–1945* (Knoxville: University of Tennessee Press, 1981), 31.

17. Ibid.

18. Carl Sandburg, *Abraham Lincoln: The Prairie Years and the War Years* (New York: Harcourt, Brace and Company, 1954). 83. Note: The original word Cartwright used was not "negro" but a much stronger, more insulting term. The author and the publisher agreed not to include the racial insult in this text. Cartwright's sentiments are clear, nonetheless.

19. Norton, *Religion in Tennessee*, 32.

20. Robert Bray, *Peter Cartwright: Legendary Frontier Preacher* (Chicago: University of Illinois Press, 2005); quoted in Wilson, "A Most Abandoned Hypocrite," 36–49.

21. Sandburg, *Abraham Lincoln*, 83–84.

22. Wilson and Davis, *Herndon's Informants*, 358.

23. Quoted in Shenk, *Lincoln's Melancholy*, 91.

24. Wilson and Davis, *Herndon's Informants*, 579.

25. Don E. Fehrenbacher and Virginia Fehrenbacher, eds., *Recollected Words of Abraham Lincoln* (Stanford: Stanford University Press, 1996), 372–74. Emphasis added.

26. Sandburg, *Abraham Lincoln*, 84.

27. Harold K. Bush Jr., *Lincoln in His Own Time* (Iowa City: University of Iowa Press, 2011), 13–14.

28. Basler, Pratt, and Dunlap, *Collected Works*, 1:367–70, 378–79, 385–86.

29. Sandburg, *Abraham Lincoln*, 99.

30. Ibid., 102.

31. Michael Burkhimer, *Lincoln's Christianity* (Yardley: Westholme, 2007), 45.

32. From the "Southwestern Christian Advocate, 1841" as quoted in William E. Barton, *The Soul of Abraham Lincoln* (Chicago: University of Illinois Press, 2005), 360–61.

33. Thomas Lewis to J. A. Reed, Springfield, IL, January 6, 1873, in *Scribner's Monthly* VI (July 1873), 339.

34. James Smith, *The Christian's Defence, Containing a Fair Statement, and Impartial Examination of the Leading Objections Urged by Infidels Against the Antiquity, Genuineness, Credibility and Inspiration of the Holy Scriptures*, 2 vols. in 1 (Cincinnati: J. A. James, 1843), 1:114.

35. Robert T. Lincoln to Isaac Markens, Manchester, VT, November 4, 1917, MS, Chicago Historical Society.

36. N. W. Edwards to James A. Reed, Springfield, IL, December 24, 1872, in *Scribner's Monthly* VI (July 1873), 338–39.

37. Wilson and Davis, *Herndon's Informant's*, 547, 549–50.

38. Richard Carwardine, *Lincoln: A Life of Purpose and Power* (New York: Random House, 2006), 37.

39. Wilson and Davis, *Herndon's Informants*, 579.

40. Ibid., 577.

41. Ibid., 524.

42. Baker, *Mary Todd Lincoln*, 125.

43. Michael Burkhimer, *Lincoln's Christianity* (Yardley: Westholme, 2007), 56.

44. Mary Lincoln to James Smith, June 8, 1870, in Justin G. Turner and Linda Levitt Turner, *Mary Todd Lincoln: Her Life and Letters* (New York: Fromm International Publishing Corporation, 1987), 567–68.

45. Barton, *Soul of Abraham Lincoln*, 319–20.

46. Temple, *From Skeptic to Prophet*, 52.

47. Basler, Pratt, and Dunlap, *Collected Works*, 2:97.

48. Barton, *Soul of Abraham Lincoln*, 321.

49. William H. Herndon to Isaac N. Arnold, Springfield, Illinois, October 24, 1883, MS, Chicago Historical Society; also Emanuel Hertz, ed., *The Hidden Lincoln: From the Letters and Papers of William H. Herndon* (Garden City, NY: Blue Ribbon Books, 1938), 90–91.

50. Fehrenbacher and Fehrenbacher, *Recollected Words*, 240.

51. Herndon and Weik, *Herndon's Lincoln*, 16.

52. Fehrenbacher and Fehrenbacher, *Recollected Words*, 240–41.

53. Allen C. Guelzo, *Abraham Lincoln: Redeemer President*, (Grand Rapids: William C. Eerdmans Publishing Company, 1999), 155.

54. Ibid.

55. Joshua Speed, *Reminiscences of Abraham Lincoln and Notes of a Visit to California: Two Lectures* (Louisville: John P. Morton, 1884), 32.

56. Fehrenbacher and Fehrenbacher, *Recollected Words*, 372–74.

CHAPTER 4: ON WINGS OF GRIEF

1. Carl Sandburg, *Abraham Lincoln: The Prairie Years and the War Years* (New York: Harcourt, Brace and Company, 1954), 195.

2. Ibid., 195–96.

3. Charles L. C. Minor, *The Real Lincoln* (Harrisonburg, VA: Sprinkle Publications, 1992), 27.

4. Ibid., 26.

5. Emanuel Hertz, ed., *The Hidden Lincoln: From the Letters and Papers of William H. Herndon* (Garden City, NY: Blue Ribbon Books, 1938), 418.

6. Justin G. Turner and Linda Levitt Turner, *Mary Todd Lincoln: Her Life and Letters* (New York: Fromm International Publishing Corporation, 1987), 180.

7. William C. Temple, *Abraham Lincoln: From Skeptic to Prophet* (Mahomet, IL: Mayhaven Publishing, 1995), 59.

8. F. B. Carpenter, *Six Months at the White House with Abraham Lincoln* (Lincoln: University of Nebraska Press, 1995), 187.

9. James T. Hickey, ed., "An Illinois First Family: The Reminiscences of Clara Matteson Doolittle," *Journal of the Illinois State History Society* LXIX (February 1976), 10.

10. Sandburg, *Abraham Lincoln*, 729.

11. Ibid.

12. Speech by Horace Mann to U. S. Congress, 1848, printed by J. Howe, Printer, 39 Merchants Row, Boston, archive.org/stream/speechofhonhorac00mann#page/n3/mode/2up (accessed March 26, 2012).

13. Roy P. Basler, Marin Dolores Pratt, and Lloyd A. Dunlap, eds., *The Collected Works of Abraham Lincoln* (New Brunswick: Rutgers University Press, 1953), 3:445.

14. Ibid., 3:204–5.

15. Don E. Fehrenbacher and Virginia Fehrenbacher, eds., *Recollected Words of Abraham Lincoln*, (Stanford: Stanford University Press, 1996), 373–74.

16. Temple, *From Skeptic to Prophet*, 141.

17. N. W. Miner, "Personal Reminiscences of Abraham Lincoln," MS, Illinois State Historical Library.

18. Douglas L. Wilson and Rodney O. Davis, eds., *Herndon's Informants* (Chicago: University of Illinois Press, 1998), 516.

19. Hertz, *Hidden Lincoln*, 408.

20. W. H. Lamon, *The Life of Lincoln* (Boston: James R. Osgood & Co., 1872), 501–2.

21. Wilson and Davis, *Herndon's Informants*, 464.

22. Basler, Pratt, and Dunlap, *Collected Works*, 4:192.

23. Ibid., 198–99.

24. Ibid., 205.

25. Ibid., 220–21.

26. Ibid., 235–36.

27. Sandburg, *Abraham Lincoln*, 197.

28. Chester Forrester Dunham, "The Attitude of the Northern Clergy Toward the South, 1860–1865," PhD diss., University of Chicago, 1939, 2.

29. Noah Brooks, *Washington in Lincoln's Time* (New York: The Century Company, 1895), 50–51.

30. Sandburg, *Abraham Lincoln*, 179–80.

31. Temple, *From Skeptic to Prophet*, 133.

32. Basler, Pratt, and Dunlap, *Collected Works*, 4:246.

33. Miner, "Personal Reminiscences of Abraham Lincoln."

34. Sandburg, *Abraham Lincoln*, 212.

35. All newspaper quotes, Ibid., 214–15.

36. Tyler Dennett, ed., *Lincoln and the Civil War in the Diaries and Letters of John Hay* (New York: Dodd, Mead & Co., 1939), 92.

37. Lloyd Ostendorf and Walter Olesky, eds., *Lincoln's Unknown Private Life: An Oral History by His Black Housekeeper Mariah Vance, 1850–1860* (New York: Hastings House Book Publishing, 1995), 158.

38. John G. Nicolay and John Hay, *Abraham Lincoln: A History* (New York: Cosimo Classics, 2009), 1:212.

39. Hertz, *Hidden Lincoln*, 409.

40. Nicolay and Hay, *Abraham Lincoln*, 212.

41. Author interview with James M. Cornelius of the Abraham Lincoln Presidential Library, Springfield, Illinois, August 16, 2011.

42. Hertz, *Hidden Lincoln*, 103.

43. William H. Herndon and Jesse W. Weik, *Herndon's Lincoln*, Douglas L. Wilson and Rodney O. Davis, eds. (Chicago: University of Illinois Press, 2006), 290.

44. Brooks, *Washington in Lincoln's Time*, 220–22.

45. Temple, *From Skeptic to Prophet*, 140.

46. Ibid., 142.

47. Future occupants of this pew would include presidents McKinley, Taft, Eisenhower, and Wilson.

48. Temple, *From Skeptic to Prophet*, 145.

49. Frank E. Edington, *A History of the New York Avenue Presbyterian Church* (Washington: New York Avenue Presbyterian Church, 1961), 13–14.

50. Lucius E. Chittenden, *Recollections of President Lincoln and His Administration* (New York: Harper & Bros, 1891), 449–50.

51. Matthew Simpson, "Under the Permissive Hand of God," May 4, 1865, in Waldo W. Braden, ed., *Building the Myth: Selected Speeches Memorializing Abraham Lincoln* (Urbana: University of Illinois Press, 1990), 82–83.

52. This was on the two-cent piece, and the bill was approved on April 22, 1864. See *U.S. Statutes at Large*, XII, 54.

53. Basler, Pratt, and Dunlap, *Collected Works*, 155–57.

54. Emanuel Hertz, ed., *Abraham Lincoln: The Tribute of the Synagogue* (New York: Bloch Publishing Company, 1927), 31.

55. Basler, Pratt, and Dunlap, *Collected Works*, 8:152–53.

56. Ibid., 8:154–55.

57. Stephen B. Oates, *Abraham Lincoln: The Man Behind the Myths* (New York: Harper Perennial, 1984), 151–52.

58. Sandburg, *Abraham Lincoln*, 576.

59. Wilson and Davis, *Herndon's Informants*, 156.

CHAPTER 5: THE HAUNTING OF GRAVES

1. Justin G. Turner and Linda Levitt Turner, *Mary Todd Lincoln: Her Life and Letters* (New York: Fromm International Publishing Corporation, 1987), 111.

2. Malcolm Cowley, ed., *The Complete Poetry of Walt Whitman* (New York: Penguin, 1976), 2:17–18.

3. William C. Temple, *Abraham Lincoln: From Skeptic to Prophet* (Mahomet, IL: Mayhaven Publishing, 1995), 182.

4. Turner and Turner, *Mary Todd Lincoln*, 189, 128.

5. Carl Sandburg, *Abraham Lincoln: The Prairie Years and the War Years* (New York: Harcourt, Brace and Company, 1954), 290.

6. Allen C. Guelzo, *Abraham Lincoln: Redeemer President* (Grand Rapids: William C. Eerdmans Publishing Company, 1999), 148.

7. Douglas L. Wilson and Rodney O. Davis, eds., *Herndon's Informants* (Chicago: University of Illinois Press, 1998), 453.

8. Ibid., 181.

9. Michael Burlingame, *The Inner World of Abraham Lincoln* (Chicago: University of Illinois Press, 1994), 57.

10. Sandburg, *Abraham Lincoln*, 290.

11. Temple, *From Skeptic to Prophet*, 182.

12. Elizabeth Todd Grimsley, "Six Months in the White House," *Journal of the Illinois State Historical Society* 19 (October 1926–January 1927), 53–54.

13. Michael Burkhimer, *Lincoln's Christianity* (Yardley, PA: Westholme, 2007), 114.

14. Michael Burlingame, ed., *With Lincoln in the White House: Letters, Memoranda, and Other Writings of John G. Nicolay, 1860–1865* (Carbondale: Southern Illinois University Press, 2000), 71.

15. William O. Stoddard, *Lincoln's Third Secretary* (New York: Exposition Press, 1955), 148–49.

16. Elizabeth Keckley, *Behind the Scenes, or Thirty Years a Slave and Four Years in the White House* (New York: Oxford University Press, 1988), 103.

17. Temple, *From Skeptic to Prophet*, 189.

18. William H. Herndon and Jesse W. Weik, *Herndon's Lincoln*, Douglas L. Wilson and Rodney O. Davis, eds. (Chicago: University of Illinois Press, 2006), 376–77.

19. William Shakespeare, *King John*, act 3, scene 4.

20. Herndon and Weik, *Herndon's Lincoln*, 376–77.

21. Noah Brooks, writing in the *Sacramento Daily Union*, December 30, 1862, 1.

22. Edgar DeWitt Jones, *Lincoln and the Preachers* (New York: Harper & Brothers, 1948), 37.

23. Walter B. Stevens, *A Reporter's Lincoln* (St. Louis: Missouri Historical Society, 1916), 11–12.

24. N. W. Miner, "Personal Reminiscences of Abraham Lincoln," MS, Illinois State Historical Library, 41, 44, 45.

25. F. B. Carpenter, *Six Months at the White House with Abraham Lincoln* (Lincoln: University of Nebraska Press, 1995), 117–19.

26. Wilson and Davis, *Herndon's Informants*, 360.

27. David Herbert Donald, *Lincoln* (New York: Simon and Schuster, 1995), 337.

28. Ibid., 338.

29. Lucius E. Chittenden, *Recollections of President Lincoln and His Administration* (New York: Harper and Brothers, 1891), 448.

30. Roy P. Basler, Marin Dolores Pratt, and Lloyd A. Dunlap, eds., *The Collected Works of Abraham Lincoln* (New Brunswick: Rutgers University Press, 1953), 7:542–43.

31. Joshua Speed, *Reminiscences of Abraham Lincoln and Notes of a Visit to California: Two Lectures* (Louisville: John P. Morton, 1884), 32–33.

32. Sandburg, *Abraham Lincoln*, 575.

33. Ibid., 576.

34. Ibid., 574.

35. Ibid.

36. Mitch Horowitz, *Occult America: White House Séances, Ouija Circles, Masons and the Secret Mystic History of Our Nation* (New York: Bantam Books, 2009), 53.

37. Arthur Conan Doyle, *The Edge of the Unknown* (New York: G. P. Putnam's Sons, 1930), 35.

38. Ibid., 54.

39. Jean H. Baker, *Mary Todd Lincoln: A Biography* (New York: W. W. Norton & Company, 1987), 218.

40. Horowitz, *Occult America*, 60.

41. Ervin S. Chapman, *Latest Light on Lincoln: And Wartime Memories* (New York: Fleming H. Revell, Company, 1917), 506.

42. Nettie Colburn Maynard, *Was Abraham Lincoln a Spiritualist? or, Curious Revelations from the Life of a Trance Medium* (Chicago: The Progressive Thinker, 1917).

43. Abraham Lincoln Online, "Meditation on the Divine Will," September

1862, http://showcase.netins.net/web/creative/lincoln/speeches/
meditat.htm.

44. Thomas Keneally, *Abraham Lincoln* (New York: Penguin Books, 2003),
120. Emphasis added.

45. Ibid., 145.

46. David Donald, *Inside Lincoln's Cabinet: The Civil War Diaries of
Salmon P. Chase* (New York: Longmans, Green & Co., 1954), 149–50.
Emphasis added.

47. Carpenter, *Six Months at the White House*, 90. Emphasis added.

48. John T. Morse Jr., ed., *Diary of Gideon Welles: Secretary of the Navy
Under Lincoln and Johnson*, 3 vols. (Boston: Houghton Mifflin, 1911),
1:142–43. Emphasis added.

49. Basler, Pratt, and Dunlap, *Collected Works*, 5:438.

50. Don E. Fehrenbacher and Virginia Fehrenbacher, eds., *Recollected
Words of Abraham Lincoln*, (Stanford: Stanford University Press, 1996),
437.

51. Reverend Matthew Simpson, DD, *Funeral Address Delivered at the
Burial of President Lincoln, at Springfield, Illinois*, May 4, 1865 (New
York: Carlton & Porter, 1865).

52. Fehrenbacher and Fehrenbacher, *Recollected Words*, 388.

53. Ibid.

54. Though Vicksburg fell on July 4, the day before Lincoln's interview with
General Sickles, the telegram announcing Grant's victory at Vicksburg
did not reach the White House until July 7.

55. William E. Barton, *The Soul of Abraham Lincoln* (Chicago: University
of Illinois Press, 2005), 327.

56. William O. Stoddard, *Inside the White House in War Times: Memoirs
and Reports of Lincoln's Secretary* (Lincoln: University of Nebraska
Press, 2000), 215–16.

57. Barton, *Soul of Abraham Lincoln*, 280.

58. Carpenter, *Six Months at the White House*, 185–86.

59. Barton, *Soul of Abraham Lincoln*, 102.

60. Tyler Dennett, ed., *Lincoln and the Civil War in the Diaries and letters
of John Hay* (New York: Dodd, Mead and Company, 1939), 121.

61. Noah Brooks, *Washington in Lincoln's Time* (New York: The Century Company, 1895), 304–5.

62. Temple, *From Skeptic to Prophet*, 251.

63. Sandburg, *Abraham Lincoln*, 445–46.

64. Ibid., 446.

Epilogue: Purposes of the Almighty

1. Charles Dickens, *American Notes* (London: Chapman and Hall, 1842), 45.

2. *Sacramento Daily Union*, March 12, 1865 (published April 10), in Michael Burlingame, ed., *Lincoln Observed: Civil War Dispatches of Noah Brooks* (Baltimore: Johns Hopkins University Press, 1998), 165.

3. *New York Herald*, March 6, 1865, 5.

4. Quoted in James M. McPherson, *Abraham Lincoln* (Oxford: Oxford University Press, 2009), 56.

5. Carl Sandburg, *Abraham Lincoln: The Prairie Years and the War Years* (New York: Harcourt, Brace and Company, 1954), 663.

6. Noah Brooks, *Washington in Lincoln's Time* (New York: The Century Company, 1895), 213.

7. Archer H. Shaw, ed., *The Lincoln Encyclopedia* (New York: MacMillan Company, 1950), 114.

8. William Safire, *Lend Me Your Ears: Great Speeches in History* (New York: W. W. Norton and Company, 1997), 469.

9. Sandburg, *Abraham Lincoln*, 665.

10. William E. Barton, *The Soul of Abraham Lincoln* (Chicago: University of Illinois Press, 2005), 326.

ACKNOWLEDGMENTS

RARE IS THE AUTHOR WHO OWES NO DEBT TO HIS high school teachers. I owe more than most.

I have the privilege of being the son of a U.S. army officer. There are many unique and valuable experiences that have come from this, but chief among them were the years I spent in the Berlin, Germany, of the 1970s. I attended Berlin American High School with hundreds of other American youth, nearly all the children of state department officials, diplomats, and intelligence analysts if they were not military brats like me. We lived, in many ways, the lives of typical American teenagers. Dates, sports, movies, dances, and mischief filled our lives. Yet we were also living behind the Iron Curtain, and the Cold War ruled us. It was not uncommon for our sleep to be interrupted by the sound of tanks clanking through the city's streets or for our fathers to disappear from our lives upon occasion with the sole explanation that they were "on alert." Some of my friends who lived nearer the Berlin Wall occasionally heard machine gun fire in the small hours of the night. When our high school teams played against other American schools, one of the two rivals had to travel through East Germany on a "duty train." These were regularly stopped by heavily armed soldiers who used dogs and mirrors to search for escapees. My civilian friends back home would only know such scenes from movies about Nazis.

We were isolated expatriates, and so we became dear to each other. We are dear to each other still. Our teachers naturally loomed large for us. The ones who influenced me were history teachers and had names like Beam, Ferguson, Sullivan, and Kilpatrick. That they were teaching just miles from armies eager to destroy all they held dear made the lessons of Western civilization more urgent, their craft perhaps more vital than they had imagined possible when they decided upon their profession.

This is what brought me to Lincoln. I remember discussing "government of the people, by the people, for the people" with Mr. Ferguson and thinking how immediate the words seemed. Our context changed everything and made Lincoln more relevant by far than the Nixons and Agnews who occupied the American stage at the time. Lincoln spoke of sacred sacrifices and the evils of slavery, of healing a nation's wounds and the better angels of our nature. Peering over the Berlin Wall into a dismal, oppressed East, we knew Lincoln's words defined the American ideal. And I loved him for it. First, I became enamored with the romantic Lincoln of patriotic lore. Then the troubled, complicated man of Herndon's many interviews. Then the disturbingly racist and political Lincoln. Finally, I simply let Lincoln be his frustrating, often unknowable, inconsistent, maddening self. But it all came to me first through devoted teachers who elected to ply their trade among the children of the Berlin Brigade. I am ever thankful.

Today our high school building no longer houses an American school. Most of our teachers are dead. There are no American troops in Berlin. Still, in my mind, I stop by the post exchange on the way home from school. I buy *pommes frites* near the Clayallee Strasse U-Bahn station. And I walk to football practice with the words of Miss Beam playing in my mind: "Lincoln lives today on the streets of West Berlin."

I was aided in my research for this book by three devoted public servants in Springfield, Illinois. The first was James M. Cornelius, curator of the Lincoln Collection at the Abraham Lincoln Presidential Library. He is a wise and gentle scholar. In fact, he is what we think of when we hear the words "Lincoln expert." He not only encouraged my pursuit of the spiritual Lincoln but read the manuscript and kindly made suggestions. Though all errors are mine, his input was invaluable. I was also well served by Timothy P. Townsend of the National Park Service. I have often thought that if I had another life to live, I would love to be a member of the Park Service stationed at some beloved historical site. Mr. Townsend set this dream aflame. He spoke with an obvious mastery about Lincoln sources, took me on a tour of the Lincoln Home, and encouraged my work with grace. We need more like him.

In Springfield I also had the privilege of meeting Dr. Wayne C. Temple. I thought at first he was merely an Illinois state archivist who had written a book about Lincoln's religion. It turns out he is the "Dean of Lincoln Scholars," a man honored as a Life Fellow by the Royal Society of Arts in England, and remembered as a valued member of General Eisenhower's staff during World War II. His counsel was like wisdom from on high, and it was a privilege merely to be in his presence.

Many others were generous with their time and insights. Dr. Mark Noll of the University of Notre Dame gave treasured advice. The amazing staff at Ford's Theatre in Washington, D.C., were generous and a credit to the cause of historical preservation. Both they and the theater they tend are national treasures. Once again Chartwell Literary Group served me with research, scheduling, editing, and counsel. Their staff, Isaac Darnall in particular, was skilled and encouraging. I don't know how I would do a book without them.

Finally, as with nearly all my books, my best counsel, most loyal opposition, most devoted advocate, and most certain guide was my wife, Beverly. It helps immensely that she is very easy to look at, but even if she weren't, she has such a sophisticated literary sense that she has become fundamental to all that I write. Her wisdom is like air for the runner, melody for the finely crafted song. She is my most welcome distraction, and I cannot imagine life or literature without her.

ABOUT THE AUTHOR

STEPHEN MANSFIELD IS A WRITER AND SPEAKER BEST known for his groundbreaking books on the role of religion in history, leadership, and politics. He first came to international attention with *The Faith of George W. Bush*, the *New York Times* bestseller that influenced Oliver Stone's film *W.* His book *The Faith of Barack Obama* was another international bestseller. He has written celebrated biographies of Booker T. Washington, George Whitefield, Winston Churchill, and Pope Benedict XVI. Known for aggressively researching his books, Mansfield worked in a brewery while writing *The Search for God and Guinness* and was embedded with U.S. troops in Iraq for his study of faith among America's warriors.

Stephen speaks around the world on topics of faith, leadership, and culture. He is also the founder of two firms, the Mansfield Group (MansfieldGroup.com) and Chartwell Literary Group (ChartwellLiterary.com). He is a frequent commentator on television news programs and an outspoken advocate for a variety of social causes. A single sentence from his book about President Obama captures the central belief that shapes his work: "If a man's faith is sincere, it is the most important thing about him and it is impossible to understand who he is and how he will lead without first understanding the religious vision that informs his life."

Stephen lives in Nashville and Washington, D.C., with his wife, Beverly, who is an award-winning songwriter and producer.

For further information, log onto MansfieldGroup.com

Clockwise from top right: The author at the Abraham Lincoln Presidential Library and Museum; with Dr. Wayne C. Temple, Chief Deputy Director of the Illinois State Archives; with Dr. James Cornelius, curator of the Lincoln Collection, Abraham Lincoln Presidential Library and Museum; at the Lincoln Home, Springfield, Illinois; the Chapel in the Lincoln Boyhood National Memorial, Lincoln City, Indiana; with Timothy P. Townsend, Historian, Lincoln Home National Historic Site.

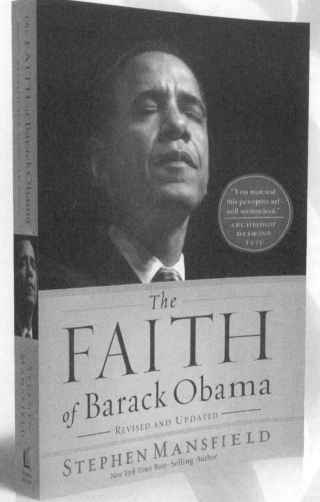

ALSO AVAILABLE FROM STEPHEN MANSFIELD

It began in Ireland in the late 1700s. The water in Ireland, indeed throughout Europe, was famously undrinkable, and the gin and whiskey that took its place was devastating civil society. It was a disease-ridden, starvation-plagued, alcoholic age, and Christians like Arthur Guinness—as well as monks and even evangelical churches— brewed beer that provided a healthier alternative to the poisonous waters and liquors of the times. This is where the Guinness tale began. Now, 250 years and 150 countries later, Guinness is a global brand, one of the most consumed beverages in the world. The tale that unfolds during those two and a half centuries has power to thrill audiences today: the generational drama, business adventure, industrial and social reforms, deep-felt faith, and the beer itself.

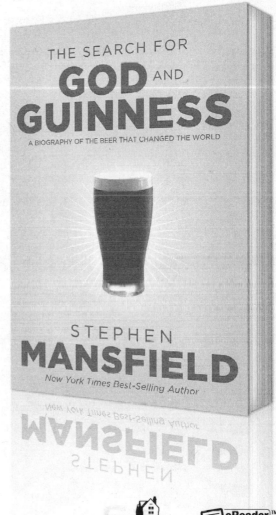

THE SEARCH FOR
GOD AND
GUINNESS
A BIOGRAPHY OF THE BEER THAT CHANGED THE WORLD

STEPHEN
MANSFIELD
New York Times Best-Selling Author